RACE ON TRIAL

VIEWPOINTS ON AMERICAN CULTURE

Edited by Catherine Clinton

Viewpoints on American Culture offers timely reflections for twenty-first-century readers. A sensible guide to knowledge in a scholarly field, something one can pick up—literally and figuratively—seems to be facing extinction. Volumes in our series will provide intellectual relief and practical solution.

The series targets topics where debates have flourished and brings together the voices of established and emerging writers to share their own points of view in a compact and compelling format. Our books offer sophisticated, yet accessible, introductions into an array of issues under our broad and expanding banner.

Sifters: Native American Women's Lives
Edited by Theda Perdue

Long Time Gone: Sixties America Then and Now
Edited by Alexander Bloom

Votes for Women: The Struggle for Suffrage Revisited
Edited by Jean H. Baker

Race on Trial: Law and Justice in American History
Edited by Annette Gordon-Reed

RACE ON TRIAL

Law and Justice in American History

Edited by Annette Gordon-Reed

OXFORD
UNIVERSITY PRESS

2002

OXFORD

UNIVERSITY PRESS

Oxford   New York
Auckland   Bangkok   Buenos Aires   Cape Town   Chennai
Dar es Salaam   Delhi   Hong Kong   Istanbul   Karachi   Kolkata
Kuala Lumpur   Madrid   Melbourne   Mexico City   Mumbai   Nairobi
São Paulo   Shanghai   Singapore   Taipei   Tokyo   Toronto
and an associated company in Berlin

Copyright © 2002 by Oxford University Press, Inc.

Published by Oxford University Press, Inc.
198 Madison Avenue, New York, New York 10016

www.oup.com

Oxford is a registered trademark of Oxford University Press

Library of Congress Cataloging-in-Publication Data
Race on trial : law and justice in American history / edited by Annette Gordon-Reed.
    p. cm.— (Viewpoints on American culture)
Includes bibliographical references.
ISBN 0-19-512279-8; ISBN 0-19-512280-1 (pbk.)
1. Discrimination in justice administration—United States—History.   2. Trials—United States.
3. United States—Race relations—History.   I. Gordon-Reed, Annette.   II. Series.
KF385.A4 R33 2002
342.73'0873—dc21   2001054875

9 8 7 6 5 4 3 2 1

Printed in the United States of America
on acid-free paper

ACKNOWLEDGMENTS

It has fallen to me, as editor of *Race on Trial*, to acknowledge all those who helped make this volume possible. There is one problem, however. Because this is a compilation of the work of multiple authors, I do not know the names of all the people in the lives of my co-essayists who provided support as they thought about and wrote their individual pieces. Under the circumstances, the best that I can do is to offer thanks, on behalf of my fellow contributors, to all the people in our lives who provided inspiration and support in the preparation of our respective essays. Presumably, you know who you are.

When it comes to Oxford University Press, things are much easier. There is no mystery about who deserves our gratitude. Without question, Susan Ferber, our editor at the press, is entitled to the lion's share of credit for bringing this project to fruition. Getting the book off the ground was not easy: there were many fits and starts—periods of intense work, followed by dormant stages of equal or greater length. It couldn't have been easy for her. Without Susan's hard work, diligence, and seemingly endless patience, we would not have completed this book. It is that simple. We cannot thank her enough.

For me, one of the best parts about being involved in this effort is that I was able to work with Catherine Clinton, the general editor of Oxford's "Viewpoints on American Culture" series. I thank her for encouraging me to become involved with this book and for her willingness to stick with one of the most inaccessible individuals on the planet—that is to say, me. The "Viewpoints" series has done interesting and important work and I am sure will continue to contribute to our national conversation in beneficial ways.

Finally, to Niko Pfund, Oxford's vice president for academic publishing: I am so glad that we have finally gotten to work together after all of these years. It has been a long time coming, and I look forward to continued associations in the future.

CONTENTS

CONTRIBUTORS

Howard Ball is Professor of Political Science and University Scholar at the University of Vermont, as well as adjunct professor at the Vermont Law School. Ball is the author of dozens of journal articles and more than twenty books, including *Courts and Politics* (1987), *Hugo L. Black: Cold Steel Warrior* (1996), *A Defiant Life: Thurgood Marshall and the Persistence of Racism* (2000), and, most recently, *The Bakke Case: Race, Education and Affirmative Action* (2000).

Gabriel J. Chin, the Rufus King Professor of Law at the University of Cincinnati College of Law, received law degrees from the University of Michigan and Yale University law schools. He is the author of "Segregation's Last Stronghold: Race Discrimination and the Constitutional Law of Immigration," *UCLA Law Review* (1996), and "The *Plessy* Myth: Justice Harlan and the Chinese Cases," *Iowa Law Review* (1996), which received the Thurgood Marshall Award from the Southwestern and Southeastern People of Color Legal Scholarship Conference.

Roger Daniels is Charles Phelps Taft Professor of History at the University of Cincinnati. Among his publications are *Debating American Immigration* (2001), *Not Like Us: Immigrants and Minorities in America, 1890–1924* (1997), *Prisoners without Trial: Japanese Americans in World War II* (1993), and *Coming to America: A History of Immigration and Ethnicity in American Life* (1990).

Thomas J. Davis, Ph.D., J.D., teaches history and law at Arizona State University in Tempe, focusing on race and the law, civil rights, as well as employment and labor law. He also teaches U.S. constitutional and legal history. Among other works, he authored *A Rumor of Revolt: "The Great Negro Plot" in Colonial New York* (1985) and coauthored *Africans in the Americas: A History of the Black Diaspora* (1994).

Annette Gordon-Reed is Professor of Law at New York Law School. She is the author of *Thomas Jefferson and Sally Hemings: An American Controversy* (1997) and coauthor (with Vernon Jordan) of *Vernon Can Read!* (2001). She is currently working on a biography of the Hemings family.

Walter L. Hixson is Professor of History at the University of Akron. He is the author of *Murder, Culture and Injustice: Four Sensational Crimes in American History* (2000). He also has published a number of works on the history of the cold war, including *Parting the Curtain: Propaganda, Culture and the Cold War, 1945–1961* (1997).

Howard Jones is University Research Professor in the Department of History at the University of Alabama. A recipient of the John F. Burnum Distinguished Faculty Award and the Blackmon-Moody Outstanding Professor Award, he is the author or editor of more than a dozen books, including *Mutiny on the* Amistad: *The Saga of a Slave Revolt and Its Impact on American Abolition, Law, and Diplomacy* (1987; rev. ed., 1997), *"A New Kind of War": Union in Peril, the Crisis over British Intervention in the Civil War* (1992), and *Abraham Lincoln and a New Birth of Freedom: The Union and Slavery in the Diplomacy of the Civil War* (1999). He is completing a book entitled "Death of a Generation: John F. Kennedy and Vietnam."

P. J. Ling is Senior Lecturer in American History in the School of American and Canadian Studies at the University of Nottingham, England. His past publications include a coedited collection (with Sharon Montieth), *Gender in the Civil Rights Movement* (1999), and a biography, *Martin Luther King, Jr.* (2001). His current research is on the classic phase of the civil rights movement (1940s–1970s) and, in particular, political education campaigns.

Denise C. Morgan is Professor of Law at New York Law School, specializing in educational policy and the law, antidiscrimination law, and civil procedure. She has written extensively in law reviews on equal educational opportunity, coauthored a guide for aspiring law professors entitled *Breaking into the Academy*, and is writing a book about the role of law in the creation of heroes within the black community.

Mark Tushnet is Carmack Waterhouse Professor of Constitutional Law at the Georgetown University Law Center. A scholar of constitutional law, he has written extensively about Thurgood Marshall and the litigation campaign that culminated in *Brown v. Board of Education*.

Peter Wallenstein teaches history at Virginia Polytechnic Institute and State University. His two hundred publications include *From Slave South to New South: Public Policy in Nineteenth Century Georgia* (1987), *Virginia Tech, Land-Grant University, 1872–1997: History of a School, a State, a Nation* (1997), and *The Encyclopedia of American Political History* (coedited with Paul Finkelman, 2001).

Xi Wang received a Ph.D. from Columbia University and is an associate professor at Indiana University of Pennsylvania, where he teaches history. He is the author of *The Trial of Democracy: Black Suffrage and Northern Republicans (1860–1910)* (1997) and *Principles and Compromises: The Spirit and Practice of the American Constitution* [in Chinese] (2000). He is also the translator of the Chinese edition of Eric Foner's *The Story of American Freedom* (2001).

RACE ON TRIAL

INTRODUCTION

Annette Gordon-Reed

It is currently popular to describe the concept of race as a social construct. Recent studies by and writings of biologists and geneticists support this idea, showing that there are no firm characteristics separating one race from another. More genetic variations exist within so-called racial groups than between them. One can truly say that our racial differences are only skin deep.

That does not settle matters. Even if race is a created fiction, the fact remains that we are all, in many ways, hostages to a variety of social constructs that are as binding, determinative—as "concrete" as any biological "reality." Even though we know the truth about race, we cannot deny its past and continuing power over the lives of millions. The rules of race have built and sustained empires, blighted lives, and destroyed civilizations. It is equally true that social rules are by no means static. Societies change their minds—create new constructs as needed, to ensure economic efficiency, in deference to new scientific discoveries, or in service of new understandings of liberty and justice. That is why it is so important to emphasize the tenuous nature of the biological bases for the concept of race. If that idea was created, we can fashion new understandings about our relationships to one another.

Law, as enunciated in legislation and judicial opinions, is a primary vehicle for setting the social rules of organized communities. It is also a chief mechanism for changing the rules of the game. Through an organic process, law creates, reflects, shapes, and sometimes contests values that individual citizens of a community hold within. It has certainly done that with respect to race in the United States. From the very beginning of the

American experiment, law was a crucial force in defining the meaning of race for individuals living on the American continent. As Europeans became a permanent and dominant fixture in what would become the United States of America, they created a system of law that sought to regulate the terms of engagement between and among Native Americans, African Americans, and European Americans.

In those early years, the idea that race, rather than culture, determined an individual's place in society became fixed. Only Africans, and to a lesser extent Native Americans, could be chattel slaves who transferred their condition to their offspring. Baptism into the Christian faith did not affect the slaves' condition. Signs of character and a willingness to assimilate European values did nothing to counteract the well-accepted belief that blood—made synonymous with race—was everything.

A crude hierarchy developed that placed whites on top and blacks on the very bottom of the social scale. Native Americans occupied a strange middle category—subject to mild tolerance, removal from proximity to whites, or outright extermination. Later, this racialized way of thinking was extended to govern the status of the large number of Asians (mainly Chinese) who came to the western states during the second half of the nineteenth century. Legislators passed various Chinese exclusion laws, thus codifying the racism of white citizens who feared the competition for labor and different culture the immigrants brought. Law, once again, encouraged inhabitants of the United States to see one another primarily in terms of race.

In his prize-winning work, *White over Black*, the historian Winthrop Jordan wisely suggested caution when studying the operation of law—created, practiced, and administered as it is by elites—as a firm guidepost to what is actually going on in a culture. Legislation and the outcomes of legal cases tell us a lot but not everything about the way people in a given society think, thought, or, most important, actually behave. Think of the age-old hostility toward interracial sex enunciated in the laws of almost every state of the Union throughout the eighteenth, nineteenth, and long parts of the twentieth centuries and then consider the visible evidence of racial mixture in the population of African Americans. Even with Jordan's proviso, cases—trials in particular—provide critical insights into the values, mores, obsessions, and aspirations (lived up to and not) of members of the community at particular moments in history.

It is with this knowledge that the essays in this volume use legal disputes in which the concept of race plays a central role to explore American attitudes, from the early days of the nation to the late twentieth century, about the proper boundaries between the races. This is by no means an exhaustive survey of all the various boundaries. The overwhelming majority of the essays deal with the engagement of black and white, since there has been no territory more contested in American history. From the days of slavery, to the cases leading up to the Civil War and Reconstruction, to the "Second American Revolution" that was the modern Civil Rights Movement, and into the post–civil rights era, U.S. courts have been the battlefield upon which the country's racial struggle has been fought.

The tenacious battle over black people's place in America has overshadowed and influenced all legal controversies involving other ethnic and racial groups in the United States. For it has long been the view that the "black race" and the "white race" are polar opposites along the continuum of the races of mankind. Native Americans, Asians, and many other ethnic groups have been placed at various points between the two polarities—sometimes closer to black, at other times closer to white. In the discussions of their fates within American life, the black-white dichotomy is never far away. For this reason, considerations of the black-white divide predominate. Presented in this volume are discussions of some of the most famous (and infamous) cases in all of American legal history. In fact, some, like *Brown v. Board of Education*, which outlawed enforced segregation in U.S. schools and suggested new possibilities for racial reconciliation, and the case that *Brown* overruled, *Plessy v. Ferguson*, which propped up Jim Crow in the American South and broadcast to the nation and to the world blacks' second-class status, have transcended the boundaries of legal history. Those cases and/or the ideas they stood for—"separate is inherently unequal" and in favor of "separate but equal"—are well-known throughout the culture at large. Then there are others, also famous, but without the iconic stature of *Brown*: *Dred Scott v. Sandford*, which determined, among other things, that blacks would never be citizens of the United States; and the *Amistad* case, which involved Africans who successfully rebelled against their captors and was made more famous by a recent Hollywood film. From the modern era, other cases reveal the still-deep divisions in our culture about what it means to be an American and whether or not certain groups will be allowed the full benefits of that appellation. *Korematsu v. United States*, which upheld the racially imposed detention of Japanese-American citizens during World War II; *Regents of California v. Bakke*, in which a fractured Supreme Court grappled with the contentious issue of affirmative action programs designed to accelerate the inclusion of blacks into the American mainstream; and *The People v. Orenthal James Simpson*, which exposed the gulf between white and black understandings about the work of modern police forces in largely black, urban areas invite considerations of what American citizens should and should not be forced to endure.

All the cases discussed in this volume, well-known and less well-known, demonstrate clearly how much time, energy, and tension have been spent on race in the United States—how it has entered into every nook and cranny of our lives. It has, for most of our history, determined who was a citizen, where we could live, what jobs we could hold, even whom we could marry—the most elemental items of human existence. Several of the essays reveal the degree to which tortured sexuality, fears about the creation of mixed bloodlines, as well as white males' desire for control (to the exclusion of black males) over the bodies of both white females and black females have been at the heart of the law's response to race in the United States.

We enter the hellish world of Celia, an enslaved Missouri woman in the 1850s, who killed her master after years of sexual abuse. At the time of Celia's ordeal, abolitionists used the rape of slave women and children to condemn the inherent wickedness of slavery. Southern apologists, then and now, characterized stories of sexual abuse as mainly hysteria on the part of zealots who wanted slavery to end immediately. The rape of slave women was rare, they argued, conducted mainly by members of the "lower orders" of whites, not upright, law-abiding white citizens. Yet the legal analysis in Celia's case presents the situation of black women under slavery very starkly. The overarching consideration was that slaves were the property of the white people who owned them, to be used for whatever purpose they saw fit. The court stated without equivocation: If Celia's master came to her cabin for sex, she had no right under the law to deny him. Whatever professed social disdain for interracial sex may have existed, the law would not step in to police it, if it meant interferring with a white man's right to use his property. I suggest that this failure to curb white men's behavior shows that freedom to have sex with slaves was an accepted and understood part of the system of slavery.

Denise Morgan's essay on the life and legal troubles of Jack Johnson, the first black man to become heavyweight boxing champion of the world, explores the incendiary and complex nature of black-white sexuality in the early twentieth century. Johnson, who was already a pariah to whites for defeating a white man in the championship match, became an even more hated figure when he openly consorted with and married a series of white women. He was the white racist's nightmare walking: an aggressive black man who physically overpowers white men and takes "their women." The law, in the form of the Mann Act, was used as a weapon to teach him a lesson. At the same time, however, Johnson was not an ideal hero to black people either, because he had so thoroughly accepted the dominant culture's adoration of white female beauty and concomitant deriding of black women's appearance. Many black people were simply appalled and ashamed by Johnson's adamant and vocal rejection of black women, even as he claimed that he was simply exercising his basic human right to the mate of his choice.

The black man as violent sexual predator fueled the prosecution and discussions of the Scottsboro cases of the 1930s. These Alabama cases, under the legal heading *Powell v. Alabama*, became an international cause célèbre to the Left during that decade and showed the southern legal system at its most racist and backward. P. J. Ling details the hysteria over black males' alleged hypersexuality; the hatred of the Jewish lawyers who defended the so-called "Scottsboro boys," most of whom were actually men; and the neo-Confederate hostility toward any scrutiny and criticism of the southern way of life (oppression of black citizens). Here was law at its worst, in its most procedurally and substantively bankrupt form. There were judges, lawyers, briefs, and arguments but virtually no chance for justice in a legal system run by and for whites in a state that saw and treated its black citizens as the enemy.

Whatever attention the Scottsboro cases received in the 1930s could not begin to approach the media circus attending what became known as the "trial of the century." *The People v. Orenthal James Simpson*, with its heady combination of race, violence, and a famous defendant, transfixed the world as people around the globe followed the trial on a daily basis and marveled at the idiosyncracies of the U.S. legal system and its distinctive racial landscape. The *Simpson* case revealed that we have not come as far as we might like to think in ridding ourselves of negative psychosexual baggage when it comes to interracial sex.

It is useful to consider the *Simpson* case along with the story of Jack Johnson and the Scottsboro cases. Before his arrest for the murder of his ex-wife, Nicole Brown Simpson, and Ron Goldman, O. J. Simpson was no Jack Johnson to white America. Instead, he was a beloved figure much admired for his prowess on the football field. Simpson presented a sunny, nonthreatening demeanor and was deemed "safe" enough to star in a series of advertisements with Arnold Palmer, the icon of one of the "whitest" sports in America: golf, played in exclusive and sometimes racially restricted country clubs.

Other aspects of the *Simpson* case reveal changes in the dynamics of race in the United States from the days of Jack Johnson and Scottsboro. By the 1990s, far from making him seem threatening, Simpson's marriage to Nicole Brown, a white woman, was in its own way reassuring, suggesting that he was just like one of the guys (white guys, that is) for whom a blonde woman is the ultimate trophy. However, as soon as Simpson got into trouble, the specter of the "black brute," which had haunted Jack Johnson's career and whipped up the sexual hysteria in Scottsboro, rose again virtually unaltered. *Time* magazine very famously put an image of Simpson on its cover with his skin color darkened at least two shades, which they justified (seemingly without the slightest embarrassment) as a way to highlight the evil of Simpson's alleged deed. Walter L. Hixson details how the racial dynamics played themselves out in the Simpson trial, suggesting that, in the end, Simpson was wrongly spared a guilty verdict by a black jury that knew all too well that the U.S. legal system was shown in the Scottsboro cases (and in many cases involving blacks in Los Angeles) to be riven by racial prejudice. Unlike the young men in the Scottsboro cases, Simpson was able to buy exceptionally strong legal counsel, a "dream team" of lawyers who understood America's racial preoccupations very well and used that knowledge to great effect. In Hixson's presentation, both the prosecution and the jury were right in their perceptions of what was at stake. He clearly believes that the evidence of Simpson's guilt was overwhelming. In the end, the Brown and Goldman families paid the price for the state of California's failure to come to grips with the "police harassment, violence, and tampering with evidence against African-Americans" that are "everyday occurrences in the United States."

At a very basic level, in *Loving v. Virginia* we confront what all the fuss seems to have been about. The issue of whether the law should allow blacks and whites to form families together has been a source of controversy since the seventeenth century, when the first colonial statutes punishing interracial sex and forbidding the recognition of interracial marriages were put in place. Many Americans would, no doubt, be surprised to find that well into the twentieth century many states, not just those in the South, had bans on interracial marriages. It was not until 1948 that the California Supreme Court struck down the state's ban on such unions. It is also worth noting that it was the American Civil Liberties Union, not other well recognized civil rights organizations like the National Association for the Advancement of Colored People (NAACP), that championed the Lovings' right to marry. As a rule, civil rights organizations, sensitive to the volatile nature of the subject of interracial sex and anxious to ensure

the success of their efforts in the areas of voting rights and school desegregation, were very keen to prove that their call for the end of segregation did not have as its objective intermarriage between the races. That
had been the charge of the white racists who resisted civil rights measures.

Peter Wallenstein's review of the precedents leading up to *Loving* reveals that the Supreme Court, even as it was expanding the rights of blacks
and others during the 1950s and 1960s, seems to have been ducking the
question of whether or not interracial marriages should receive the protection of the U.S. Constitution. Marriage, as one of the lower court judges
in the *Loving* case declared, had long been the province of individual
states—which may well have accounted for some of the Court's hesitancy
to deal with this area of the law. But by 1967, American society had
changed enough to warrant action to grant protection of this most private of human choices: the right to decide whom to marry and with whom
to have children. Not everyone had, however. Just two years before man
walked on the moon, a Virginia lower court judge, reviewing the *Loving*
case, felt no compunction about writing in his judicial opinion, "Almighty
God created the races white, black, yellow, malay, and red, and he placed
them on separate continents. And but for the interference with his arrangement there would be no cause for such marriages. The fact that he
separated the races shows that he did not intend for them to marry."

The strengths and weaknesses of law as a mechanism for dealing with racial
differences come through very clearly in many of the essays in this volume. At times, we see the law as a force for progress, rising above the
prejudices of the majority to protect the rights of disadvantaged minorities. Mark Tushnet suggests that this has not been the predominant tendency, at least not within the U.S. Supreme Court. In his essay on *Brown
v. Board of Education*, Tushnet observes that the Court, throughout "nearly
all of its history," has "developed constitutional law in ways that preserved
the status quo or obstructed change sought by political liberals." In *Brown*,
the Supreme Court placed itself squarely on the side of what was viewed
as social progress and in doing so "prodded all sorts of groups and individuals to cast their political claims in constitutional terms." The case
ushered in a "rights revolution" that, rightly or wrongly, encouraged citizens to see law and litigation as a means of achieving their political and
social aims. Tushnet emphasizes the contingent nature of the road to
Brown and its aftermath. It was the product of a well-planned and well-
executed strategy by a group of lawyers who brought the individual cases
that were eventually tried together under the name of *Brown*. Once the

case reached the Court, more strategy and planning were needed—this time among the justices—to engineer a unanimous vote that would serve as an opinion of law and an important social statement about the direction in which American society should head. Given the problems in implementing *Brown*, Tushnet suggests that the case's most lasting effect was cultural rather than specifically legal.

Howard Jones's essay draws the same conclusion about the *Amistad* case. Although the decision actually turned on recondite provisions of several international treaties on shipment of slave property, and the Africans who mutinied technically were not slaves, the case became a referendum on slavery as practiced in the American South. Jones notes that the captive Africans were, from the very beginning, thought of as slaves, "by both southerners and northerners . . . primarily because of their color." Jones argues that the New England supporters of the Africans successfully made the case a competition between the "natural rights" formulations of the Declaration of Independence and the "property rights in slavery guaranteed by the Due Process Clause of the Constitution." Former president John Quincy Adams argued that the only law that applied to the case was the Declaration, because the controversy at its heart was about the natural rights of all mankind. Although the decision to allow the Africans to return to their homeland was based on international law, Chief Justice Joseph Story's reference to "eternal principles of justice" indicates some acceptance of Adams's view. *Amistad*, like *Brown*, was an important cultural statement that reflected its historical period. In the eyes of many, the Supreme Court had struck a blow in favor of freedom over slavery in the very volatile years leading up to the Civil War.

If *Brown*, *Loving*, and *Amistad* show law operating as a force for progress and change, there are other moments when the law emerges as a blind enforcer of the status quo, justifying and tolerating the most heinous circumstances. What is most striking is how ordinary citizens, and those aspiring to be citizens, looked to the courts as the primary means of achieving their various goals. Xi Wang perceptively notes that *Dred Scott* was more than just a "failed devastating judicial decision" and considers the powerful story of the "enslaved Dred Scott and his wife, Harriet" who "persistently pursued their freedom." Wang highlights the agency of the Scotts, showing that they were keenly aware of how contemporary politics might aid their cause. Their suit for freedom was timed to take advantage of the atmosphere created by the looming contest between the North and South over slavery. In the end, however, it was the Supreme Court's own eye toward the brewing political controversy that killed the

Scotts' chances for freedom. Chief Justice Roger B. Taney's now infamous majority opinion in 1857, Wang says, "legalized slavery nationwide," sending both a legal and a cultural message, and was an early metaphorical "shot" at those who would end slavery before the first shots at Fort Sumter were fired.

The agency of disadvantaged individuals comes to the fore again in *Plessy v. Ferguson*. Thomas J. Davis introduces a fascinating group of citizens who engineered the legal confrontation that turned into *Plessy*. The *Comité des Citoyens* challenged Louisiana's system of Jim Crow public accommodations, but not because they were primarily interested in assuring that blacks and whites could ride on trains together. Instead, the *Comité*, which consisted of racially-mixed blacks who "rejected what they saw as the false dichotomy" between black and white, wanted to do away with the state's power to define an individual's racial identity. Well before the modern view of race as a social construct, members of the *Comité* knew, based on their own lives, that racial categories were fluid and had more to do with maintaining social power than anything else. At that moment in history, the Court was unable to accept this notion and insisted in 1896 that race "represented 'distinctions based upon physical differences.'" Accordingly, race was a fixed, immutable, and rational fact of life. It was, therefore, entirely reasonable for the law to take account of this reality.

Although the struggle between black and white preoccupies most of the discussions on race in the United States, other discrete minority groups have borne the brunt of the doctrine of white supremacy. Asian Americans, first Chinese and later Japanese, and other ethnic groups ran up against the wall of racial prejudice in the United States. Gabriel Chin tells us the story of Takuji Yamashita and his poignant and valiant struggle to become a practicing lawyer in Washington. Yamashita emigrated from Japan and became, he thought, a naturalized U.S. citizen in 1902. His application for a license to practice law was denied when the supreme court of Washington held that only "whites and persons of African descent were eligible to become naturalized" American citizens, and only naturalized American citizens were eligible to hold attorney's licenses in the state of Washington. In this instance, individuals who were adjudged neither white nor black were the most disadvantaged when it came to citizenship rights. Chin's essay ends with news of a much delayed and bittersweet recognition of the wrong that was done to a man who believed in the American system but was rendered a permanent alien from the country he loved on account of his race.

"All residents of this nation are kin some way by blood and culture to a foreign land. Yet they are primarily and necessarily a part of the new and distinct civilization of the United States. They must accordingly be treated at all times as the heirs of the American experiment and as entitled to all the rights and freedoms guaranteed by the Constitution." With those words, Justice Frank Murphy's 1944 dissenting opinion in *Korematsu v. United States* puts the predicament of Asian Americans in clear view. Although persons of African descent, however much reviled, had been settled on the American continent since 1565 and had developed a population that had grown into the millions, the majority of white Americans had little exposure to Asians. The nation was divided into three racial groups, based on appearance: white, black, and red. The addition of another group, with distinctive physical characteristics that separated them from black and white, threw confusion and fear into the mix. A popular television commercial in the 1980s showed that the confusion persisted. It presented two Olympic athletes, a Caucasian female and an Asian male. The female tries to make conversation in the halting and overly deliberate manner employed by people when they think someone they are talking to doesn't understand their language. She asks the young man if they have a particular brand of American coffee in his homeland. He responds, "In Spokane, Washington [Takuji Yamashita's home state]? Of course we do." The young white woman did not recognize her own countryman because he was a person of Asian descent.

In the 1940s, many Americans, including a majority of the Supreme Court, did not recognize their countrymen either. Approximately 11,000 Japanese Americans, presumed to be disloyal, were interned in camps along the West Coast. Roger Daniels's treatment of the Japanese internment cases shows the tenuous nature of life for visible minorities in times of national crisis. The *Korematsu* decision, which upheld the detention of U.S. citizens strictly on the basis of race, has long been recognized as one of the low points in modern Supreme Court jurisprudence. Although the government acted against citizens of German and Italian descent, the numbers interned were nowhere near the level of those of Asian descent. There is no question that the Japanese were seen as more "foreign," more "alien" because of their appearance and non-Western cultural background. That had been the basis of the Chinese exclusion laws passed in the second half of the nineteenth century. Tragically, the prejudice that Asians were incapable of being assimilated into U.S. society was still in place as late as the 1940s.

Finally, Howard Ball's essay on *Regents of the University of California v. Allan Bakke* is sure to be provocative. Affirmative action combines a recognition of past injustices to blacks with an attempt to redress those errors in modern times. It says, in effect, that we are inexorably tied to our past. Americans are said to have very short historical memories, which may account for at least some of the unease over the concept of affirmative action. Have whites today really benefited from the racial hierarchy on display in the cases discussed in *Race on Trial*? Has the legacy of the long-standing ideology of white supremacy affected blacks in ways that should influence public policy today? Ball apparently is not convinced of either proposition, and his investigation of the case from Allan Bakke's perspective sheds light on the view of whites who prefer not to be involved with social experiments designed to counteract the effects of America's racially charged past. The *Bakke* court's splintered opinion ultimately reaffirmed the concept of affirmative action, even as it gave opponents hope that ways might be fashioned to mount an effective attack on such programs in the future. By employing the notion of a color-blind society, critics of the concept suggest that we now live in a world where race does not and should not matter.

The cases explored in the essays that follow show how race in the United States is woven into the fabric of American life. They help explain where we have been, where we are now, and what our future might be. They explore how competing definitions of race and clashing concepts of citizenship have shaped our nation's history and will continue to leap into the headlines. Shifting definitions and battles over redefining race grab our attention whenever the legal system and popular culture rush headlong into one another. The trials discussed in this volume cover more than one hundred and fifty years of U.S. history. Many of the plaintiffs and defendants in these landmark cases knew that their court battles were not just for themselves, that they would help shape the contours of society for years to come.

As America continues to redefine itself, the issues raised in this book will prove instructive in telling us what to hope for and what we must, at all cost, struggle to avoid. Pausing to consider these pivotal and defining moments when race went on trial allows us to better discern the dimensions of race and justice and to better chart a course to discover who we are and who we want to become.

1

THE IMPACT OF THE *AMISTAD* CASE ON RACE AND LAW IN AMERICA

Howard Jones

The U.S. Supreme Court's March 1841 decision to free the black captives of the *Amistad* marks the only instance in history in which captured Africans brought to the New World won their freedom and returned to their homeland. Indeed, this series of events constituted the first civil rights case to reach the highest tribunal in the land. Although the ruling turned on a technicality, it had lasting importance because black people had testified in antebellum American courts and won their freedom on the basis of innate human rights. In accordance with the defense team's argument, Joseph Cinqué (whose name was Sengbe Pieh in his native Mende language) and his companions were "kidnapped Africans" who had the inherent right of self-defense in killing their captors and winning their liberty. The abolitionists had taken the lead in this case, highlighting the evils of the African slave trade and slavery itself in their effort to arouse national sentiment for emancipating all slaves. That the *Amistad* blacks went free allowed the abolitionists to herald the Court's decision as a triumph of freedom based on higher law and a major stroke against the racial discrimination that permeated the American legal system and underlay slavery and society in general.

The *Amistad* case only tangentially involved the issue of slavery, and yet that issue remained critical throughout the deliberations. The essence of the *Amistad* controversy lay in the timeless conflict between human rights and property rights, which grew into a struggle for civil rights that reached the Supreme Court. Without mentioning slavery, the advocates for the blacks argued for their rights as human beings and thereby posed a profound challenge to the peculiar institution by attacking the very basis of its existence: one group's use of color and race to justify the exploitation of another group. The *Amistad* decision for freedom ignored these man-made social barriers in administering a subtle but ultimately powerful blow to slavery.

The irony in the *Amistad* case is that even though the captives were never slaves, both southerners and northerners treated them as such, primarily because of their color. Every sentiment expressed, whether for or against these black people, arose within the context of slavery considerations, driving the abolitionists together while mobilizing the opposition to them and thereby thrusting the *Amistad* story into the mainstream of American history.

The chief determinant in the *Amistad* episode was the blacks' status on their arrival in the United States. If legally held slaves from Cuba, they had to be returned as property to their owners under Pinckney's Treaty of 1795. But if victims of the illegal African slave trade, they had entered the United States as free people, kidnapped in violation of both Portuguese law and the Anglo-Spanish treaties of 1817 and 1835. The captain and his cohorts aboard the Portuguese slave ship *Tecora* had therefore committed a crime in transporting more than 500 West Africans through the "middle passage" to Cuba. The illegal voyage continued with their clandestine, nighttime entry on the island, where Spanish officials customarily accepted payoffs rather than enforce the prohibitions against importing captured Africans.

Once in Cuba, a strange metamorphosis occurred: because slavery itself was legal, in practical terms the *Tecora*'s captives became "slaves" indigenous to the island. The Spanish Crown had recently decreed that children born of slaves after 1820 would be free; but the law, like the Anglo-Spanish stipulations against the African slave trade, proved unenforceable. The mixed commission assigned the task of suppressing the illegal practice was hamstrung by the law itself: its members lacked jurisdiction over blacks who reached the island and could only make decisions affecting those Africans confiscated and held on board anti–slave-trade patrol vessels. In the case of the *Amistad*, the slave dealers smuggled their cargo through the jungles and into Havana, where they stored the blacks in oblong and often roofless enclosures known as barracoons, used as sleeping quarters at night and auction blocks by day. Late in June 1839, two Spanish dons, Pedro Montes and José Ruiz, purchased fifty-three of the captives at $450 apiece, including Sengbe Pieh and four children under eleven years of age (three of them girls), and chartered the *Amistad* to transport them to two plantations near Puerto Principe, located 300 miles away from Havana on the northern part of the island.

An examination of this initial stage of the story reveals a string of illegalities. The Portuguese ship captain had violated both his government's laws and the two Anglo-Spanish treaties against the African slave trade in purchasing the blacks and transporting them to Cuba. That he did so in the stealth of night further confirmed his illegal actions. The Spanish officials' refusal to enforce the laws against the entry of this illegal cargo onto the island placed them in virtual complicity with the Portuguese. And, finally, those Cuban officials running the auction, as well as the two Spaniards who bought the fifty-three blacks, could not claim ignorance of their being native Africans, since at least four were too young to have been born before 1820 and could not have been slaves. But Montes and Ruiz were seasoned slave dealers who masqueraded the newly purchased blacks as slaves native to Cuba by altering their names on the ownership papers. Each African (most of them Mende) received a new Spanish name that they could neither pronounce nor recognize. Sengbe Pieh, for example, became Joseph Cinquéz until the z gradually faded from the name to become Cinqué.

Early on the morning of July 1, 1839, Cinqué led a rebellion on the *Amistad* as it was en route to Puerto Principe. The blacks killed the cook and captain in the melee, and two sailors jumped overboard and drowned in the twenty miles of water that separated the ship from shore. The mutineers later testified that they had killed the cook after his boast that the blacks' captors intended to cannibalize the Africans. The captain, they explained, had killed one of the blacks, which unleashed a frenzy that led to his death by strangulation. The blacks spared the lives of the two Spaniards, ordering them to navigate the vessel to Africa.

During the day, Montes and Ruiz complied with Cinqué's orders by sailing into the sun, but at night they shifted the vessel's direction northward until, more than sixty days later, it anchored off Long Island, New York, in August 1839. While Cinqué and others foraged for provisions on land, Lieutenant Richard W. Meade of the U.S.S. *Washington* spotted them. Thinking them pirates, he alerted his commanding officer, Lieutenant Thomas R. Gedney, who ordered the capture of the forty-three surviving blacks, the vessel, and its cargo and prepared to tow his cache into an admiralty court, where it might grant him salvage or prize rights (and hence a monetary reward) on the property he had seized.

From the moment the *Amistad* blacks reached America, the violations of law mounted rapidly. Their voyage out of Havana and toward the plantations in northern Cuba was illegal, of course, because it marked a continuation of the original voyage on the *Tecora* out of Africa. But once the blacks rebelled and seized control of the *Amistad*, they changed the entire situation by initiating a new and lawful voyage aimed at returning home to Africa. They were in command of their own destiny—and hence *not* slaves—on their arrival in the United States. They controlled the vessel and held the two Spaniards in captivity. They were engaged in no illegal activity ashore when seen by Meade. And yet, because Cinqué and the others were black and appeared to be pirates, Gedney felt justified in seizing the ship, cargo, and alleged slaves. Cinqué and those with him amassed some resistance but quickly surrendered to the well-armed Americans. His only concerns mercenary, Meade showed no interest in how the ship and cargo had gotten to this place. Had he taken his captives into the free state of New York, they would have been legally viewed as human beings and not subject to salvage law. He instead took them to nearby New London, Connecticut, a state in which slavery was still legal.

Had it not been for the abolitionists led by Lewis Tappan, the *Amistad* story would have ended quietly in admiralty court proceedings, with Gedney and his colleagues sharing the salvage award and the court returning the *Amistad*, its captives, and the remaining contents in the hold to their so-called owners. But Tappan, a wealthy New York businessman and evangelical Christian who openly advocated racial amalgamation, considered the *Amistad*'s arrival a "Providential occurrence" that would unite the abolitionists in their righteous cause.[1] Neither gradual emancipation nor compensation to owners was acceptable to these abolitionists, who believed slavery a sin. Many Americans dismissed this fringe group as wild-eyed radicals who were ready to ignore the law and upend society rather than permit the existence of an institution that only they considered to be a moral wrong in need of instant correction. Although numerous Americans were moderately antislavery, they rejected the abolitionists' call for an immediate end to slavery and the recognition of racial equality. Tappan intended to use the *Amistad* captives to draw attention to the great impasse between natural law (higher law) and positive law (man-made law). The natural rights doctrine of freedom ensured in the Declaration of Independence stood in stark contrast with the property rights in slavery guaranteed by the Due Process Clause of the Constitution. How could a self-professed republic support both liberty and slavery?

Tappan joined forces with Joshua Leavitt, an attorney and the editor of the *Emancipator*, and Simeon Jocelyn, minister of New Haven's first racially integrated church, in forming the "*Amistad* Committee," which in turn organized the legal defense team for the captives. At its heart was Roger S. Baldwin, a Connecticut attorney already renowned as a visionary, humanitarian, and abolitionist who was willing to work for little or no wages in the name of righteousness. He and his colleagues, Seth Staples and Theodore Sedgwick, decided to argue for the blacks' freedom as "kidnapped Africans" who had an inherent right of self-defense in winning their freedom from unlawful captivity—even if that meant killing their captors.

Baldwin first sought a writ of habeas corpus, which would force the Spaniards to charge the blacks with piracy and murder and thereby incur the obligation to produce justification for accusing them of a crime; failing that, the court would set them free. Court compliance with Baldwin's request, the abolitionists believed, would constitute tacit admission to the blacks' existence as human beings and not property in slaves. Baldwin could then use the court proceedings to expose the inhumanities of the slave trade and slavery itself while raising moral issues stemming from the natural rights exalted in the Declaration of Independence. As one abolitionist put it, the central question in the case was "whether an African [was] a *man*, and of course entitled to all the rights of humanity."[2]

At this point, however, the case became even more complex. Ruiz and Montes brought suit for the return of their property, and authorities in New Haven kept the blacks in jail, to await a decision of the grand jury of the U.S. Circuit Court on the Spaniards' property claims and whether or not the evidence was sufficient for the blacks to stand trial for murder and piracy. In the meantime, Gedney filed a libel suit for salvage of the *Amistad* and its cargo, including the blacks. He and his men, argued the suit, deserved compensation for their "meritorious service" in saving the Spaniards' property from total loss. Soon afterward, the Spanish government appealed to the reciprocity provisions in Pinckney's Treaty of 1795, which stipulated the return of one signatory's merchandise entering a port of the other for reasons beyond control. More important, the Spanish minister in Washington eventually declared that the U.S. government must return the blacks as "assassins," so they could stand trial in Cuba for piracy and murder. Compliance with this demand, the abolitionists warned, would lead to a "judicial massacre."[3]

Politics, as usual, was no stranger to these diplomatic and legal issues. President Martin Van Buren sought reelection in the fast approaching campaign of 1840 as candidate for a Democratic party comprised of a shaky coalition of northerners and southerners. He knew that he could maintain party unity only by steering clear of any matter relating to slavery and that whatever stand he took on the *Amistad* issue could cost him his office. He therefore chose to comply with the Spanish government's demands and return the blacks to Cuba. According to the Constitution, his spokespersons blandly pointed out, treaties were part of the supreme law of the land and therefore took precedence over all other issues. Van Buren's position is more understandable when seen in light of the danger posed by Britain to America's long-standing interests in Cuba. If evidence showed that Spain had flaunted its treaties with England against the African slave trade, the London government would gain a pretext for intervening in Cuba.

When circuit court proceedings opened in the state capital of Hartford, the presiding judge, Associate Justice Smith Thompson of the U.S. Supreme Court, at first seemed inclined to favor the argument of the defense. Baldwin appealed for the blacks' freedom on the basis of their free status on arrival in the United States, rather than the color of their skin, and requested asylum for them in the United States. Thompson appeared to agree. He first ruled that Connecticut lacked jurisdiction in the case because Gedney had captured the vessel and cargo in New York and the alleged murders and piracy had taken place "on board a Spanish vessel, with a Spanish crew and commander." The so-called evidence was too weak to justify a grand jury indictment, which meant that the captives would not stand trial on capital charges. But the momentary sense of victory proved to be just that when Judge Thompson rejected the defense's request for a writ of habeas corpus. Although Thompson personally found slavery morally repugnant, he recognized that it was approved by law and that granting such a writ would constitute an admission to the blacks' status as free people, entitled to equal justice. As he put it, justice emanated only from the law, "however painful it might be." Although the case appeared to focus on slavery, he asserted, the court refused to make a decision on the "abstract right of holding human beings in bondage."[4] He denied the writ and ruled that a suit would have to be filed in the district court to determine whether or not the blacks were Spanish property.

The issuance of a writ of habeas corpus would have had enormous ramifications, as Thompson surely recognized. Approval of a writ would have necessitated the blacks' immediate release without resolving the question of whether they were slaves and would have given them status as human beings endowed with a divine right of liberty that they could protect by any means. Such a decision, of course, would have encouraged American slaves to break their bonds as a moral right, as well as offered an invitation to enslaved blacks anywhere in the world to rebel and expect asylum in the United States. By implication, even when the laws of a land condoned slavery, the higher law of morality would have taken precedence in condemning the institution. In the realm of diplomacy, the United States would have taken the tenuous position of offering freedom to a group of rebellious blacks that had arrived on its shores, while at the same time it criticized the British practice of freeing slaves in the Caribbean who had made it there after escaping from America. Furthermore, the liberation of the *Amistad* captives would have provided ample public notification of Spanish violations of their anti–slave-trade treaties with the British government, which could then have intervened in Cuba and threatened not only Spanish interests but those of the United States as well.

And yet, Thompson's refusal to issue a writ did not mark a total defeat for the abolitionists. He had adhered to the law, while sending a shrewd signal to Tappan and others that the only way to end slavery was to work within the legal system in changing that law. The widespread publicity accorded the case had made many Americans aware of the sordid nature of the slave trade and of slavery itself. The abolitionists had succeeded in exposing the hypocrisy of a self-professed republic that advocated both liberty and slavery. If they had not completely awakened the national conscience, they had led more Americans to ponder the morality of human bondage and, in that sense, inched the nation a bit closer toward the end of slavery.

On appeal by defense, the case went before the district court, which also sat in Connecticut and whose presiding judge was Andrew Judson. The prospects for success looked grim. Judson was an avowed racist who had fought openly for white supremacy. But he was also a realist and an ambitious politician. Many people in Connecticut had developed an affinity for the black captives, visiting them in their quarters or watching them exercise daily on the New Haven Green, and had come to see them as human beings who posed no threat to society. And yet, Judson also realized that the White House expected a friendly decision, which meant a speedy return of the blacks to Cuba in accordance with Pinckney's Treaty. The Van Buren administration was so confident of the outcome that it stationed a naval vessel in New Haven waters, ready to transport the blacks back to Cuba *before* they could exercise their constitutional right of appeal.

Judson was on a political tightrope and, appropriately, made a political decision. The abolitionists had made it difficult to ignore the truth about the *Amistad* blacks' origins and simply comply with the wishes of the White House. The defense team had located a native of Sierra Leone who spoke Mende and was on a British naval vessel docked in New York.

James Covey, a former slave, secured his captain's permission to appear in court and translate the captives' story into English. The most poignant moment came when Cinqué described the middle passage and demonstrated the horrors of a slave ship by crouching on the floor as if shackled in chains. Judson was convinced that the captives were from Africa. He first affirmed the right of the district court to handle the case by ruling that Gedney had seized the *Amistad* on the high seas and was entitled to salvage. But then, after a pause that allowed observers to note his drawn and pale demeanor, Judson shocked everyone by declaring the blacks to be native Africans, kidnapped from their homeland and entitled to win freedom by whatever means necessary. Salvage rights did not extend to the blacks. Judson then muddled the case by citing an 1819 law that authorized the president to return slaves who had illegally entered the United States to their homeland. This decision clearly contradicted Judson's initial statement that the blacks were kidnapped Africans; they had never been slaves and hence did not fit this law. For the moment, however, this problem escaped observers on both sides of the issue. By freeing the captives, Judson hoped to satisfy his peers; and by ordering the blacks' return to Africa, he sought to relieve the president of having to make a decision.

But Judson's political maneuverings succeeded only in infuriating the Van Buren administration and keeping the case alive. The president's son expressed its bitter reaction when he irately denounced Judson's failure to recognize the political implications of the case. The White House appealed the case to the Circuit Court, where Judge Thompson again presided and refused to dismiss the appeal because, he declared, the central question involved both the American and Spanish governments. "I say again, as I have said a hundred times, that however repugnant slavery may be, sitting here as a Judge, I must recognize that the laws of this country do admit the right of property in men."[5] The case then went to the final arbiter in the land, the U.S. Supreme Court, where Chief Justice Roger B. Taney presided over eight justices, the majority of whom had owned or presently owned slaves.

Although the abolitionists' chances for victory were not good in early 1841, they had made great strides in legal history. Blacks had testified on their own behalf, helping to establish their civil and legal rights as human beings. To underscore this point, Tappan and his supporters had worked with the blacks to bring kidnapping charges against Ruiz and Montes, both of whom fled the United States rather than appear in court. But the abolitionists made their biggest advance in human rights by winning a hearing by the U.S. Supreme Court. In the first civil rights case to go before that august body, they intended to argue for the universal, divine right of freedom, regardless of race, color, creed—or law.

The appointed hour before the U.S. Supreme Court became a symbolic battle between presidents when the abolitionists secured the legal services of John Quincy Adams, former president and current congressman from Massachusetts. Seventy-three years of age, almost deaf, and absent from the courtroom for three decades, Adams only reluctantly accepted the invitation. He had a well-deserved reputation as a crotchety, maverick politician who had many times in his career broken party loyalties by supporting a cause that he thought was just—most notably, fundamental liberties. He was not an abolitionist, but he hated slavery. More important, his image was that of an unyielding proponent of morality and ethics. No less significant, Adams had privately advised the blacks' defense team in the early stages of the case and was well aware of the issues. Baldwin had done a magnificent job in court, but he lacked the national stature of Adams and graciously surrendered the lead to the former president, known as "Old Man Eloquent."

Adams delivered an eight-and-a-half-hour argument that stretched over two days and ranged over a number of sometimes extraneous topics. He launched a major attack on the president for interfering in the case and denounced every instance of slavery throughout history as the product of sheer force, before calling for the freedom of the *Amistad* captives on the basis of the higher law found in the Declaration of Independence. All the surviving blacks were on trial for piracy or murder, with the exception of the four youths considered incapable of such crimes, he argued; and yet, they had all been held captive for eighteen months because of the "utter injustice" of the executive branch of the U.S. government operating in collusion with the Spanish government in Madrid. The White House had not dispensed justice, Adams indignantly proclaimed; it had wrongfully considered Montes and Ruiz the only two aggrieved parties. "The sympathy of the Executive government, and as it were of the nation, in favor of the slave-traders, and against these poor, unfortunate, helpless, tongueless, defenceless Africans, was the cause and foundation and motive of all these proceedings."[6]

The case, Adams asserted, was an anomaly in that no law was applicable to it—except the Declaration of Independence, which asserted that every man was "endowed by his Creator with certain inalienable rights" and that "among these are life, liberty, and the pursuit of happiness."[7] He dismissed the Spanish minister's call for the captives' return on the grounds that Meade and Gedney had no right to board the *Amistad* because the Africans were in control of the vessel in peacetime and were, by international law, entitled to hospitality from the host country. Adams asked the Court to dismiss the appeal on the basis of the U.S. government's acting in error. Gedney had no legal right to seize the blacks in New York or to take them to Connecticut. The U.S. government then compounded its infractions of the blacks' rights by insisting that the American legal system lacked jurisdiction because their offense had taken place on a foreign vessel. The only acceptable procedure, according to the White House, was to adhere with treaty stipulations and return the captives to the Spanish government. Again, Adams argued, this claim had no basis in law.

Adams also used the floor of the Supreme Court to counter the angry protests made by southerners, insisting that the case had no bearing on the South. "It is a question of slavery and freedom between foreigners; of the lawfulness or unlawfulness of the African slave trade; and has not . . . the remotest connection with the interests of the southern states."[8] Those who claimed otherwise, Adams asserted, sought to arouse sentiment between the sections in an effort to pressure the Court to refrain from suppressing the African slave trade.

Technically, Adams was correct in denying any relevant connection between the *Amistad* case and the South's concern over slavery. The captives were, according to their defense attorneys, kidnapped Africans, never slaves, and appealed for their freedom on these grounds. But slavery was by no means a separate and distinct matter. By discussing the incompatibility of slavery with the life and liberty emphasized in the Declaration of Independence, Adams had belied his own claim that slavery was not an issue. Although Adams disclaimed any interest in joining the abolitionists, his argument justified any people's revolt for freedom when illegally held and was therefore as dangerous to proponents of slavery as those presented by the abolitionists.

The Supreme Court associate justice assigned to the case, Joseph Story, agreed with the defense and, with the concurrence of all but one of his colleagues (who offered no explanation for his dissent), freed the blacks as "kidnapped Africans." Story refused to explore Adams's charges against Van Buren, probably because the evidence proved more circumstantial than conclusive, but he readily dismissed the administration's claim that the courts had no right to examine the ship's papers for authenticity. The papers, Story declared, were fraudulent—meaning that the captives had been held in violation of the law and therefore had an inherent right to use any means necessary to escape. He overturned Judson's decision authorizing the president to return the blacks to Africa, since the congressional act of 1819 referred only to slaves entering the United States, and the *Amistad* blacks were never slaves. Most important, Story referred to the "eternal principles of justice" in declaring the inherent right of self-defense against illegal captivity.[9]

Despite the Supreme Court's decision to free the *Amistad* blacks, problems remained in securing their return to Africa. Some observers thought that damages were due for the captives' eighteen months of incarceration. Adams and Baldwin conceded that they had no legitimate grievance on this point, since the courts had adhered to the legal process in rendering their decisions. Adams sought equity in the form of the U.S. government's financing the blacks' voyage home, but President John Tyler, a Virginia slaveholder, refused on the basis of Story's ruling that the 1819 law did not provide authorization to do so. The freed blacks spent the next eight months following the Supreme Court decision in Farmington, Connecticut, where abolitionists helped them secure lodging and work and raised funds for transportation home through exhibitions and public displays. Church groups—both black and white—helped fund a vessel to carry the Africans across the Atlantic. In January 1842, after an absence of nearly three years, the thirty-five surviving *Amistad* captives returned home to Africa.

The legacy of their experience in America remains clear. The *Amistad* case exposed the contradictions between morality and the law and helped to build pressure for revoking the statutes protecting slavery. Blacks and whites had worked together throughout the ordeal, demonstrating the value of cooperation in matters involving both race and law. And the black captives had gone free, signaling a victory for the American legal system. Furthermore, the *Amistad* decision contributed to the public's growing knowledge of the slave trade and slavery, thereby helping to lay the basis for the abolition of slavery by the Thirteenth Amendment more than two decades later. The *Amistad* case also brought focus to the central issue of human decency toward fellow human beings, reminding many Americans of the need to regard all people as equal, regardless of color or race. Those white Americans who visited the *Amistad* captives came away with the feeling that, at least in the case of these blacks, there was a common bond of humanity that crossed the arbitrary lines of distinction drawn by man. The abolitionists took advantage of this fleeting moment by hailing the captives' freedom in every available public forum.

So many times in history the perception of truth is more important than the reality. Even though the *Amistad* case resulted in no immediate legal changes, it freed the blacks and left the public impression that the American judicial system had dealt a severe blow to slavery by exalting the sanctity of freedom. The *Amistad* captives actually went free on a strictly legal basis: their incarceration had been a distinct violation of Portuguese law and the Anglo-Spanish treaties against the African slave trade. Indeed, the Supreme Court made clear that their status as "kidnapped Africans" effectively removed the slavery issue from the case. But the perception remained that the decision rested on moral principles and constituted a landmark ruling against slavery. Black people had brought suit on behalf of their rights as human beings and, whether on the basis of law or morality, went free. Story had (inadvertently?) furnished the abolitionists with justification for claiming a victory over slavery when he declared the captives free on the basis of the "eternal principles of justice." If they found equality before the courts, the momentum would develop for their achieving the same status outside the courts. Once people of color could claim equal protection under the law, they would predictably use their civil rights victory to help undermine the institution of slavery.

NOTES

1. Tappan, quoted in Howard Jones, *Mutiny on the* Amistad: *The Saga of a Slave Revolt and Its Impact on American Abolition, Law, and Diplomacy*, rev. ed. (New York: Oxford University Press, 1997), 81.

2. Ibid., 64.

3. Ibid., 30, 160, 161, 168.

4. Ibid., 71, 74, 76.

5. Thompson, quoted in the *New York Commercial Advertiser*, 2 May 1840.

6. John Quincy Adams, *Argument of John Quincy Adams, before the Supreme Court of the United States, in the Case of the United States, Appellants, vs. Cinque, and Others, Africans, Captured in the Schooner* Amistad, *by Lieut. Gedney* (New York: Benedict, 1841), 4, 6–7.

7. Ibid., 88.

8. Ibid., 87.

9. Quoted in Jones, *Mutiny on the* Amistad, 191.

2

THE *DRED SCOTT* CASE

Xi Wang

On the morning of Friday, March 6, 1857, a large crowd gathered in the chamber of the Supreme Court of the United States, anxiously waiting for the delivery of the Court's decision on the *Dred Scott v. John F. A. Sandford* case. Just two days earlier, the new president, James Buchanan, in his inaugural address, had assured the nation that the imminent Court decision would "speedily and finally" settle the issue of slavery in territories that deeply divided the nation.[1] The justices appeared, led by the 79-year-old chief justice, Roger B. Taney, who would be speaking for the Court. Taney's voice was barely audible, but when he finished reading the 55-page opinion of the Court, the attentive audience had unmistakably captured three important points. First, Dred Scott, the slave from St. Louis, Missouri, who had initiated the suit for freedom for himself and his family some eleven years earlier, would continue to remain the property of his alleged owner, John F. A. Sanford.[2] Second, no person of African descent, whether being free or in bondage, could ever be considered a citizen of the United States. Third, the Missouri Compromise of 1820, a federal law that had prohibited slavery from the unorganized territories of the Louisiana Purchase (1803), was unconstitutional because the right to own slave property was guaranteed by the Constitution.[3]

There was little doubt that all nine of the justices sitting on the bench—five southerners and four northerners—sensed the gravity of the case since each of them submitted an opinion. The six justices who joined Taney in the majority opinion perhaps had hoped that the decision would settle the slavery issue once and for all. Few of them, however, predicted that, instead of depleting the intense sectional hostilities, their decision would push the nation to the verge of a bloody civil war. None, perhaps, had foreseen that their decision would be reversed by the Civil War and the subsequent constitutional revolution within just a decade.

Because of its intimate connections to the Civil War, the most tragic ordeal endured by the nation during the nineteenth century, the *Dred Scott* decision has been one of the most intensively studied Supreme Court decisions. For some, it was a classical example of the abuse of judicial power by a politically minded Court majority that attempted to impose its sectionalism over nationalism. For others, it was an unfortunate mistake by the Court to apply a judicially faithful interpretation of the Constitution to a vastly changed political circumstance. Still for others, it demonstrated the inevitable fatality of the pre–Civil War constitutionalism characterized by an innate ambiguity over the issues of freedom and slavery.[4] But the *Dred Scott* case was not merely about a failed and devastating judicial decision. Its implications went far beyond the confinement of jurisprudential theory and practice. As revealed by modern scholarship, the *Dred Scott* case was a larger and more profound story about how the enslaved Dred Scott and his wife, Harriet, persistently pursued their freedom under extraordinarily difficult circumstances. It was a story about the determination and perseverance with which the Scotts and their abolitionist supporters had struggled to advocate freedom over slavery as the nation experienced its vigorous geographic expansion. Finally, it was a story about how a different group of Americans tried to employ the badly politicized constitutional mechanisms to define the intriguing relationship between race, slavery, and the political boundaries of the American nation.[5]

This chapter explores the history of the *Dred Scott* case with a focus on the centrality of race in the process. It examines a number of issues, including: How did the case evolve? Why did Dred Scott decide to initiate a suit for freedom after being a slave for forty-some years? How was it possible for him, who could neither read nor write, to pursue the litigation over such an extended period to the highest court in the land? Who were Dred Scott's advocates? And, more important, how were the case and its decision related to the political upheavals of the 1850s and how did the case transform from a simple lawsuit for freedom into a devastating catalyst for the Civil War?

Although Dred Scott is considered the most famous litigant known in American constitutional history, his true identity is not completely known. Like many other victims of slavery, Dred Scott had been deprived of not only his rights as a human being but also of his history. Only after his case made national news in 1857 was Dred Scott noticed by contemporary newspapers and weeklies, which described him as a person of "very dark skin" and modest statute. A St. Louis newspaper portrayed him as a man with a "strong common sense," "illiterate but not ignorant."[6] But his contemporaries, as well as modern scholars, were not able to find any reliable record to ascertain the accurate information about Dred Scott's birth and early life. All historians can say is that he was born in Virginia of slave parents sometime around 1800 and was originally owned by Peter Blow, a Virginia planter.[7] When Dred Scott became a slave for the Blow family is unknown, but his association with the family must have been a long one, since in 1857 Dred Scott referred to the children of Peter Blow as "them boys" with whom he had been "raised."[8] The Blow family first moved to Alabama before relocating in 1830 to Missouri, the only slave state that was allowed by the Missouri Compromise of 1820, which excluded slavery from the Louisiana Purchase land north of latitude 36°30'. Dred Scott was one of six slaves that had accompanied the Blow family when it finally settled in St. Louis. Sometime during 1833, Scott was sold to John Emerson, a physician residing in the city. It was unclear who sold Scott to Emerson since Peter Blow himself died in 1832 and left his estate (including his slaves) to his two daughters and two sons.

A native of Pennsylvania, Emerson was about the same age as Dred Scott. He had studied medicine at the University of Pennsylvania and had been seeking an appointment in the U.S. Army since he settled in St. Louis in 1831. Two years later, Emerson received his commission as an assistant surgeon in the army and was ordered to report for duty at Fort Armstrong in Illinois, which was situated on an island in the Mississippi River some three hundred miles north of St. Louis. As a practice permitted for military officers at that time, Emerson purchased Scott to be his body servant. Illinois had been organized from the Old Northwest Territory (which encompassed the present states of Ohio, Indiana, Illinois, Michigan, Wisconsin, and the eastern portion of Minnesota), and its constitution of 1818, following the antislavery provision of the Northwest Ordinance of 1787 (originally enacted by the Confederation Congress and reenacted by the U.S. Congress in 1789), prohibited slavery within its boundaries. Thus, when Emerson and Dred Scott arrived at Fort Armstrong as master and slave on December 1, 1833, Emerson's ownership of Scott was voided under the Illinois law.

Soon after he arrived at Fort Armstrong, Emerson began to file a series of requests for transfer or leave of absence because of a "syphiloid disease." In 1836, he received his transfer order, not to St. Louis, as he had wished, but to Fort Snelling, which was located on the west bank of the upper Mississippi River near what is now St. Paul, Minnesota. Originally part of Wisconsin Territory and, after 1838, Iowa Territory, the region lay within the non-slaveholding boundaries of the Louisiana Purchase as defined by the Missouri Compromise. Shortly before Emerson and Scott departed for Fort Snelling, Congress created the Wisconsin Territory (which encompassed most of the present-day states of Wisconsin, Minnesota, and Iowa) by enacting the Wisconsin Enabling Act, which reaffirmed the antislavery restrictions of the Northwest Ordinance of 1787. Thus, when Emerson took Dred Scott to Fort Snelling in 1836, he brought slavery into an area where slavery had been explicitly forbidden by at least three congressional laws. By then, he had held Scott as a slave in Illinois, a free state, for more than two years.

Emerson found life at Fort Snelling equally miserable, and before long he requested a leave of absence to escape the irritability of cold weather and the nuisance of rheumatism. For Dred Scott, however, Fort Snelling was a major turning point in his life. Soon after arriving, Scott met Harriet Robinson, a slave girl of perhaps half his age owned by Lawrence Taliaferro, the resident American Indian agent and the largest slaveowner in the vicinity. It is unclear whether Taliaferro sold Harriet to Emerson or gave her to Dred for a wife, but the two slaves were allowed to marry shortly after meeting. As local justice of the peace, Taliaferro himself performed the ceremony uniting Dred and Harriet, adding a legal recognition of the Scotts' marriage, which later became a focal point for the Scotts' lawyers to argue for their freedom. The Scotts remained married until Dred Scott's death more than two decades later.[9]

Between October 1837 and October 1838, Emerson made two moves, first to Jefferson Barracks in St. Louis and then to Fort Jesup in western Louisiana. Instead of taking Dred and Harriet with him, Emerson left them at Fort Snelling and hired them out to officers there as he had done since the couple's marriage. At Fort Jesup, Emerson met and married Eliza Irene Sanford, a young woman from St. Louis. After the marriage, Emerson sent for Dred and Harriet, supposedly to use them as house servants for his newly established family. But barely had the Scotts, who traveled alone, arrived in Louisiana when Emerson received a transfer order to return to Fort Snelling. The Emersons and their slaves quickly began the passage on the steamboat *Gypsey* to Fort Snelling via St. Louis. On the trip from St. Louis to Fort Snelling, Harriet gave birth to a girl named Eliza. The child was born on the river far above the northern boundary of Missouri and well into free territory.

After another two years at Fort Snelling, Emerson was ordered to go to Florida, where the army was fighting against the Seminole Indians. Irene Emerson did not accompany her husband and instead went to live on her father's estate, a large farm with slave labor, near St. Louis. The Scotts remained with Irene Emerson and may have been used as slave labor by her father. For Dred Scott, returning to St. Louis in 1840 ended his seven-year sojourn in free territory. He would never set foot on free soil again.

After two difficult years in Florida, Emerson was discharged from the army and returned to St. Louis. In the spring of 1843, he moved to Davenport, Iowa Territory, hoping to start a private medical clinic there. But before year's end, he died of consumption, leaving behind his young widow and a one-month-old daughter.[10] In his will, Emerson left everything to his wife but made no mention of Dred and Harriet. He named his wife's brother, John F. A. Sanford, a businessman who traveled between St. Louis and New York, an executor of his will, although Sanford was never involved in executing the will. Irene Emerson sold off some of the land that she inherited, but she kept Dred and Harriet as slaves, using them as workers on her father's farm or hiring them out for wages. At one time, Dred was used by Irene Emerson's brother-in-law, a military officer, who took him as far as Texas. When Dred Scott returned, he attempted to buy freedom for himself and his family from Irene Emerson, but she refused.[11] According to Dred Scott, this happened right before he and his wife initiated their suits for freedom.[12]

On Monday, April 6, 1846, Dred and Harriet Scott submitted two separate petitions, respectively signed with an "X," via their lawyer, Francis B. Murdoch, to the St. Louis Circuit Court. In the petitions, the Scotts, believing that they were "entitled to" freedom under the facts of their sojourns, asked the court to allow them to sue and to establish their "right to freedom."[13] The court granted their request for the "leave to sue," following the similar petitions filed previously in the court.

Why did Dred and Harriet decide to institute a suit for their freedom at this time? This question has triggered several plausible speculations.[14] First, the Scotts' action might have been a response to Irene Emerson's treatment of them after her husband's death, which might have ended their hope for eventual freedom that the Scotts might have been promised. Second, the Blow family, which from the beginning of the suit provided financial aid for the Scotts, might have encouraged them to sue for freedom since Dred Scott had reconnected with the family after his sojourn in free territories. Third, Scott himself by this time could have conceived the idea of gaining freedom on the basis of extensive travels and experience in the free territory, and his growing family (his second daughter, Lizzie, was born around the time the suit began) certainly made gaining autonomy more urgent. Fourth, the Scotts might have learned about the way of gaining freedom from the black communities in St. Louis.[15] The last speculation is particularly powerful because Harriet, who filed her suit individually because slave marriage was not recognized, was a member of the Second African Baptist Church, founded by Reverend John Anderson in February 1846. Anderson was born a slave but later purchased his freedom and became a typesetter for Elijah P. Lovejoy, an antislavery editor in Alton, Illinois. No solid evidence has been found to support any of these speculations, but there is little doubt that by this time the Scotts had discovered that they could gain freedom through the courts.

In hindsight, the timing of the suits could not be more coincidental as the development of national politics was concerned. The Scotts filed the suits for freedom about a month before the beginning of the war with Mexico, a subsequent event following the U.S. annexation of Texas in 1845. The undoubted prospect of winning the war prompted northerners in Congress to propose in August 1846 the so-called "Wilmot Proviso" (named after David Wilmot of Pennsylvania, who introduced the proposal), which banned slavery in all the territories that the United States might acquire as a result of the war. The Wilmot Proviso, which was killed in the southern-dominated Senate, revived sectional disputes over the issue of slavery in the territory and helped initialize such northern antislavery efforts as the Free Soil Movement, which was later incorporated into the Republican party before the final decision was made on the *Dred Scott* case.

But in 1846, the *Scott* cases were inconsequential. In fact, the freedom suits submitted by Dred and Harriet Scott were not so unusual in the Missouri courts. A few years after Missouri became a state, the Missouri Supreme Court, in *Winny v. Whitesides* (1824), freed a slave who had been taken to Illinois. In the following thirteen years, the Missouri courts heard about ten similar cases, always deciding in favor of the slave litigants. Missouri, according to legal historian Paul Finkelman, was "one of most liberal states in the nation on this question."[16] The earlier Missouri rulings were based on the legal theory, first articulated in the English case of *Somerset v. Stewart* (1772), that the status of a "slave" was so contrary to the common law and natural law that it could only be supported by specific positive legislation. The *Somerset* ruling, which granted freedom to a slave who was taken into England and demanded freedom, thus set the precedent that when a master took a slave into a jurisdiction that lacked laws establishing slavery, the slave reverted to his natural status as a free person. Once he gained the status of a free person, he remained free. The "once free, always free" principle was, however, compromised later by another English case, the *Slave, Grace* (1827), by which the English High Court ruled that once a slave returned to a slave jurisdiction then the law of England would no longer be in force and his status would once again be determined by the laws of the slaver jurisdiction.[17] The Missouri courts, however, had generally ignored the *Grace* ruling, at least during the time when the Scotts filed their suits.

On June 30, 1847, *Dred Scott v. Irene Emerson* was tried in the Circuit Court of St. Louis County, and Scott was represented by Samuel M. Bay, who took over the Scotts' cases from Charles D. Drake, who had earlier replaced Murdoch. After the testimonies of a score of witnesses, including Henry Taylor Blow (the son of Peter Blow), the Scotts' employers at Fort Snelling, and Samuel Russell (the Scotts' employer in St. Louis right before they filed the suits), Scott lost the case because his lawyer failed to present a key witness who would prove that Irene Emerson was Scott's owner. Scott's lawyer quickly asked for a new trial, which was granted by the Missouri Supreme Court over Irene Emerson's rejection.

At the second trial, held on January 12, 1850, Scott's lawyers, Alexander P. Field and David Hall (who took over the case in 1848), used the same reasoning their predecessor Bay had used in the first trial, that is, under the Ordinance of 1787 and the Missouri Compromise, Scott's residence in Illinois and Wisconsin Territory effectuated his freedom. This time, the lawyers presented a key witness who testified to Irene Emerson's ownership of Dred Scott. Following the circuit court judge's instruction that if the jurors determined Dred Scott had in fact lived in a free state or territory they should find him free, the jury awarded Dred Scott his freedom. Irene Emerson refused to accept the decision and appealed to the Missouri Supreme Court on February 14, 1850.

It was two years before the Missouri Supreme Court announced its decision. During this interval, the two individual Scott cases were combined under the name *Scott v. Emerson*. Irene Emerson left for Massachusetts where, in November 1850, she married Calvin Clifford Chaffee, a Springfield physician who held antislavery beliefs and later became a Republican congressman. John F. A. Sanford, Irene Emerson's brother, began to act on her behalf in defending the case. Dred and Harriet Scott and their two daughters were put in the custody of the St. Louis County sheriff to be hired out for wages. The wages earned by the Scotts would be held by the sheriff and later distributed to those who, after the litigation was over, won the suit.

In the meantime, national and state politics experienced some drastic changes that would affect the Missouri Supreme Court's decision. At the national level, Congress once again deadlocked over the issue of whether slavery should be allowed in the territory acquired as a result of the Mexican War, which ended in 1848. Only after extensive political negotiations did Congress accept the Compromise of 1850, which admitted California as a free state, left the question of slavery in the newly created Utah and New Mexico territories to be determined by popular sovereignty (decision of the residents), ended the slave trade in Washington, D.C., and enacted a tougher fugitive slave law. Neither the North nor the South was completely satisfied with the compromise, which served only as a temporary solution to the increasingly tense sectional strife. Responding to national political developments, proslavery forces in the Missouri state legislature elected Henry S. Geyer (who later was one of Sanford's lawyers before the U.S. Supreme Court) to the U.S. Senate to replace Thomas Hart Benton, the state's representative in the Senate for more than thirty years. Benton owned slaves but refused to endorse the extreme sectionalism advocated by South Carolina senator John C. Calhoun.

Reflecting the changes of political mood in the state and the nation, the Missouri Supreme Court decision, announced on March 22, 1852, reversed the lower court and declared that Scott was still a slave. Completely ignoring its earlier decision on *Winny v. Whitesides* in which the court ruled that residence by a slave in free territory entitled that slave to freedom upon return to Missouri, Justice William Scott rendered a number of new principles: (1) every state has the right to determine the scope of application of its comity (which means the respect for the law of other states); (2) a state cannot take away the property of its own citizen by the command of other states' law; and (3) slavery was a godly business to place uncivilized Negroes "within the pale of civilized nations." Justice Scott made no attempt to hide how much the recent national politics over slavery—the Compromise of 1850 and intensified sectional hostilities—had justified the reversal of the court's stance. Since "a dark and fell spirit in relation to slavery" had come and meant to bring "the overthrow and destruction of our Government," he stated, the state must "assume her full responsibility for the existence of slavery within her limits."[18]

The Scotts had lost not only their nearly six-year-old fight for freedom but also their lawyers. David Hall died in 1851, and Alexander P. Field left for Louisiana. But the Scotts and their supporters did not give up their hopes. Roswell M. Field, the Scotts' new lawyer, tried a different avenue to revive the Scotts' freedom suits. Field, a native of Vermont who was strongly antislavery, took up the case possibly because of persuasion from

Charles Edmund LaBeaume, a brother-in-law of Peter Blow's sons and also a lawyer, who had joined the Blow family in shouldering the legal cost for the Scotts in the previous trials. Believing that the Missouri Supreme Court was wrong to disregard all legal precedents, Field hoped to win freedom for the Scotts by obtaining an opinion from the federal courts.[19]

On November 2, 1853, the now-famous case of *Dred Scott v. John F. A. Sanford* was filed in the Circuit Court of the United States in the District of Missouri. Sanford, a resident of New York, was named as the defendant mainly because he, instead of Irene Emerson Chaffee, now owned the Scotts, though historians later pointed out that no document could be found to demonstrate the transfer of ownership from Irene Emerson. Dred and Harriet Scott and their daughters, all covered in the federal case under Dred Scott's last name, asked for $9,000 in damages instead of $10 as originally demanded in the state case.[20] Six months later, Sanford responded with a plea in abatement, in other words, a request asking the court to stop the case. Since Scott, as a descendant of slaves of "pure African blood," was not a citizen in Missouri and therefore had no right to sue, argued Sanford, the court had no jurisdiction over the case and should throw it out of court.[21] Dismissing Sanford's plea, U.S. Circuit Court judge Robert W. Wells upheld Dred Scott's right to sue by saying that "every person born in the United States and capable of holding property was a citizen having the right to sue" in federal courts.[22] Wells consciously avoided addressing the issue of whether a black person was entitled to full citizenship under the Constitution, but his ruling heightened the issue of citizenship for blacks, which had not been addressed during the previous trials.

The optimism generated from Judge Wells's decision, if there was any, was short lived. When the case came to trial on May 15, 1854, Wells instructed the jury to decide the case on the basis that "the law is with the defendant" since, as he explained, Scott had not been declared free by the Illinois court and, under the circumstances, Missouri's law would prevail. Wells derived his rationale from the Supreme Court's ruling in *Strader v. Graham* (1851), which declared that a slave living in a free state would be reversed to slavery once he voluntarily returned to a slaveholding state. In other words, for a slave who had lived in a free territory or state, his status as a freeman was only temporary, while his status as a slave was permanent and unchangeable once he left the free territories. The jury accordingly returned the verdict in Sanford's favor.[23] As expected, Scott's lawyer, Field, took the case to the U.S. Supreme Court.

In the meantime, Field and Scott's advocates began to look for stronger legal, financial, and public opinion support for the case. As part of that endeavor, Scott's supporters selected July 4, 1854, as the date to release a twelve-page pamphlet, signed by Dred Scott with an "X," to appeal for public assistance for "a poor black man and his family." In telling the story of his life and the earlier trials, Dred Scott launched a politically loaded attack on the irrationality of the law dividing slavery and freedom in federal territories. Once blacks crossed the border into slaveholding Missouri, "My right to be free was gone; and that I and my wife and my children became nothing but so many pieces of property." Scott pleaded to the public for support:

> I have no money to pay anybody at Washington to speak for me. My fellow-men, can any of you help me in my day of trial? Will nobody speak for me at Washington, even without hope of other reward than the blessings of a poor black man and his family? I do not know. I can only pray that some good hear [*sic*] will be moved by pity to do that for me which I cannot do for myself; and that if the right is on my side it may be so declared by the high court to which I have appealed.[24]

By the end of the year, Montgomery Blair, a Washington-based lawyer who had practiced in St. Louis, accepted Field's invitation to join the counsel for Dred Scott. Additionally, Gamaliel Bailey, editor of the antislavery newspaper *National Era*, agreed to underwrite some of the court costs. Meanwhile, Sanford retained Missouri's proslavery U.S. senator, Henry S. Geyer, and, most impressively, Reverdy Johnson, a close friend of Chief Justice Roger B. Taney and one of the nation's most distinguished constitutional lawyers.

The case of *Dred Scott v. John F. A. Sandford* was filed in the Supreme Court on December 30, 1854, but due to the overload of the Court dockets, the first oral argument was not ordered until February 1856. Political developments during the intervening period fundamentally redefined the historical position of the case. In January 1854, Illinois senator Stephen Douglas, who chaired the Committee on Territories, proposed to replace the Missouri Compromise with popular sovereignty to determine the issue of slavery in the newly created Kansas and Nebraska territories, both being part of the original Louisiana Purchase and located north and west of Missouri. The Kansas-Nebraska Act, which Congress passed on May 22, 1854 (one week after the *Dred Scott* trial took place in the federal circuit court), opened areas north of latitude 36°30′ where, for more than thirty-five years, slavery had been prohibited by the Missouri Compromise. Fearing that slavery would legally spread into all of the unorganized federal

territories, northern states organized anti-Nebraska protests that eventually led to the formation of the Republican party, the first major political
party demanding the termination of further spread of slavery in the name
of freedom. Against this political backdrop, the *Dred Scott* case suddenly
assumed particular importance. After 1856, Dred Scott became a familiar
name to Americans who followed national events.

During the first oral argument before the Supreme Court, which took
place from February 11 to 14, 1856, Scott's lawyers focused on the citizenship question, insisting that the Scotts' residence in free territories and
state qualified him to be a citizen of the United States. Montgomery Blair
argued that since free blacks were permitted to hold property and carry
commerce under the U.S. laws, "they must be embraced in a class of
citizens." Sanford's lawyers, however, almost ignored the citizenship question and focused instead on the constitutionality of the Missouri Compromise, subtly shifting the gravitation of the *Dred Scott* case from the
Scotts' claim for freedom to the present political controversies.[25] After
arguments were heard, the Court voted to postpone the decision and
ordered a reargument for December of that year. Although some justices
claimed that the goal of the postponement was to keep the case out of
the 1856 presidential race, the Republicans (for instance, Abraham Lincoln) later suggested later that such a move was a deliberate conspiracy
to overturn the Missouri Compromise. Although James Buchanan, the
Democratic candidate who carried the election with the promise to re-
store peace in civil war–ridden Kansas, carefully avoided the issue of
slavery, the deep-seated sectionalism continued to drive the nation apart.
On his part, the outgoing president, Franklin Pierce, openly denied Congress the power to restrict slavery in the territories and pointed to the
Supreme Court as the final arbitrator on the matter.[26]

Emerging from the two oral arguments were a number of issues for the
Court to decide, including (1) was the plea in abatement before the Court
(in other words, did the Court have jurisdiction over the case?); (2) could
Dred Scott, a "Negro of the African race," be a citizen of the Untied States?;
(3) did Congress have the power to prohibit slavery in the territories (or,
was the Missouri Compromise constitutional)?; and (4) was Missouri ob-
ligated to recognize Dred Scott's freedom based on his residence in either
Illinois or the Wisconsin Territory?

Dred Scott's lawyers' main objective was to win freedom for Dred Scott
and his family. Blair even invited George Ticknor Curtis, a high-powered
Boston lawyer and brother of Justice George Rabbins Curtis, to join the
Scotts' team during the second oral argument. But the make-up of the

Court was quite discouraging. Of the nine justices on the High Court, five—James M. Wayne of Georgia, John Catron of Tennessee, Peter V. Daniel of Virginia, John A. Campbell of Alabama, and Chief Justice Roger B. Taney of Maryland—came from slave states, and five of them came from slaveholding families, although Taney and Wayne no longer personally owned slaves. The southern justices were Democrats and die-hard supporters of slavery (Campbell resigned his seat in 1861 to serve the Confederate government as assistant secretary of war). Chief Justice Taney was not only a firm supporter of the right to own slaves but also a foe of racial equality. As Andrew Jackson's attorney general in 1831, Taney had argued that blacks, "even when free," were a "degraded class" that would only receive privileges as a result of "kindness and benevolence rather than right."[27] The remaining four justices—John McLean of Ohio, Robert C. Grier of Pennsylvania, Samuel Nelson of New York, and Benjamin R. Curtis of Massachusetts—were northerners. Grier and Nelson, both Democrats, did not want to give Dred Scott freedom or deal with the status of slaves in free territories. Thus, the seven Democrats—five southerners and two northern doughfaces (that is, northerners who did not oppose slavery)— made up a clear majority. Although Curtis was not a Democrat, he had earlier defended the right of a master to bring a slave into Massachusetts in a state court case and supported the constitutionality of the Fugitive Slave Act of 1850. Only McLean openly opposed slavery.

The Court did not have to decide all of the issues before it and could have avoided a decision that would involve any current political issues. One way to do so was to dismiss the appeal for lack of jurisdiction, basing it on the ruling of *Strader v. Graham* (1851), in which the Court held that, with the exception of runaway slaves who had to be returned to their owners, every state had complete authority to decide for itself the status of all people within its borders. In this way, the Court could simply reaffirm an established principle and decide the case with little controversy. Initially leaning to that direction, it instructed Nelson to draft an opinion that was to serve as the "Opinion of the Court." Nelson indeed dealt very narrowly with the case by simply upholding the lower court ruling that Scott had "reverted" to slavery under Missouri law.

But, during the month of February 1857, the "bitter sectionalism" of Chief Justice Taney, according to historian Don Fehrenbacher, shifted the course of history. Urged on by his southern colleagues on the bench and President-elect James Buchanan, who wanted a Court ruling on the constitutionality of the Missouri Compromise, Taney decided to write a comprehensive opinion that would address all the issues before the Court. He and the southern clique believed that the proslavery majority on the bench could eventually settle the issue of slavery in the territories that had virtually crippled the legislative and executive branches of the government.

As a result, Taney's opinion, as delivered on March 6, 1857, was not only a thorough proslavery manifesto but also an ambitious attempt to redefine the nature of American nationhood. Given the political situation and his personal views on slavery, Taney's discussion of the issue of slavery in territories was expected, but what was unexpected was that he devoted the bulk of the opinion to Dred Scott's claim of citizenship, which was considered by some justices not even legitimately before the Court. But for Taney, this question was equally, if not more, important as the territorial question. His purpose, as revealed by his opinion, was to offer a racialized definition of U.S. citizenship that would permanently exclude blacks regardless of their status.

Taney used the plea in abatement to establish the connection to the citizenship question and then raised a question:

> Can a Negro, whose ancestors were imported into this country, and sold as slaves, become a member of the political community formed and brought into existence by the Constitution of the United States, and as such become entitled to all the rights, and privileges, and immunities, guarantied by that instrument to the citizens?[28]

Taney's answer to the question was no. To reason his answer, Taney developed his own theory of federal citizenship. In his view, citizenship was established when the Constitution was adopted, but at that time, "the civilized and enlightened portions of the world" regarded Africans as being "an inferior order" and "so far inferior" that "they had no rights which the white man was bound to respect." It was considered "for his benefits," Taney reasoned, for an African to "justly and lawfully" be reduced to slavery. The idea that "all men are created equal," according to Taney, never meant to embrace "the enslaved African race," whose rights "were not even in the minds of the framers of the Constitution."[29]

Taney recognized the power of the states to confer citizenship but insisted that state citizenship could not automatically be converted into federal citizenship. Only Congress could confer federal citizenship after the Constitution was established, Taney stressed, but the laws passed by Congress after the adoption of the Constitution—such as the naturalization law of 1790—never intended to include blacks into the body of citizens. The heart of Taney's ruling on this question was not simply to deny slaves any opportunity for citizenship, but to deny people of African descent—whether born free or having gained freedom through emancipation or other means—the chance to become U.S. citizens. Such a denial would prevent free blacks from claiming the protections of the Fifth Amendment, which were not limited to U.S. citizens. Thus, from the perspective of citizenship, Taney ruled that, since Dred Scott was not a citizen of Missouri "within the meaning of the Constitution," he was not entitled to sue in the federal court and the case should have been dismissed by the lower court for lack of jurisdiction.[30]

In addressing the territorial issue, Taney reversed the order of Dred Scott's travels in the free territories and first dealt with his residence in Fort Snelling, so that he could invalidate the Missouri Compromise with a full-fledged assault. He first dismissed as irrelevant the constitutional provision that empowered Congress to "make all needful rules and regulations" for the federal territories and argued that since the federal government was a union founded by "sovereign and independent within their own limits in their internal and domestic concerns," Congress could not "legislate without restriction" in its governance of the territories.[31] Most important of such restrictions was placed within the Fifth Amendment, which specifically prohibited Congress from depriving any person of life, liberty, and property without due process of law. To support his argument that the Constitution had "distinctly and expressly affirmed" the right of property in a slave, Taney cited the two provisions from the Constitution: the slave trade clause (which allowed the continuation of importing slaves from Africa for twenty years after the Constitution was adopted) and the fugitive slave clause (which required that all fugitive slaves be returned to their owners). The Constitution, in Taney's view, gave Congress no other power over slavery except "the power coupled with the duty of guarding and protecting" the rights of the owner to own slaves. Well aware of the abolitionist rhetoric about universal freedom and the humanity of blacks, Taney mindfully warned that "laws or usages of other nations, or reasoning of statesmen or jurists upon the relations of master and slave" could be used to "enlarge the powers of the Government" to "take from the citizens the rights they have reserved."[32] Thus the Missouri Compromise, a federal law that deprived a U.S. citizen of his liberty or property "merely because he came himself or brought his property into a particular Territory of the United States," was "not warranted by the Constitution." Thus, "neither Dred Scott himself, nor any of his family, were made free by being carried into this territory" under this law.[33]

After ruling on Scott's residence at Fort Snelling, Taney quickly dismissed Dred Scott's claim for freedom on the grounds that he had lived in Illinois, a free state. Using his own opinion in *Strader v. Graham* (1851), Taney ruled that Scott's status would be determined by "the laws of Missouri" once Scott returned to Missouri.[34]

Taney received full support from Justice Wayne, who wrote a short concurring opinion, and Justice Daniel, who further argued that emancipation could not make a slave a citizen because the conferring of citizenship was an act of sovereignty that no slave owner or other individual could perform.[35] Upholding Taney's ruling on the grounds of reversion and reattachment, Justice Catron differed from the chief justice on the question of congressional power to govern territories, even though he believed that such power did not by default include the power to prohibit slavery. On the unconstitutionality of the Missouri Compromise, Catron went even further than Taney by arguing that the act had denied citizens of all the states "an entire equality of rights" on the Louisiana Purchase land which, in his view, was a common property of all the states.[36]

Taney's other supporters were the two northern Democrats. Justice Nelson, who originally had been designated to write the Court opinion, had avoided the two major issues that Taney had addressed—black citizenship and the constitutionality of the Missouri Compromise. He simply used the *Strader v. Graham* ruling to deny Scott's claim to freedom. Congress possessed no power to regulate or abolish slavery within the states. Grier, who wrote the shortest opinion, supported Taney's ruling on the plea in abatement and Nelson's denial of Dred Scott's freedom.[37]

Of the two dissenting justices, McLean's opinion was openly antislavery. He argued that slavery was strictly a state or local institution that received no national or constitutional sanction. In this line of reasoning, he believed that the right of Dred Scott to sue was not even legitimately before the Court because slavery could only be established through positive law. An active Republican, McLean made no effort to hide his political opinion. Using the *Somerset* principle, he argued that Dred Scott became free when his master took him to Illinois and Wisconsin. Once he became free, he was free forever. But McLean's most important pronouncement was his progressive interpretation of the American Revolution, which opened a new epoch of freedom in human history, an ear devoid of prejudicial European views on race.[38]

Justice Curtis's opinion, sixteen pages longer than Taney's majority opinion, challenged Taney's ruling on black citizenship. In Curtis's view, federal citizenship originated under the Confederation government, which left the issue entirely in the hands of the states, and was synonymous with state citizenship by that time. Since free blacks in five states (New Hampshire, Massachusetts, New York, New Jersey, and North Carolina) were recognized as citizens of their respective states under the Confederation government, they were therefore also the citizens of the United States when the Constitution was adopted in 1789. Rejecting as erroneous Taney's usage of African ancestry and slave background to deny blacks citizenship, Curtis declared that he found "nothing in the Constitution" that defined citizenship or intended to take it away from "any class of persons who were citizens of the United States at the time of its adoption."[39] As to Dred Scott's freedom, Curtis used quite a different perspective by arguing that the antislavery laws of the federal government could be applied to Emerson when he, as military personnel, took Scott to Fort Snelling "in a public capacity in the service of the same sovereignty that made laws." In Curtis's view, both Emerson's consent of Dred Scott's marriage to Harriet and the inaction of the Missouri courts to invalidate the Scotts' marriage when they returned to Missouri (which did not recognize slave marriage) consisted of a de facto "act of emancipation."[40] On the territorial question, Curtis argued that Congress was empowered to govern the territories and possessed the power to prohibit, but not to protect, slavery. Rejecting the principle of reattachment, Curtis concluded that the lower court's ruling be reversed and a new trial ordered.

The repercussions of the *Dred Scott* ruling were beyond anyone's imagination. The reactions toward the decision were sharply divided by geopolitical lines. Northern Republicans and abolitionists interpreted the Court decision as a green light to the nationalization of slavery and a part of the conspiracy of "Slave Power." The *New York Independent* critiqued Taney's ruling on Negro citizenship as based on "a deliberate falsification of the Constitution and of history."[41] The *New York Tribune* called the Court ruling a denial of "the rights of Human Nature" that "know no distinction founded on this difference of origin and color."[42] The South welcomed the decision not as merely a triumph of southern politics but ironically as a triumph of nationalism. The decision, according to the *Charleston Mercury*, put "our claim to equality of privilege" in the Union.[43]

Taney, who was known as an advocate of states' rights, had used the nation's highest tribunal to legalize slavery nationwide. For northern Republicans, this very bold move demonstrated how the national government could be used to transform a sectional institution and the ideology behind it into a national institution and ideology. If the Court could declare slavery a constitutionally sanctioned institution in the territories, the institution could also be declared unconstitutional or illegitimate. The key was to control the branches of the federal government from which such decisions are made. In this sense, the *Dred Scott* decision intensified not only the sectional dispute over slavery but also powerfully pushed the Republican party to fight more vigorously to capture the national leadership. More perceptive than most, black abolitionist Frederick Douglass grasped the real implication of the *Scott* decision. Separating the Constitution from "its administration," Douglass argued that the Constitution "knows all the human inhabitants of this country as 'the people'" and makes "no discrimination in favor of, or against, any class of the people . . . without reference to color, size, or any physical peculiarities;" thus, the Constitution could be used to support the abolitionists' cause for liberty. He called on northern voters to exercise their voting power to force a new interpretation of the Constitution and promised that "when this is done, the wounds of my bleeding people will be healed . . . [and] the glorious birthright of our common humanity, will become the inheritance of all the inhabitants of this highly favored country."[44]

The legitimacy of the *Dred Scott* decision became the most important subject in the 1858 Illinois senatorial race between Stephen Douglas, the author of the Kansas-Nebraska Act, and Abraham Lincoln, the most profound mind of the Republican party. While Douglas tried to dismiss the impact of the decision by saying that local laws could ignore the protection of slave property, Lincoln believed that the decision had actually forced the nation to choose between slavery and freedom—not only to vindicate the freedom that had existed in the nation's past, but to preserve it as the nation's future, because "this government cannot endure, permanently half slave and half free."[45]

Lincoln lost the senatorial race, but his opposition to the *Dred Scott* decision and advocacy for freedom provided a powerful ideological language that critically united the Republican party in winning the presidential election of 1860. Viewing Lincoln's election and Republican control of Congress as the fatal blows to the institution of slavery, the South seceded from the Union. Only after four years of bloodshed in the battlefield, which claimed the lives of 620,000 Americans, was the question of slavery finally settled. The Thirteenth Amendment, ratified in 1865, permanently abolished slavery throughout the United States. Three years later, the Fourteenth Amendment for the first time conferred U.S. citizenship on "all the persons who were born or naturalized in the United States." The Fifteenth Amendment, ratified in 1870, conferred voting rights on the newly freed black males. These three amendments thus eradicated Taney's decisions on the original intent of the Constitution, black citizenship, and the legality of slavery and established the foundation of what Lincoln called "a new birth of freedom" for the nation.

Dred Scott did not live to see the Civil War and the enactment of the new constitutional order. Nor did Sanford, his alleged owner, who died as an inmate in an asylum in New York City two months after Taney's decision. Soon after the decision, the identity of Irene Emerson (now Mrs. Irene Chaffee) as the true owner of the Scotts was revealed. Her secret was a devastating embarrassment for her husband, Calvin C. Chaffee, an avowed abolitionist and U.S. congressman from Springfield, Massachusetts. Finding it impossible for them to continue to keep the Scotts as slaves, Calvin Chaffee arranged to transfer the Scotts to Taylor Blow (the son of Scott's original owner, Peter Blow). The Chaffees, however, still collected all the wages that the Scotts earned during these years. On May 26, 1857, Dred and Harriet Scott appeared in the Circuit Court of St. Louis County with Taylor Blow, who formally freed them. On September 17, 1858, fifteen months after he was freed, Dred Scott died of tuberculosis in St. Louis. Harriet died shortly thereafter.

For nearly a century, Dred Scott's grave in Section 1, Lot No. 177, of Calvary Cemetery in St. Louis remained unmarked and unnoticed. Not until 1957 was a new tombstone erected. On one side of the tombstone, it is inscribed:

> DRED SCOTT
> BORN ABOUT 1799
> DIED SEPT 17, 1858
> Freed from slavery by
> His friend Taylor Blow

And on the other side:

> DRED SCOTT
> SUBJECT OF THE DECISION OF
> THE SUPREME COURT OF THE
> UNITED STATES IN 1857 WHICH
> DENIED CITIZENSHIP TO THE
> NEGRO, VOIDED THE MISSOURI
> COMPROMISE ACT, BECAME
> ONE OF THE EVENTS THAT
> RESULTED IN THE CIVIL WAR[46]

NOTES

1. James Buchanan, Inaugural Address, 4 March 1857, in vol. 4 of *A Compilation of the Messages and Papers of the Presidents*, ed. James D. Richardson (New York: Bureau of National Literature, 1897), 2962.

2. The correct spelling of the defendant's name is "John F. A. Sanford," and the misspelling of his name in the official Supreme Court report was never corrected by the Court.

3. *Dred Scott v. John F. A. Sandford*, 60 U.S. (Howard 19) 393 (1856). Hereafter cited as *DSvS*.

4. For representation of these traditional discussions, see John Lowell and Horace Gray, *A Legal Review of the Case of Dred Scott, as Decided by the Supreme Court of the United States* (Boston: Crosby, Nichols, 1857); George Ticknor Curtis, *Constitutional History of the United States* (New York: Harper & Brothers, 1896); James Ford Rhodes, *History of the United States from the Compromise of 1850*, vol. 2 (New York: Harper & Brothers, 1892); Edward S. Corwin, "The *Dred Scott* Decision, in the Light of Contemporary Legal Doctrines," *American Historical Review* 17 (1911): 52–69; and Horace H. Hagan, "The *Dred Scott* Decision," *Georgetown Law Journal* 15 (1926): 95–114.

5. For the authoritative modern account of the *Dred Scott* case, see Don E. Fehrenbacher, *The* Dred Scott *Case: Its Significance in American Law and Politics* (New York: Oxford University Press, 1978). Other valuable studies include Walter Ehrlich, *They Have No Rights: Dred Scott's Struggle for Freedom* (Westport, Conn.: Greenwood, 1979); Kenneth C. Kaufman, *Dred Scott's Advocate: Biography of Roswell M. Field* (Columbia: University of Missouri Press, 1996); and Paul Finkelman, Dred Scott v. Sandford: *A Brief History with Documents* (Boston: Bedford, 1997).

6. *St. Louis Daily Evening News*, 3 April 1857; quoted in Fehrenbacher, Dred Scott *Case*, 240, and Ehrlich, *They Have No Rights*, 182–83.

7. Historians estimate Dred Scott's birth date from 1795 to 1809. The most solid evidence on this was found in an 1818 property tax record, which listed Scott as being "over sixteen years old." But historians concur that there is no agreed-upon birth date of Dred Scott, which perhaps explains why his tombstone marked his date of birth as "Born about 1799." Paul McStallworth, "Scott, Dred," in *Dictionary of American Negro Biography*, ed. Rayford W. Logan and Michael R. Winston (New York: Norton, 1982), 548; Ehrlich, *They Have No Rights*, 9, 185; Kaufman, *Dred Scott's Advocate*, 22, 2n; Finkelman, Dred Scott v. Sandford, 10.

8. Ehrlich, *They Have No Rights*, 11.

9. Of the four children born to them, two sons died in infancy but two daughters became parties in the suit for freedom in 1846.

10. Fehrenbacher, Dred Scott *Case*, 248.

11. Fehrenbacher, Dred Scott *Case*, 249–50; Kaufman, *Dred Scott's Advocate*, 118. Also see Ehrlich's question on Dred Scott's journey to Texas in *They Have No Rights*, 26–29.

12. According to Fehrenbacher, Dred Scott told a newspaper reporter many years later about this incident, but it was not confirmed by Irene Emerson, who refused to talk about the *Dred Scott* case for the remainder of her life. Fehrenbacher, Dred Scott *Case*, 250.

13. Petition of Harriet, a woman of color, dated 6 April 1846, to the Hon. John M. Krum, judge of the St. Louis Circuit Court; petition of Dred Scott, dated 6 April 1846, to the Hon. John M. Krum, judge of the St. Louis Circuit Court; *Dred Scott* Case Documents Exhibit, docs. #1 and #2 (University of Washington Libraries website: www.libraries.wsustl.edu/dredscott/, accessed 1 March 2001), originals in the Dred Scott Collection, Missouri Historical Society.

14. For extensive discussion of these speculations, see Fehrenbacher, Dred Scott *Case*, 251–53; Ehrlich, *They Have No Rights*, 35–27; and Kaufman, *Dred Scott's Advocate*, 136–41.

15. Kaufman, *Dred Scott's Advocate*, 145.

16. Ehrlich, *They Have No Rights*, 41–42; Finkelman, Dred Scott v. Sandford, 20.

17. *Somerset v. Stewart*, 1 Lofft 1 (King's Bench, June 1772); for discussion of this case, see William M. Wiecek, *The Sources of Antislavery Constitutionalism in America, 1760–1848* (Ithaca, N.Y.: Cornell University Press, 1978), 20–39; *The Slave, Grace*, 2 Hagg. Admir. (G.B.) 94 (1827).

18. *Scott v. Emerson*, Mo. 576 (1852), 586; also see Fehrenbacher, Dred Scott *Case*, 264–65; Finkelman, Dred Scott v. Sandford, 22–23.

19. Ehrlich also suggests that Field might have learned about the Scott case from Arba N. Crane, a young lawyer working in Field's office. Crane happened to meet and conversed with Dred Scott who, employed as a janitor, was cleaning up the office. This incident was recalled by Crane almost fifty years after the Scott decision and has not been firmly confirmed by other evidence. Ehrlich, *They Have No Rights*, 74–75.

20. Walter Ehrlich, "Was the *Dred Scott* Case Valid?" *Journal of American History* 55, no. 2 (September 1968): 256–65; Ehrlich, *They Have No Rights*, 82–83; Fehrenbacher, Dred Scott *Case*, 271, 276; Kaufman, *Dred Scott's Advocate*, 185–86.

21. Fehrenbacher, Dred Scott *Case*, 276; Kaufman, *Dred Scott's Advocate*, 186.

22. Law Record B., Circuit Court of the United States for the District of Missouri (1853–1854), ms., 273, 276; quoted in Ehrlich, *They Have No Rights*, 84.

23. Ehrlich, *They Have No Rights*, 85–87; Fehrenbacher, Dred Scott *Case*, 279.

24. The twelve-page Dred Scott pamphlet, originally kept in the Law School Library at the University of Missouri at Columbia, was reported missing, thus the only available source of the pamphlet is the quoted paragraphs of the pamphlet that are presented in a footnote in volume 13 of *American State Trials*, which contains detailed narratives and summaries of *Dred Scott* case–related trials, especially at the lower courts. "The Trial of the Action of Dred Scott (a Slave) against John F. A. Sanford for Flase Imprisonment and Assault, St. Louis, Missouri, 1854," in *American State Trials: A Collection of the Important and Interesting Criminal Trials Which Have Taken Place in the United States, from the Beginning of Our Government to the Present Day*, ed. John D. Lawson, vol. 13 (St. Louis: Thomas Law Book, 1921), 243–45, footnote 4; also see Fehrenbacher, Dred Scott *Case*, 280; Kaufman, *Dred Scott's Advocate*, 197.

25. Ehrlich, *They Have No Rights*, 91–97; Fehrenbacher, Dred Scott *Case*, 285–93; Kaufman, *Dred Scott's Advocate*, 203; Finkelman, Dred Scott v. Sandford, 27–28.

26. Franklin Pierce, Annual Message, 2 December 1856, in *Compilation of the Messages and Papers of the Presidents*, 6:2934.

27. Unpublished opinion of Attorney General Taney, quoted in Carl Brent Swisher, *Roger B. Taney* (New York: Macmillan, 1935), 154.

28. *DSvS*, 403.

29. *DSvS*, 405–7, 410–12.

30. *DSvS*, 419–20, 423, 427.

31. *DSvS*, 448.

32. *DSvS*, 451.

33. *DSvS*, 450, 451, 452.

34. *DSvS*, 452–53.

35. *DSvS*, 481–82. Daniel argued that state governments might bestow civil and political privileges upon anyone they chose, but "they could not add to or change in any respect the class of persons to whom alone the character of citizen of the United States appertained at the time of the adoption of the Federal Constitution." Since blacks in 1787 were not included in the social compact, Scott was not "politically a person" at all. Daniel's opinion, in spite of its reactionary nature, was later used to justify the enactment of the Fourteenth Amendment, which established not only federal citizenship via congressional power but also reversed the order of primacy of citizenships. Daniel went as far as to deny any fundamental difference between the Constitution and its predecessor, the Articles of Confederation, and argued that under the Constitution the federal government was "simply the agent or trustee for the United

States," which could not breach the trust of these individual states. *DSvS*, 489.

36. *DSvS*, 518–29.

37. *DSvS*, 457–65, 469.

38. *DSvS*, 529–64.

39. *DSvS*, 576.

40. *DSvS*, 598.

41. *New York Independent*, 19 March 1857.

42. Editorial, *New York Tribune*, 25 March 1857.

43. "The Dred Scott Case—Supreme Court on the Rights of the South," *Charleston (S.C.) Mercury*, 2 April 1857.

44. Frederick Douglass, "The *Dred Scott* Decision: An Address Delivered, in Part, in New York, New York, in May 1857," in *The Frederick Douglass Papers: Series One: Speeches, Debates, and Interviews, Volume 3: 1855–1863*, ed. John Blassingame and John R. McKivigan (New Haven, Conn.: Yale University Press, 1985), 163–83, esp. 177–83. (This pamphlet was an expanded version of Douglass's discussion of the *Dred Scott* decision in his speech delivered on 14 May 1857 in New York. For the original speech, see the same volume, 143–50.)

45. Abraham Lincoln, "A House Divided," speech at Springfield, Illinois, 16 June 1858, in *The Collected Works of Abraham Lincoln*, vol. 2, ed. Roy P. Basler (New Brunswick, N.J.: Rutgers University Press, 1953), 461.

46. Ehrlich, *They Have No Rights*, 185.

3

CELIA'S CASE

Annette Gordon-Reed

If one were to start, there would be no end to the horror stories that could be told about the nightmare of American slavery. Although the institution was a marked catastrophe for a people, the fundamentally tragic nature of slavery unfolded, in historian Walter Johnson's apt phrase, "soul by soul."[1] Each enslaved man, woman, and child could tell his or her own unique tale of suffering during a time when law, culture, economics, and religion—the pillars that sustain a society—worked in concert against the humanity of black people. For the most part, the stories of individuals who lived in bondage are lost from the historical record. That is why each story that has survived must be treated as the rare, and thus valuable, artifact that it is.

The story of Celia, a slave woman whose last name is unknown to us, is one such story. Celia escaped the anonymity of slavery in the manner of the downtrodden throughout the ages: she had an encounter (in her case, a fatal one) with the legal system. We know of Celia because she was a slave who did the one thing most feared by southern slaveowners: she resisted the terms of her enslavement by using deadly force. She killed her master after years of sexual abuse. The record of her trial, and the newspaper accounts based on it, tell us the details of Celia's short and brutish life.

Celia's case also speaks with devastating clarity about the way in which the law during the period of American slavery served as a blueprint for white supremacy, reflecting and refining the desires of southern whites. As Melton A. McLaurin has shown in his 1991 biography, *Celia: A Slave*, Celia's predicament provides the perfect vehicle for exploring the intersection of law, politics, culture, and sexual hierarchies in the antebellum period. Even the setting—Missouri—a state that played such a prominent role in the country's sectional disputes about slavery, serves as a dramatic backdrop for the events that shaped Celia's life and death.[2]

Most particularly, however, Celia's case highlights the special plight of enslaved black women, whose bodies were used for manual labor and for the sexual gratification of white men. For this reason, Celia can be seen as an archetype of the enslaved woman. But it is important to keep in mind that the real pain of Celia's life took place at an individual level. Behind every court case, despite whatever greater meaning the issues presented may have for society at large, is a story of the struggle of individual people. We must never forget the person behind the symbol. It is, after all, the humanity of Celia—this particular individual soul—that speaks to us across the years.

According to the two most comprehensive accounts of her life, Celia was approximately fourteen years old in 1850 when Robert Newsom, a farmer in Callaway County, Missouri, purchased her.[3] Newsom had done well at the business of farming, owning 800 acres of land, with a smaller portion of it under cultivation. He was a widower with four adult children, two daughters and two sons. In addition to Celia, Newsom owned five other slaves, all of them male.[4] Although we do not know the extent of Celia's possible contacts with enslaved people in the surrounding area, it is safe to say that she had no real female companionship at Newsom's farm. Neither Newsom's daughter Virginia, who lived at the farm with her children, nor his youngest daughter Mary, also in residence, could have fulfilled this role. Even had there not been a vast difference in their social positions, the role that Celia came to play in Robert Newsom's life likely would have precluded a truly close relationship between the three females. A picture emerges, then, of a young girl living in almost total isolation from either family members, who could have provided comfort, or from female friends who would have been capable of empathizing with her situation.

And what was Celia's situation? She lived under the power of Robert Newsom, who had raped her on the way home after he had purchased her. From the very first day, it was clear that Newsom viewed Celia, in McLaurin's phrase, as "his property and his concubine."[5] In truth, Celia's role as concubine cannot be properly separated from her role as an item of Robert Newsom's property—a fact that ultimately determined the outcome of Celia's fate in the Missouri legal system.

It should come as no surprise that those who felt entitled to use human beings as items of capital for their economic gratification would also view the use of their human property for sexual gratification as part and parcel of their rights as owners. A central tenet of the Western system of property rights, to which Newsom certainly would have subscribed, is that property exists to be put to whatever use the owner chooses, so long as a given use does not interfere with another property owner's use and enjoyment of his or her property. The right can only be curbed in furtherance of some extremely important public policy goal.

There actually was an enunciated policy goal that one would think might have had some bearing on Celia's circumstances. The racial dimensions of American slavery complicated Newsom's and other male slaver owners' perceptions about their property-based right to be involved sexually with their female slaves. Despite its prevalence, southern society professed extreme disdain for sex across the color line, which suggests that there should have been a strong interest in placing some limits on the use of slaves as sexual objects. But, interestingly, these limits were to be achieved by the soft push of social opprobrium rather than through positive laws that could exact any serious punishment. Deterrence, apparently, was never really a serious option. If one wanted to engage in interracial sex and maintain one's position in society, discretion was all that was required.

By the time Celia arrived in Newsom's household in 1850, the issue of southern white men's abuse of slave women was a point of vulnerability in the great debate about slavery. Thomas R. R. Cobb, a noted southern apologist for slavery, was sensitive to the points that the abolitionists had scored on the question of the misuse of enslaved women. He suggested that perhaps one day an enlightened legislature should provide some degree of protection for black women by punishing their rapists.[6] But his proposed remedy never was adopted. The rape of a slave woman was considered a trespass against the master's property. As it is impossible to trespass upon one's own property, there was no conceptual framework within traditional property law to justify a limit on this particular exercise of a property right. To date, there is no recorded instance of a white man, master or otherwise, being punished for raping a slave woman.[7]

Celia endured Newsom's abuse for five years, during which she bore two children, with whom she lived in a cabin that Newsom built for her not far from the main house. At some point, exercising a degree of autonomy, Celia became involved with another of Newsom's slaves, a man named George. The community on Newsom's farm was quite small. George had actually moved in with Celia for a time. So he must have known of Celia's situation when he began his relationship with her. Not surprisingly, George resented Celia's involvement with Newsom and at some point demanded that Celia cease having sexual relations with her master.[8]

George's hostile reaction to the sexual contact between Celia and Newsom is understandable. He was attempting to build a life with her. Just as Celia's powerlessness in the face of Newsom's depredations makes her life symbolic, George's position, as lover/husband unable to protect his loved one, is symbolic as well. Of the many psychological cruelties of slavery, the inability of parents to protect children, of husbands and wives to protect one another, must have been one of the most profound.

Still, under the circumstances, it is difficult to understand why George thought that his demand was tenable. How exactly was Celia to make the break with Newsom? Newsom owned her, and the facts of their interactions (his initial rape of Celia and the building of the special house for her) suggest that Newsom fully intended for the relationship to last as long as he wanted under his own terms. Recorded instances of slave women successfully resisting overtures from masters exist, but these "successes" would have depended on the personality of the individual man. Was Newsom the type of person to retreat in the face of resistance or was he not? Nothing in the record suggests that he was the type to retreat. In fact, the events surrounding his death suggest the very opposite.

Despite the reality of her circumstances, Celia took George's concerns very seriously and began to take steps to extricate herself from the relationship with Newsom. There is evidence that she spoke with one of Newsom's daughters about the matter, although no record exists of what the daughter did or did not do in response to Celia's entreaties.[9] Only one person could end Celia's torment peacefully—Robert Newsom himself. In June 1855, Celia, pregnant again and ill, told him not to come to her cabin for sex anymore.

Defiant, Newsom determined to exercise his rights as a property owner. Celia suspected trouble and prepared to defend herself with a large stick. When Newsom arrived that evening, Celia resisted his advances. During the altercation, Celia struck him with the stick. The first blow merely injured (and no doubt surprised) Newsom. When he continued to come toward her, she struck him again in the head. The second blow, according to Celia, killed him.

What Celia did next reveals the extent of her desperation and raises some question as to whether or not her description of the events of that evening was completely truthful. After waiting a while, she decided that her only option was to burn Newsom's body in her fireplace. She built a fire large enough for this purpose and spent the rest of the night reducing Newsom's corpse to ashes. When the body finished burning, Celia removed and hid the remaining bones. She disposed of some of the ashes herself during the night. When morning came, in an act that was stunning in its coolness and that "revealed the depth of her hatred for Newsom and his kin,"[10] Celia asked Newsom's grandson to help her remove ashes from her hearth. The boy gathered up the remains of his grandfather's body and deposited them some distance from Celia's cabin.

Later in the day, Newsom's family became concerned when they could not find him. His children, aided by local neighbors, conducted a search. As time passed, they probably began to fear the worst and decided to find out if anyone else might know of Newsom's whereabouts. The first person they spoke to was Celia's companion, George. During the course of the interrogation, George implicated Celia. The search party then went to Celia's home and questioned her about Newsom.

After first denying that she knew anything about Newsom's disappearance, Celia eventually confessed to killing him and detailed how she had disposed of the body. Upon learning of their father's fate, Newsom's children gathered up the remains of their father to prepare for the legal proceedings that would follow.[11]

The progress of Celia's case through Missouri's legal system shows how much white members of southern slave society needed to believe that their dominion over the lives of their human property was not truly despotic. After all, once Celia confessed to her crime in the presence of white people who could swear before law to the details of her confession (and who had ample proof of her guilt), it would have been a simple matter to have killed her on the spot, in much the same way that a mad or dangerous horse would be put down. Had the search party, with Newsom's heirs at law giving permission or undertaking to do it themselves, decided to inflict corporal punishment upon Celia and "accidentally" killed her in the process, it is unlikely that they would have suffered any penalty.[12]

Instead, the Newsoms and their neighbors decided to let the family tragedy play itself out in the Missouri courts. We can never know with certainty why they made the more restrained choice, given the horrific dimensions of the way in which Newsom's body was disposed of. We do know, however, that the power to take an action does not always translate into the will to do so. These particular individuals simply may not have had the stomach for killing a human being, even one whose humanity they regularly ignored.

Perhaps the Newsoms were influenced by their knowledge that they didn't have to be the ones to take Celia's life. The family, and the neighbors who helped search for Robert Newsom, understood the society in which they lived. They had every reason to be confident in the likely outcome of Celia's murder trial. Under the circumstances, the family took no real gamble in letting the legal process run its course. "We'll give her a fair trial and then we'll hang her" seems to have been the order of the day. A trial conducted in a system that was truly prepared to do justice to both parties, Celia and Robert Newsom, would have contained an element of uncertainty. But there would not have been much uncertainty here. Celia, under the control of Newsom's family and neighbors, had confessed to killing Newsom. What question could there be about the trial's result?

Along with whatever internal constraints guided their responses to Celia's killing of their father, it is likely that external forces influenced the Newsoms' behavior. They were part of a southern society that was extremely self-conscious about the criticisms of its way of life. The legal commentary, newspapers, and political discourse of the day suggest that southerners were anxious to prove that they operated under a culture of restraint imposed by the rule of law in the same manner as other societies they would have recognized as civilized. Therefore, a case like Celia's would have to be brought to the legal system—the enslaved woman would become a defendant in a legal case.

Celia's situation reveals one of the great paradoxes of southern slave society. There was an inherent contradiction between viewing slaves as chattel and likening them to horses and other beasts of burden while at the same time recognizing that slaves were sentient beings in ways that non-human property could never be. That is why Celia could be bought and sold as an item of property, like livestock, and at the same time be held responsible under law for her actions in a manner that a cow or horse would not.

Of course an ordinary slave owner's deference to the legal process in cases involving the murder of a member of his class would have provided benefits beyond sending a signal to outsiders that a legitimate rule of law existed within the southern slave system. An on-the-spot execution of Celia, the destruction of an item of property, would flirt with chaos, the very antithesis of one of the basic societal functions that property law exists to serve, the promotion of stability. Even in a culture in which masters dominated slaves, taking the law into one's own hands would be disfavored. The overall welfare of southern society depended on every person adhering to the same standards. It is to any society's advantage to have all disputes about property, human or otherwise, resolved under the auspices of the prevailing legal system.

The handling of Celia's case bears out legal commentator Grant Gilmore's prediction that "in hell, there will be nothing but law, and due process will be meticulously observed."[13] The investigation and trial highlights the meaninglessness of procedure in a culture devoted to goals other than achieving substantive justice. Nearly all of the familiar trappings of a legal case were present. A version of a complaint was filed against Celia. A warrant was issued for her arrest. There was an inquest. An indictment was handed down. Counsel was appointed for Celia. There was a judge and a jury. Witnesses were called and testimony was heard—all elements that would be familiar to a modern observer. But there was one essential difference. The defendant in this case was a slave. Doing justice to her interests as a human being was never of true concern.

It is often said that not presenting a legal case is like telling a story. Celia did not have the opportunity to help shape her legal narrative because she could not participate in the proceedings that would decide her fate. Like all slaves, she was under a disability: she could not testify in court against a white person. In this, Missouri law followed a universal precept of the southern slave system.[14] Therefore, Celia's motive for her actions could not properly be put before the jury. Nor could she speak with her own voice and hope to win the sympathy of the jury.

The judge in the case, William Hall, appointed counsel to represent Celia. By all indications, these men—John Jameson as lead counsel, Nathan Kouns and Isaac N. Boulware as co-counsel—worked diligently on behalf of their client up until the very end. After entering a plea of not guilty, they proceeded to build a case for that verdict.

Defense counsel's strategy was to make Newsom's sexual abuse of Celia the ultimate (and justifiable) cause of his death. On cross-examination of one of the state's witnesses, Jameson established that the relationship between Celia and Newsom was sexual and nonconsensual on Celia's part.[15] No doubt this was done to make the all-male jury sympathetic to Celia's plight and, perhaps, to make them less likely to identify with Newsom. Thus, it was important to put before the jury the fact that Newsom's abuse of Celia was long-standing and had begun when Celia was a young girl.

But was Newsom's sexual abuse of Celia enough to justify a verdict of not guilty? Was it justifiable homicide? That was the essential issue in Celia's case. Did a slave have the right to use deadly force to resist rape?

Legal precedents in southern states established that slaves did have the right to self-defense.[16] Even if a Missouri court were to take that view, the problem for Celia's lawyers was that Newsom had come to Celia's cabin not to kill her, but to rape her. The challenge was to find some way around the strict limitations that were placed on the slave's right to defend his or her physical autonomy. Celia's lawyers tried several avenues of attack.

After establishing for the jury and the members of the community who attended the trial that Newsom had been having sex with Celia against her will, Jameson then moved to show that Celia was not guilty of intentional murder because she had not intended to kill Newsom. Under this formulation, Celia would be guilty of manslaughter and would escape a death sentence. One of the prosecution's witnesses, Jefferson Jones, testified on cross-examination that Celia had told him that when she struck Newsom she had not intended to kill him "but only to hurt him."[17] The prosecution objected. The judge sustained the objection, most likely on the grounds that it was hearsay.

Hearsay is an out-of-court declaration offered to prove the truth of the matter asserted. Jones testifying in court that Celia said that she had struck Newsom with no intent to kill him could not be used as evidence that Celia had no intent to kill Newsom. Hearsay is typically not allowed as evidence because the person who makes the out-of-court statement should be the one giving the testimony, not the person who merely heard it and repeated it. The out-of-court declarant should be available for cross-examination. Of course, it would have been impossible to cross-examine Jones about the substance of Celia's intent.

Modern rules of evidence allow for numerous exceptions to the hearsay rule. One exception is that if the individual making the out-of-court statement is unavailable—either dead or incapacitated for some reason—the hearsay statement may be allowed. In this case, Celia was "unavailable" because the law would never have allowed her (as a slave) to give testimony against Newsom (a white man). There was no way to effectively deal with the question of whether or not Celia was in fact attempting to use non–deadly force in repelling Newsom's attack.

Jameson also tried to raise doubt in the jurors' minds about whether Celia had acted alone, or if she had really been involved at all, despite her confession. Celia maintained until the end that no one had helped her kill Newsom or dispose of the body. Her lawyers brought in expert testimony to cast doubt on the notion that acting alone, Celia, several months pregnant and ill at the time of her fight with Newsom, could have disposed of the body all by herself. But this line of inquiry went nowhere.

Jameson was unable to get beyond the court's determination to sustain all of the prosecution's objections to the physicians' testimony.

Finally, attempting to grasp the one slender thread available to him, Jameson tried to show that Celia feared for her life during the course of her struggle with Newsom. He would have known that there were some precedents suggesting that slaves could use deadly force to prevent being killed, even against a master. Jameson seems to have tried to break the altercation between Celia and Newsom into two parts, which was the best strategy that could be employed given the facts of the case and the law as it existed. Under this theory, Celia had no intent to kill Newsom with the first blow. She was merely attempting to stop him from forcing her to have sex. When Newsom did not retreat and continued to come toward her, it was reasonable for Celia to believe that he was going to do more than just respond to her in kind. Jameson argued that she feared that Newsom, angered by the blow she had struck, was going to kill her.

Jameson questioned Thomas Shoatman on this point. Shoatman had been with Jefferson Jones when Celia was interrogated before her arrest. He testified that Celia had mentioned that after her first strike, Newsom "threw his hands up."[18] He interpreted this as a threatening gesture. He said that Celia had told them that she had struck Newsom to keep him from "having sexual intercourse with her."[19] The prosecution objected. Again the judge sustained the objections and directed that the quoted language be stricken from the record. There would be no record of Celia's reason for hitting Newsom the first time, or the second time.

Having been deprived of the strongest argument that could be made—that Celia was acting in self-defense—Celia's lawyers had one last chance to save her life. At the end of a trial, the defense and the prosecution have the opportunity to craft instructions that the judge gives to the jury to use during deliberation. If the defense lawyers' instructions are accepted, there is a good chance of acquittal. Conversely, if the prosecution's instructions are given to the jury, chances are great that the defendant will be found guilty. Despite the procedural impediments thrown their way, the instructions Celia's lawyers drafted on her behalf attempted to drive home the notion that Celia had the right to act to protect herself against forced sexual intercourse. They relied on a Missouri statute that allowed "any woman" to use deadly force to protect her honor. Celia's counsel argued that "any woman" was meant to include slave women as well.[20]

The prosecution, mindful of the defense lawyers' attempts to put Celia's motive and her possible fear for her life before the court, presented instructions that required the judge to reiterate that there was no evidence that she was acting in fear for her life, nor should the jurors consider what might have been her motive in killing Newsom. They objected to the defense instructions that invited the jury to find that Newsom's death was justifiable homicide and offered a set of instructions that put the master's rights and power over his slaves front and center. "If Newsom was in the habit of having intercourse with the *defendant who was his slave* and went to her cabin on the night he was killed to have intercourse with her or for any other purpose" (emphasis added),[21] he was allowed to do so and therefore Celia's actions could not be justifiable homicide. Writing about Celia's case in modern times, Judge Leon Higginbotham observed, "The instructions suggest that the trial judge believed that under Missouri law a slave woman had no sexual rights over her own body and thus had to acquiesce to her master's sexual demands."[22]

Not only did Judge Hall adopt the prosecution's instructions, he also sustained its objections to the defense's instructions on the question of Celia's motive for killing Newsom. He also accepted the prosecution's procedural instructions, which gave Celia no reasonable prospect for acquittal. The case went to the jury, and just as members of the Newsom family probably knew from the beginning, Celia was found guilty of the murder of Robert Newsom and sentenced to hang.

Although the prospects for reversal were slim, Celia's lawyers filed an appeal to the Missouri Supreme Court. Because Judge Hall refused to issue a stay of execution, there was some question as to whether Celia would be executed before the Supreme Court could hear and decide on her appeal.

Apparently some public sympathy for Celia's plight existed, and her lawyers let the members of the Supreme Court know that Celia's trial had divided the white community. While she awaited execution, she managed to escape from jail with the help of sympathetic members of the community. These individuals hid Celia for several weeks until after the date of her scheduled execution passed and then returned her to jail. A new date of execution was set, and Celia's fate was in the hands of the Missouri Supreme Court.[23]

The members of the Missouri Supreme Court had before them the record of Celia's trial, with all the testimony of the witnesses as well as the record of the jury instructions drafted by the prosecution and counsel for the defense. Along with the trial record, Celia's lawyers sent a letter setting forth the circumstances surrounding the case. In sum, the judges were well aware of the circumstances of Celia's life and confrontation with Newsom. But the Court was as unmoved as the twelve men who had found her guilty. They rejected the appeal. Celia was executed on December 21, 1855.[24]

Despite how twenty-first-century observers view the circumstances of Celia's life, the conduct of her trial, her death, the events that unfolded, and how they were resolved should not be shocking considering the society into which Celia was born. McLauren makes the comparison between Celia's case and that of another famous decision that came out of Missouri: *Dred Scott*. He suggests that the arguments raised by Celia's lawyers were much more daring than those offered in *Dred Scott* because acceptance of those arguments would have had results more far-reaching than if Dred Scott had prevailed in his case.[25] This is undoubtedly true, but it is important to consider why. Jameson and his co-counsel offered a theory of law that ran counter to the very meaning of slavery. They were saying, in effect, that slaves had honor and free will that their masters were duty bound to respect. How could this be if Celia was Newsom's slave? Resort to analogy is the lifeblood of legal reasoning. If Celia's right to protect her honor allowed her to kill her master, why wouldn't it have allowed her to prevent the sale of her children? Or protect her from being beaten with a lash? Or from being forced to work when ill? Or a myriad of other indignities and cruelties that were integral to the institution of slavery? To argue that Celia was a woman like any other in Missouri society was certainly daring, but it was an ineffectual form of daring. There was little chance that the arguments Celia's lawyers made could have prevailed.

It was one thing to countenance a slave's natural will to self-defense when faced with deadly force. Some judges viewed this almost as an involuntary reaction that was present in all living creatures. Even a horse might fight to prevent being killed. The will to self-protection was built in and could not be overborne by human agency. The concept of honor was another matter, as it could be cultivated. How could this sensibility exist, or be recognized in law, in a person who was owned by another? Celia's lawyers' insistence that she did have honor that could be protected from her master was in a very deep sense extralegal. It was akin to saying that Robert Newsom did not own Celia but, under the law, he did.

What impresses the most about the actions of Jameson and his co-counsel was not the brilliance or the daring of their strategy. Celia's case was not terribly complicated; it was known from the beginning what had happened and why it had happened. What stands as a testament to their actions as lawyers was the thoroughly professional manner in which they pressed their client's case under circumstances that would have caused lesser men to give up before they started. As lawyers who worked within the confines of the legal system of their day, Celia's lawyers did the best that they could with very little. Their efforts show how limited a role the law could play in ameliorating the gross moral injustice that was the American slave system. Once human beings were designated as property in a society that viewed the right to private property as a bedrock value, there was little chance that appeals to sympathy on their behalf could override the self-interest that every property owner or potential property owner had in safeguarding the power that comes with the ownership of property. Celia's interest had to yield to the interests of the community.

It is probably true that Celia's case will never be as well known as the other landmark cases involving slavery that made it to the U.S. Supreme Court. Celia's story should be remembered, however, because it shows without equivocation the ultimate meaning of slavery in America. Celia's body, like that of all slaves, was a form of property. An appeal that rested on the value of her soul had no place in a legal system devoted to protecting the right of men like Robert Newsom to enjoy their property as they saw fit. As history bears out, the law was simply not the vehicle for resolving the injustices made so clear by Celia's unhappy life.

NOTES

1. Walter Johnson, *Soul to Soul: Life inside the Antebellum Slave Market* (Cambridge, Mass.: Harvard University Press, 1999), which details the tragedy of New Orleans slave auctions and trafficking in human beings.

2. Melton A. McLaurin, *Celia: A Slave* (Athens: University of Georgia Press, 1991), xii–xiv, 22–23.

3. Hugh P. Williamson, "Document: The State against Celia, a Slave," *Midwest Journal* 8 (1957): 409; McLaurin, *Celia*, 11. My discussion of this case relies on both of these works for the account of the lives of Celia, Robert Newsom, and the proceedings before the Missouri courts.

4. McLaurin, *Celia*, 9–11.

5. Ibid, 22.

6. Thomas R. R. Cobb, *An Inquiry into the Law of Negro Slavery in the United States of America. To Which Is Prefixed, an Historical Sketch of Slavery* (Philadelphia: Johnson, 1858), 98–100.

7. See Thomas D. Morris, *Southern Slavery and the Law, 1619–1860* (Chapel Hill: University of North Carolina Press, 1996), 304–5 (discussing slave women's lack of protection again sexual violence).

8. McLaurin, *Celia*, 22–30; Williamson, "State against Celia," 409.

9. McLaurin, *Celia*, 31–32.

10. Ibid., 36.

11. Ibid., 45–47; Williamson, "State against Celia," 410. Williamson

reproduces testimony from the witnesses in the case, including that of Newsom's daughter Virginia, who told of finding her father's "bones under the hearth of the cabin," having "turned [a] large stone over to find them. . . . I have more bones in a box which I have kept myself."

12. Morris, *Southern Slavery and the Law*, 161–62, 182–208.

13. Grant Gilmore, *The Ages of American Law* (New Haven, Conn.: Yale University Press, 1977), 111.

14. Morris, *Southern Slavery and the Law*, 228.

15. McLaurin, *Celia*, 95–96.

16. Mark Tushnet, *The American Law of Slavery, 1810–1860: Considerations of Humanity and Interest* (Princeton, N.J.: Princeton University Press, 1981), 108–39; Ruth Wedgewood, "The South Condemning Itself: Humanity and Property in American Slavery," review of *People without Rights: An Interpretation of the Fundamentals of the Law of Slavery in the U.S. South*, by Andrew Fede, *Chicago-Kent Law Review* (1993): 1393.

17. McLaurin, *Celia*, 102.

18. Ibid.

19. Ibid.

20. See Williamson, "State against Celia," 416, quoting Missouri Statutes of 1845, Article II, Section 14.

21. McLaurin, *Celia*, 109.

22. Leon Higginbotham, *Shades of Freedom: Racial Politics and Presumptions of the American Legal Process* (New York: Oxford University Press, 1996), 101.

23. McLaurin, *Celia*, 124–25.

24. Ibid.

25. Ibid., 111–13.

4

RACE, IDENTITY, AND THE LAW

Plessy v. Ferguson

Thomas J. Davis

On Tuesday, June 7, 1892, Homer Adolph Plessy bought an East Louisiana Railway ticket for first-class passage from New Orleans to Covington, Louisiana, and boarded a scheduled 4:15 P.M. train at the Press Street station. The thirty-year-old shoemaker had no intention, however, of taking the two-hour trip. He went to play his part in a pre-scripted drama designed to put the law of race on trial.

The immediate law in question was an 1890 Louisiana statute commonly called the Separate Car Act, which decreed that "all railway companies carrying passengers in their coaches in this state, shall provide equal but separate accommodations for the white, and colored races." It further provided that "no person or persons shall be permitted to occupy seats in coaches, other than the ones assigned to them, on account of the race they belong to." The penalty for violating the law was a $25 fine or not more than twenty days in prison.[1]

The Citizens' Committee to Test the Constitutionality of the Separate Car Act chose Plessy to play his part in a carefully planned legal confrontation. French-speaking Creoles dominated the committee, which they called the *Comité des Citoyens*. Often referring to themselves as *gens de couleur*, or "people of color," the Creoles celebrated their mixed African, European, and Indian descent. They considered themselves neither black nor white, neither one race or another, and they vehemently objected to black-white segregation that denied their separate identity. Plessy embodied the common Creole self-view: His appearance belied his black blood;

by looks he was white, but the law said he was black, and he said he was both and neither.

Who was to decide Plessy's identity, the identity of any person of mixed heritage, or the identity of any person, period—the person or the government? That was the ultimate legal question the *Comité des Citoyens* wanted to test. Legally enforced separation of persons by race depended on the government's deciding racial identity. If the government by law could no longer decide who was who on the basis of race, the decision of where a person belonged would lie with the individual, not with the government. The committee hoped to reach that end and thus stop the widening law of segregation that had come to replace the law of slavery as a tool of white supremacy.

Like the law of slavery in the United States, the law of segregation fixed a system of identity that marked a person either as white or as not white. The simple dichotomy incorporated notions of white supremacy and racial purity. It made white the standard and made anything less than white substandard and separate. It did not completely ignore the reality of persons of "mixed community"—the phrase the U.S. Supreme Court used to avoid "mixed race," a fact that contradicted the doctrine of racial dichotomy.[2] The law simply put the offspring of the interbreeding called miscegenation on one side of the dichotomy. A "mixed" person was not white: The precise measure of mixture that moved a person from one side to the other differed, however, from state to state. And "mixed" persons not infrequently sued in court to be moved to the white side of the two-part system. Creoles such as Plessy and members of the *Comité des Citoyens* rejected what they saw as a false dichotomy. Their mixed heritage was for them a matter of pride, of self-identity; it was also in the 1890s increasingly a matter of access to government services, public accommodations, and equal rights.[3]

The end of the law of slavery with ratification of the Thirteenth Amendment in 1865 left a vacuum in the law of race and rights. Slavery had kept whites and blacks in legally separate places. It hung as a badge even on blacks or people of color who were not or never had been slaves, for under slavery they had virtually no rights. As U.S. Supreme Court chief justice Roger B. Taney asserted in his infamous *Dred Scott* decision in 1857, "They had no rights which the white man was bound to respect."[4] The Thirteenth Amendment did not clarify what rights blacks and people of color would have after slavery.

The nation's first civil rights act sought some clarity. Passed in 1866, it sought to secure the right "to make and enforce contracts, to sue, be parties, and give evidence, to inherit, purchase, lease, sell, hold, and convey real and personal property, and to full equal benefit of all laws and proceedings for the security of person and property."[5] The continuing challenge to enforce such rights gave rise to the Fourteenth Amendment in 1868, with its guarantee of "equal protection of the laws." The Fifteenth Amendment in 1870 further outlawed "race, color, or previous condition of servitude" as a bar to voting. Such rights were thought of at the time as political rights because they involved a person more or less directly with the political system—with the operation of government in the courts, at the ballot box, or in some other public function.

Securing political rights generated violent resistance, as the Ku Klux Klan and other white vigilantes showed. But reaction to demands for so-called social rights was even more bitter. Outside of slavery, blacks and whites had not in large numbers commonly worked together or associated with each other before the Civil War. That was true even outside the slave states. In describing African American experience in the so-called free states from 1790 to 1860, historian Leon F. Litwack noted that "in virtually every phase of existence, Negroes found themselves systematically separated from whites." And the separation ran the length and breadth of society. Blacks "were either excluded from railway cars, omnibuses, stagecoaches, and steamboats or assigned to special 'Jim Crow' sections; they sat . . . in secluded and remote corners of theaters and lecture halls; they could not enter most hotels, restaurants, and resorts, except as servants; they prayed in 'Negro pews' in white churches," Litwack explained.[6]

After the war, few whites appeared ready to change their pattern of not associating in public with blacks or other people of color. Congress itself long resisted addressing changes that were regarded as social rights. It relented only after Massachusetts's long-time Republican senator and civil right champion Charles Sumner died in March 1874, paying him a tribute by passing parts of a bill he had pushed since 1869.

In the Civil Rights Act of 1875, Congress entitled "all persons . . . to the full and equal enjoyment of the accommodation, advantages, facilities, and privileges of inns, public conveyances on land or water, theaters, and other places of public amusement."[7] Blacks and people of color hailed the new law, for they had long clamored against being "deprived of the privileges of these public arrangements."[8]

African Americans embraced the new law and fought to have it enforced. The 1875 act allowed persons to sue if they were discriminated against, and blacks and people of color did sue. Hotels, restaurants, and theaters received their share of complaints, but the focus fell on public transportation companies, railroads, steamships, and streetcars. Finding another place to sleep, eat, or be entertained appeared less of a problem than finding another means of effective transportation. Thus faced with taking the means offered or having no means at all to get where they wanted to go in a timely or convenient manner, blacks and people of color insisted on "the full and equal enjoyment of the accommodation" that they paid for and that the law promised on common carriers that provided public transportation.[9]

Even before the 1875 act, blacks had pressed to have common carriers recognize their legal equality. Their insistence infuriated many and moved the *New York Times* in June 1874 to retort that whenever blacks "believe their rights assailed or threatened, a rush is made to some court or other for redress."[10] What the newspaper described as the "pleasures of court proceedings" were not confined to the South. Just the year before the *Times*'s comment, Iowa was the scene of a major case against Jim Crow transportation in which the Iowa Supreme Court vindicated the legal principle on which blacks insisted. The Iowa court declared that "all persons, unobjectionable in character and deportment, who observe all reasonable rules and regulations of the common carrier, who pay or offer to pay first-class fare, are entitled, irrespective of race or color, to receive . . . first-class accommodations."[11]

Louisiana's black and Creole communities had early campaigned to have equal rights recognized "irrespective of race or color," and they succeeded somewhat early during the Reconstruction era. Louisiana's new state constitution in 1868 provided that "all persons shall enjoy equal rights and privileges upon any conveyance of a public character . . . without distinction or discrimination on account of race or color," a principle the state's civil rights act of 1869 reinforced.[12]

Limits on enforcement quickly developed, however, as the case of Mrs. Josephine DeCuir showed. A plantation owner in south-central Louisiana, DeCuir booked first-class passage on the Mississippi steamer *Governor Allen* in July 1872. When she appeared in New Orleans for her trip upriver, the captain denied her a regular first-class berth, instead assigning her to separate quarters as a Negro. DeCuir sued and won at trial and on appeal to the Louisiana Supreme Court. Steamer captain John C. Benson appealed the judgment further. He died before the U.S. Supreme Court decided the case in January 1878, when the executor of his estate, Eliza Jane Hall, won on his behalf in the case that became known as *Hall v. DeCuir*. The nation's High Court held that state laws, such as Louisiana's, could not regulate any transport engaged in interstate commerce, at least not to any degree that burdened such commerce.[13]

DeCuir lost not only her case but also the grounds for suing at all. The U.S. Supreme Court decided that a state could not outlaw racial segregation on interstate common carriers because all power to regulate interstate commerce belonged to Congress. Justice Nathan Clifford cut even deeper against state antisegregation power. In a separate opinion in *Hall v. DeCuir*, Clifford wrote that any common carrier had not merely the right but the duty to use "reasonable discretion" in accommodating passengers in such a way "as will promote, as far as practicable, the comfort and convenience of his whole company." Under Clifford's standard, common carriers could make their own rules, including rules segregating passengers by race, as long as the rules were "reasonable" or Congress did not say otherwise.

Congress had said otherwise in the Civil Rights Act of 1875. But that offered DeCuir no solace, for the act was not in effect at the time of her ordeal aboard the *Governor Allen*. And the act soon offered little solace to others as well, for in 1883 the Supreme Court ruled that Congress had overstepped, or at least misstated, its powers in seeking to outlaw racial discrimination in public accommodations. Congress had gone beyond what was public, to reach what was private, and thus intruded into the area of social rights, the Court said.

Congress rested the Civil Rights Act of 1875 on the Fourteenth Amendment, but the Court declared in the *Civil Rights Cases* of 1883 that Congress's power under the amendment reached only to state action, not to the actions of private persons such as the owners and operators of hotels, inns, restaurants, theaters, or common carriers. With a glance back to *Hall v. DeCuir*, the Court invited Congress to use its commerce power if it truly wished to regulate public accommodations, but Congress refused the invitation for more than eighty years.[14]

The decisions in the *Civil Rights Cases* and *Hall v. DeCuir* left few apparent restraints on Jim Crow transportation practices. No valid federal law outlawed the practices, and no state law appeared able to reach them, at least aboard interstate carriers. The result was that separate accommodations increasingly appeared after 1883.

The emerging rule of law allowed carriers to separate their passengers by race but required that they "treat all passengers paying the same price alike," as a federal judge in Tennessee noted in an 1885 challenge to Jim Crow on a railroad. The challengers argued that if they paid the same money, they should get the same accommodation. The judge agreed but explained that "equal accommodations do not mean identical accommodation"; they meant "substantially" the same. He agreed with the challengers that "there is no equality of right, when the money of the white man purchases luxurious accommodations amid elegant company, and the same amount of money purchases for the black man inferior quarters."[15]

The Tennessee challenge reflected a new turn in state law to mandate racial segregation on common carriers. Often singled out for passing in 1881 the first Jim Crow transportation act, Tennessee in fact acted initially to assure that "all colored passengers who pay first class passenger rates" would have first-class cars "subject to the same rules governing other first class cars."[16] The act contrasted with those of the nine states, including Tennessee, that between 1887 and 1892 went beyond leaving common carriers to their own rules by mandating racial segregation of passengers by law.[17]

Louisiana was one of the nine that passed Jim Crow car acts. Between 1869 and 1890, the state had moved from outlawing racial segregation on common carriers to requiring it. Blacks and Creoles in the Pelican State aggressively challenged the change. And that is where Homer Adolph Plessy entered history. He arrived, however, as an alternate. The first choice of the Citizens' Committee to Test the Constitutionality of the Separate Car Act was Daniel F. Desdunes, the 21-year-old son of a prominent New Orleans Creole family. In February 1892, the committee had arranged a case involving Desdunes. He purchased a first-class ticket to go from New Orleans to Mobile, Alabama, on the Louisville and Nashville Railroad. He took a seat in a car for whites and, by prearrangement that identified him as other than white, he was arrested and charged with violating the Separate Car Act.[18]

Even before choosing Desdunes, the committee had raised $1,400 for legal fees and retained two attorneys. James C. Walker, a New Orleans Creole experienced in criminal law, was to handle preliminary matters in Louisiana. Senior counsel was Albion W. Tourgée, an Ohio-born Union army veteran who served as a North Carolina judge during Reconstruction and gained national reputation for exploits on behalf of freedmen as depicted in his autobiographical novel, *A Fool's Errand by One of the Fools* (1879). Advising on strategy from his law practice in western New York State, Tourgée was to carry the case to the U.S. Supreme Court—at least that was the aim.

Before *State v. Desdunes* could follow the path the committee planned for it, a dead end appeared. The Louisiana Supreme Court in May 1892 decided the case of *Abbott v. Hicks*. Appearing to learn from its 1878 error of ignoring the federal interstate commerce power in *Hall v. DeCuir* and not wanting to be overruled again by the U.S. Supreme Court, the Louisiana high court ruled that the state's Separate Car Act did not "apply . . .

to interstate passengers."[19] Desdunes's ticket from New Orleans to Mobile made him such a passenger. That fact led Criminal District Court judge John H. Ferguson to dismiss the case.[20]

Walker, Tourgée, and the committee reconsidered their strategy. Having the Separate Car Act declared unenforceable on interstate carriers was not the victory they wanted. They wanted to destroy the act's foundation—the idea that government could by law identify persons by race and require or allow separate or different treatment of persons on the basis of race. To reach that foundation, they wanted a case that would go to the U.S. Supreme Court and challenge not only the act's operations but also its racial presumptions. To get to the High Court, the legal team and the committee agreed to challenge the Separate Car Act's operation on an intrastate carrier. Thus Plessy purchased his first-class ticket for a trip entirely within Louisiana.

On June 7th, Plessy went to the Press Street station to play his part. He presented himself to board a coach for whites only. As with Desdunes, the committee prearranged for Plessy to be identified and arrested. East Louisiana Railway conductor J. J. Dowling confronted Plessy in the whites' coach and directed him to the colored car. Plessy refused to go, and also by prearrangement, Dowling summoned New Orleans police detective Chris C. Cain, who arrested Plessy and took him for booking at New Orleans's Fifth Precinct Station on Elysian Fields Avenue, about a half-mile from the Press Street station. The committee's test case to challenge the constitutionality of legally mandated or *de jure* race-based segregation was about to begin: It was not the first and sadly not the last such case.

The district attorney indicted Plessy in Orleans Parish Criminal District Court on July 20, 1892, on the criminal charge of violating the Separate Car Act. Plessy refused to enter a plea. He refused also to respond to court questions about his race. Instead, following his script, Plessy's local counsel, James C. Walker, challenged the court's authority to hear the case on the grounds that the Separate Car Act violated the U.S. Constitution. The plan was to establish a federal case so that the issues the Citizens' Committee wanted addressed would reach the U.S. Supreme Court.

Orleans Parish assistant district attorney Lionel Adams prosecuted Plessy's case and apparently cooperated with Plessy's attorneys to preserve issues important to the test case. Why Adams acted as he did is not clear; he may have been sympathetic toward the committee or merely carrying out a sense of duty to see the law properly tested. Part of Adams's cooperation extended to not specifying Plessy's race in the indictment.

That left the issue for the court to decide, because Plessy himself had re-fused to identify himself by race.

Judge John H. Ferguson heard the case of *State v. Plessy* in the Orleans Parish Criminal District Court, as he had heard the committee's failed Desdunes case earlier. Ferguson also apparently cooperated with the committee's plan. In fact, defense attorney James Walker described him as a "friend." Ferguson advised Plessy of the charges and consequences he faced on the indictment and on refusing to plead to the facts or state his race. Ferguson postponed judgment to allow the case to go forward on the challenge to the legal basis of the law. The challenge went directly to the Louisiana Supreme Court as an application for a ruling on Plessy's behalf, and thus in November 1892 the case became *Ex parte Plessy*.[21]

The defense shifted its position between criminal court and the state supreme court. Facing Ferguson, Plessy stood silent in identifying his race. Had he identified himself by race, it would have become a fact for Ferguson to decide. The issue then would have become whether Ferguson was right or wrong, not whether the law itself was right or wrong. Although the initial silence was necessary then to reach the state supreme court, once there the defense risked being turned back to trial court if the issue of race remained unanswered. So, to keep the state high court from merely re-turning the matter to Ferguson for a decision about Plessy's race, the defense identified Plessy for the court as "seven-eighths Caucasian and one-eighth African blood" and said further "that the mixture of colored blood was not discernible in him."[22]

The defense presented the Louisiana Supreme Court a fourteen-point petition on Plessy's behalf, but the court reduced all to a single claim that "the statute in question establishes an insidious distinction and discrimi-nation between citizens of the United States, based on race, which is ob-noxious to the fundamental principles of national citizenship." Speaking for a unanimous court that included Chief Justice Francis T. Nicholls, who as governor signed the Separate Car Act into law in 1890, Justice Charles Fenner swept away all arguments on Plessy's behalf against the law.

Fenner cited the U.S. Supreme Court's decision in the *Civil Rights Cases* as settling that "the denial of equal accommodations in inns, public con-veyances, and places of public amusements imposes no badge of slavery or involuntary servitude," meaning that there was no valid Thirteenth Amendment argument against the segregation act. Nor did the Fourteenth Amendment provide any grounds for Plessy's attack. According to Fenner, "Statutes or regulations enforcing the separation of the races in public conveyances or in public schools, so long, at least, as the facilities or accommodations provided are substantially equal, do not abridge any privilege or immunity of citizens, or otherwise contravene the Fourteenth Amendment." Repeating the prevailing doctrine of the day that equal application, that is, separate but equal treatment, satisfied the Equal Protection Clause of the Fourteenth Amendment, Fenner further declared that the segregation act "impairs no right of passengers of either race, who are secured that equality of accommodations which satisfies every reasonable claim."[23]

With this decision, the Louisiana Supreme Court upheld race as a legitimate basis for governmental distinctions. It saw no acceptable alternative. "To hold that the requirement of separate, though equal, accommodations in public conveyances, violated the fourteenth amendment, would, on the same principles," Fenner recognized, "necessarily entail the nullity of statutes establishing separate schools, and of others, existing in many states, prohibiting intermarriage between the races." If race was not a legitimate basis for any one legal distinction, then it was not a legitimate basis for any legal distinction, the court agreed.[24]

Plessy's supporters hoped for the exact result they got: A final adverse ruling by Louisiana's highest court opened the way for an appeal to the nation's highest court. The Supreme Court of the United States was from the beginning the forum in which Plessy, his attorneys, and the *Comité des Citoyens* wanted a hearing on race as a basis for legal discrimination.

It took about three months to prepare Plessy's case for filing at the U.S. Supreme Court. At the end of February 1893, all was in order. The Citizens' Committee to Test the Constitutionality of the Separate Car Act and attorneys Walker and Tourgée agreed on all points, including the decision to engage the Washington, D.C., attorney Samuel F. Phillips. A personal friend of Tourgée's, Phillips had served as the U.S. solicitor general—the nation's chief trial lawyer—and had argued the *Civil Rights Cases* in 1883, albeit on the losing side defending antidiscrimination provisions in the Civil Rights Act of 1875.

The tangle of the Supreme Court's calendar pushed its hearing of *Plessy v. Ferguson* to April 1896, more than three years after the filing. Such was swift justice. But the schedule did allow the two sides to prepare fully.

Washington attorney Alexander Porter Morse argued for Louisiana on behalf of state attorney general Milton J. Cunningham. The state's case was presented as a simple matter. The Supreme Court itself had already decided the issues in the *Civil Rights Cases*. Moreover, in another 1883 case, *Pace v. Alabama*, the Court had upheld race or color as a basis for the state's making distinctions that reached the most fundamental rights, for it there had allowed Alabama to outlaw interracial sex and marriage.[25] The existing law supported no part of Plessy's defense; the man had broken the law and should pay the punishment provided: That was Louisiana's argument.

The argument Walker, Tourgée, and Phillips crafted on Plessy's behalf was not so simple. It ranged widely in revisiting the history and intention of the Thirteenth and Fourteenth amendments and the principles of the Declaration of Independence, concluding that race was not a legitimate basis for decisions that government could either make or sanction. Underlying the argument ran a profound theme that questioned race itself as an undeniable category of fact.

Plessy's defense rejected the binary, either/or dichotomy of the Louisiana Separate Car Act's "white and colored races." It went further to suggest a view of humanity as a stretching, open continuum rather than as clumps of closed categories. It offered the person of Plessy as physical evidence of whether race was a clear matter of fact. In his appearance and lineage he confounded the prevailing notion of race as a physical fact of mutually exclusive groups. Plessy's defense sought to put on trial the very notion of grouping humanity in so-called natural divisions dubbed races.

The defense had prepared Plessy's identity as the central issue from the start by having Plessy refuse at his criminal trial to identify himself as either white or colored. The defense wanted to argue that Plessy's race—and race itself—was indefinable. It was a risky strategy that ran contrary to deeply held consensus. It certainly ran contrary to existing state law. A radical idea for its day, it left the defense open to easy attack.

The defense's central issue allowed the question to become whether Plessy *was* colored or white. But that was not the issue the defense wanted to address, because it would not test *de jure* racial segregation's underlying rationale. The defense wanted to argue not for or against the legal fact of Plessy's being colored or white but against the fact that any law could reasonably categorize Plessy as either colored or white.

If the issue became one merely of legal fact, the defense was lost because the issue would be treated simply as fact-finding controlled by existing law. The case, or at least any part that turned on Plessy's race, would rest with Louisiana, for its courts to decide under state law, because as states had controlled the law of slavery, states also controlled the law of race.

Plessy's defense denounced any and all discretion for law to recognize or sanction race. It advanced a single proposition: No reasonable law could exist to categorize Plessy, or anyone else, as colored or white or as a member of any race because race was indefinable; it was not a physical fact but, rather, a social construct. Differing state laws themselves showed the many ways race was manufactured. A person the law in North Carolina said was black under its rule that "any visible admixture of black blood stamps the person as belonging to the colored race" might be white in Ohio, where the law used the rule of "the preponderance of blood." That showed race simply was not a rational category, according to Plessy's defense.[26]

The U.S. Constitution permitted no distinctions among its citizens, the defense further argued. The Thirteenth and Fourteenth amendments clearly outlawed race as a legal distinction. Using a phrase that would often be repeated, Tourgée argued for the defense that the U.S. Constitution was "color-blind." For government to recognize color or race in any way led, he argued, to "invidious distinction and discriminates between citizens of the United States . . . which is obnoxious to the principles of national citizenship . . . [and] perpetuates involuntary servitude." Thus, the defense concluded, laws that used race to draw distinctions among citizens were not only unreasonable but unconstitutional.[27]

The U.S. Supreme Court decided *Plessy v. Ferguson* on May 18, 1896, five weeks after the oral argument. Justice Henry Billings Brown of Massachusetts delivered the seven-to-one decision, almost contemptuously dismissing Plessy's defense that the law of race was unreasonable and unconstitutional. Brown announced that the Court's majority found no legal problem with Louisiana's Separate Car Act.

In recognizing race and in requiring "equal but separate" accommodations based on race, Louisiana acted completely within its power to express "the established usages, customs and traditions of the people," Brown ruled. Louisiana did no more than recognize the reality of race, which represented "distinctions based upon physical differences." Any law recognizing such distinctions was not unreasonable: What was unreasonable, in Brown's view, was arguing that race did not in fact exist, that race was not real.[28]

Race was a fact of life and of law, Brown insisted. Louisiana's segregation act merely recognized facts that, according to him, "must always exist so long as white men are distinguished from the other race by color." Neither the recognition nor the distinction was unconstitutional, for they had "no tendency to destroy the legal equality of the two races," Brown said. In a classic blame-the-victim reversal, he asserted that "the underlying fallacy of [Plessy's] argument . . . [was] the assumption that the enforced separation of the two races stamps the colored race with a badge of inferiority. If this be so," he declared, "it is not by reason of anything found in the act, but solely because the colored race chooses to put that construction upon it."[29]

Thus twisting the core of Plessy's defense, Brown refused to put either race itself or Plessy's race on trial. If Plessy's race was "a question of importance," then Plessy should have the proper court determine "whether, under the laws of Louisiana, . . . [he] belongs to the white or colored race", Brown declared. To him and his fellow justices in the Court's majority, the case was clear-cut: Separate but equal was constitutionally unassailable.

The lone dissenter on the Court was Justice John Marshall Harlan of Kentucky. As he had in the *Civil Rights Cases* in 1883, Harlan vigorously challenged his fellow justices in *Plessy v. Ferguson* to see that, by recognizing race, law created classes among citizens, which, he insisted, violated the nation's fundamental principles. "Our constitution is color-blind, and neither knows nor tolerates classes among citizens," Harlan declared. His view of the United States was as a place where "the law regards man as man, and takes no account of his surroundings or of his color when his civil rights as guarantied by the supreme law of the land are involved."[30]

Although Harlan embraced Plessy's attack on *de jure* racial segregation, even he abandoned Plessy's assault on the law of racial identity. Like his fellows on the Supreme Court, Harlan accepted the concept of race, the idea of humanity grouped by "distinctions based upon physical differences." Where Plessy's defense insisted that race did not exist as fact, Harlan insisted only that the Constitution restricted government from recognizing race as a basis for any public action.

Despite the Citizens' Committee to Test the Constitutionality of the Separate Car Act having succeeded in bringing its case to the highest court in the land, it had lost. It spent thousands of dollars in what was from the beginning an uphill struggle against at least a decade of settled case law and generations of thinking about race.

So, more than four-and-a-half years after his arrest, Homer Adolph Plessy appeared again in Orleans Parish Criminal District Court. On January 11, 1897, he pled guilty to having violated the Separate Car Act, paid a $25 fine, and walked back into obscurity until a two-line notice of his death at 5:10 A.M. on Sunday, March 1, 1925.[31] But his case was not forgotten.

The immediate response to *Plessy v. Ferguson* recognized that it had routinely affirmed what was already decided. The "case settles the question of the validity of a State law requiring . . . the separation of the white and colored races," the *Virginia Law Register* reported.[32] The decision embraced the status quo. The *American Law Review* commented that the *Plessy* decision merely agreed with "other decisions both in the Federal and in the State tribunals."[33]

Other law commentators noted with approval the Court's consistency in separating "political equality" from so-called social rights. They applauded Justice Brown's comment that "if one race be inferior to the other socially, the Constitution of the United States cannot put them on the same plane." The *New Orleans Times-Picayune*, one of Louisiana's most widely circulated newspapers, hailed the decision for upholding "social distinctions." "Equality of rights does not mean community of rights," the paper insisted. "The laws must recognize and uphold this distinction; otherwise," it said, "if all rights were common as well as equal there would be practically no such thing as private property, private life."[34]

Segregation was the way of life, not only in the South but in the United States, the *Times-Picayune* claimed. Racial separation was a matter of the personal recognition and choice basic to U.S. values, the paper editorialized. To outlaw segregation, it said, "would be absolute socialism, in which the individual would be extinguished in the vast mass of human beings, a condition repugnant to every principle of enlightened democracy." The *Virginia Law Register* commented more boldly that segregation was not merely the American way, it was nature's way. "It will continue until the leopard changes his spots and the Ethiopian his skin. Nature has ordained it," the law journal declared.[35]

As with Justice Harlan's lonely dissent, a few raised their voices against the chorus signing hymns praising the Court's decision. The *Rochester (N.Y.) Democrat and Chronicle* echoed Harlan and Plessy's defense in insisting that laws separating citizens on the basis of race were unreasonable. "It would be just as reasonable for the states to pass laws requiring separate cars . . . for descendants of those of the Teutonic race and those of the Latin race," the western New York newspaper retorted. The *New York Tribune* similarly declared that there was "no more reason for separate cars for whites and negroes than for Catholics and Protestants. It is unfortunate, to say the least, that our highest court has declared itself in opposition to the effort to expunge race lines in State legislation," the newspaper lamented.[36]

The decision failed to quiet opponents of "separate but equal." Continuing to resist hardening racial lines, they fought the fundamental inequality with initially small, scattered, but persistent success that in time moved the U.S. Supreme Court increasingly to hold that separate was not equal. In 1946, the National Association for the Advancement of Color People

(NAACP), which was founded in 1909–1910 to consolidate and continue the work of local groups such as the Citizens' Committee to Test the Constitutionality of the Separate Car Act in the 1890s, moved the Court to reclaim ground obscured by the *Plessy* decision. In *Morgan v. Virginia*, the Court struck down a state law requiring segregation on common carriers in the state, at least when the carriers were engaged in interstate commerce. *Brown v. Board of Education* in 1954 signaled the coming end of the *Plessy* doctrine. For a unanimous Court, Chief Justice Earl Warren declared that "in the field of public education, separate but equal has no place." An erupting groundswell followed to shatter *de jure* segregation. In 1956, the Court fully confronted segregation on common carriers as the defense in *Plessy* had argued sixty years earlier. As a result of a year-long black boycott of buses the seamstress Rosa Parks initiated and the NAACP and others sustained in Montgomery, Alabama, the Court in *Gayle v. Browder* fully accepted that no law could require segregation on public transportation.[37]

The *Plessy* defense had finally won, but not on the ground it had most wanted. The courts from highest to lowest continued to ignore the reality of race and underlying questions such as who was to decide Homer Plessy's identity, the identity of any person of mixed heritage, or the identity of any person, period—the person or the government? The law has shifted to ambivalence; it has allowed a degree of self-identification but has persisted in allowing government to recognize race as a category for public action—a result that has not recognized race as indeterminate, as Plessy's defense had insisted, but that has rendered the law of race indeterminate. The ambiguity has continued to unsettle the nation because it continues to put race on trial.

NOTES

1. 1890 La. Acts 152. For details and direction to sources of information, the discussion presented is heavily indebted to Charles A. Lofgren's masterful *The Plessy Case: A Legal-Historical Interpretation* (New York: Oxford University Press, 1987) and the rich collection of materials in Otto H. Olsen, comp., *The Thin Disguise: Turning Point in Negro History; Plessy v. Ferguson, a Documentary Presentation, 1864–1896* (New York: Humanities, 1967).

2. *Plessy v. Ferguson*, 163 U.S. at 538, 552 (1896).

3. Rodolphe Lucien Desdunes, *Our People and Our History*, trans. Sister Dorothea Olga McCants (1911; repr., Baton Rouge: Louisiana State University Press, 1973); Ariela J. Gross, "Litigating Whiteness: Trials of Racial

Determination in the Nineteenth Century South," paper delivered at the American Society for Legal History Annual Meeting, Minneapolis, Minn., 1997. My thanks to Professor Gross for sharing her work with me.

4. *Scott v. Sandford*, 60 U.S. 393, 408 (1857).

5. 14 Stat. 27 (9 April 1866).

6. Leon F. Litwack, *North of Slavery: The Negro in the Free States, 1790–1860* (Chicago: University of Chicago Press, 1961), 97.

7. 18 Stat. 335 (1 March 1875).

8. "A Black Delegation Addresses U.S. President Ulysses S. Grant on Civil Rights," *Washington, D.C., New National Era*, 18 January 1872.

9. Stephen J. Riegel, "The Persistent Career of Jim Crow: Lower Federal Courts and the 'Separate but Equal' Doctrine, 1865–1896," *American Journal of Legal History* 28 (January 1984): 25.

10. *New York Times*, 2 June 1874, 1.

11. *Coger v. North Western Union Packet Company*, 37 Iowa 145, 147 (1873).

12. La. Const. art. 13 (1868); 1869 La. Acts 37.

13. *DeCuir v. Benson*, No. 7,800, 8th District Court for the Parish of Orleans (1872–1873); *DeCuir v. Benson*, No. 4,829, Louisiana Supreme Court Archives, Earl K. Long Library, University of New Orleans; *DeCuir v. Benson*, 27 La. Ann. 1 (1875); *Hall v. DeCuir*, 95 U.S. 485, 487–489 (1878).

14. *Civil Rights Cases*, 109 U.S. 3 (1883).

15. *Logwood v. Memphis & C.R.*, 23 F. 318, 319 (C.C.W.D. Tenn. 1885).

16. 1881 Tenn. Pub. Acts 211, 212.

17. Lofgren, *Plessy Case*, 21–22.

18. Case file for *State v. Desdunes* (case No. 18,685, Section A, Criminal District Court, Parish of Orleans, 1892), photocopy in Archives and Manuscripts Department, Earl K. Long Library, University of New Orleans.

19. *The State of Louisiana ex Rel. W. C. Abbott v. A. W. O. Hicks, Judge, et al.*, 11 So. 74, 44 La. Ann. 770, 778 (1892).

20. Case file for *State v. Desdunes* (case No. 18,685, Section A, Criminal District Court, Parish of Orleans, 1892), photocopy in Archives and Manuscripts Department, Earl K. Long Library, University of New Orleans.

21. *State v. Plessy; Ex parte Plessy*, 45 La. Ann. 80 (1892); Lofgren, *Plessy Case*, 42.

22. Petition for Writs of Prohibition and Certiorari, filed 22 November 1892, in Plessy La. Case File; Lofgren, *Plessy Case*, 56.

23. 45 La. Ann. at 83.

24. 45 La. Ann. at 87.

25. 106 U.S. 583.

26. 163 U.S. at 552.

27. See 163 U.S. 537, 560–561, 559 (Harlan, J., dissenting).

28. 163 U.S. at 550, 543.

29. 163 U.S. at 551.

30. 163 U.S. at 559 (Harlan, J., dissenting).

31. Plessy obituary, *New Orleans Times-Picayune*, 4 March 1925, 8.

32. *Virginia Law Register* 2 (1896): 347.

33. Ibid.; *American Law Review* 30 (1896): 784.

34. 163 U.S. at 552; *American Law Review* 30 (1896): 784; *Central Law Journal* 43 (1896): 129; *Michigan Law Journal* 5 (1896): 298; New Orleans *Times-Picayune*, 19 May 1896, 1.

35. *New Orleans Times-Picayune*, 19 May 1896, 1; *Virginia Law Register* 2 (1896): 347.

36. *Rochester (N.Y.) Democrat and Chronicle*, 20 May 1896, 1; *New York Tribune*, 19 May 1896, 1.

37. *Morgan v. Virginia*, 313 U.S. 409 (1946); *Brown v. Board of Education*, 347 U.S. 483, 494 (1954); *Gayle v. Browder*, 352 U.S. 903 (1956).

5

JACK JOHNSON VERSUS THE AMERICAN RACIAL HIERARCHY

Denise C. Morgan

Asserting a strong sense of individuality—by exercising the right to excel at what, to live where, and to love whom one desires—has been a punishable offense for black Americans for most of the history of the United States. Even after the abolition of race-based slavery, Jim Crow laws constrained the ability of black Americans to act upon their individual desires by limiting their social, political, and economic mobility. In addition to legal impediments, white Americans used the threat of lynching and rape to deter such assertive behavior.[1] The system of racial segregation and subordination that prevailed in the United States from the end of the Civil War through the middle of the twentieth century was maintained by the ever present threat and the consistent reality of violence.[2] Thus, men and women who have had the courage or the audacity to act upon their strong sense of individuality have been seen as heroes in the black community. They have offered reassurance that the human spirit can overcome racial adversity and have helped to dispel the myth of black inferiority.

But all heroes are not the same. Those heroes who have simultaneously exposed the fallacy of the American racial hierarchy of white over black and have embraced their connections to other black Americans have inspired particular pride in the black community. Rather than using their individual successes to argue that race does not matter, those men and women have acknowledged the continuing social and political significance of race in the United States. They have recognized that their individual successes or failures affect the strength of the black community and, correspondingly, that the strength of the black community affects the opportunities available to all black Americans.

In contrast, reluctant heroes—those who find it difficult to reconcile their sense of individuality with membership in a subordinated community—have tended to have more complex relationships with the black community. Those men and women also have helped to dispel the myth of black inferiority by excelling in their respective fields, but they have simultaneously reinforced that myth by renouncing their connections to other black people. While black Americans have cheered the individual successes of their reluctant heroes, they have also resented those men and women and been angered by their lack of responsibility to the black community.

The difficulties that both white and black Americans had with Jack Johnson, the first black man to win the world heavyweight boxing championship, resulted from his status as a reluctant hero. Johnson was hated by white Americans for exhibiting a strong sense of individuality, for excelling in a sport that had previously been closed to men of his race, and for asserting his right to love the three white women whom he married. And although black Americans admired his courage and felt vindicated by his success in the ring, they were troubled by the ways that his uncompromising individuality distanced him from the black community and by the fact that white Americans used his behavior as an excuse to seek reprisals against that community.

Like many black "firsts," Johnson's place as the first black man to win the world heavyweight boxing championship would likely have been filled at an earlier date by another man, but for the myths of racial inferiority that naturalized the denial of opportunities to people of color in the United States.[3] Despite those ambivalent feelings, black Americans joined together in support of Johnson when he became the target of a racially motivated criminal investigation. The display of solidarity by the black community is, on one level, merely an indication of the depth of black Americans' distrust of the racially-biased criminal justice system. But, more significantly, their response shows the affirmative importance of race to black Americans. In its effort to dislodge the American racial hierarchy and to disprove the myth of black *biological* inferiority, the black community has consistently appealed to race as a basis of *social and political* solidarity. Thus, although Jack Johnson spent his life working to prove the insignificance of race, his story also serves to highlight the ways that race does matter.

During the early years of Jack Johnson's boxing career, at the turn of the century, practitioners of anthropometry worked to find scientific evidence of biological differences between people of different races. Implicit in their search was "the preordained conclusion that, in virtually all ways that mattered to a civilized world, 'the Negro' was inferior to whites and so were his mulatto offspring."[4] In 1906, just two years before Johnson's championship fight against Tommy Burns, Dr. Robert Bennett Bean published a study in the popular press that purported to show that the frontal lobes of the brains of white people were larger than those of blacks.[5] From this evidence, Bean concluded that whites were inherently better suited to tasks involving higher mental functions. Similar claims of racial difference were routinely used to justify excluding people of color from access to opportunity and privilege and to explain inequalities in the social, political, and economic power of different racial communities.

The myth of black inferiority substantially affected all areas of life, including sports. In boxing, it was widely accepted that black men made poor fighters because they were cowardly and because their weak stomachs made them susceptible to body blows.[6] In addition, it was believed that "only athletes from the colder Northern latitudes had enough stamina to remain strong during the course of a long boxing match."[7] Race was also used to justify the denial of opportunities to blacks. Despite the supposed existence of biological impediments to the success of black fighters—or perhaps because on some level of consciousness white fighters knew that their claim to racial superiority was unfounded—the color line was frequently invoked to stop interracial matches. Indeed, Jack Johnson's fight against Tommy Burns on December 26, 1908, marked "the first time in modern history that a heavyweight title holder [would meet] a negro on equal footing in a battle for premier honors."[8]

To black Americans, the match was about much more than one man's shot at the heavyweight title; it was an opportunity to disprove the myths of biological inferiority that worked to disempower the entire black community. However, it was not Johnson's bravery in the ring or his strong stomach that earned him the opportunity to fight Burns for the title but his ability to disguise his boxing talent.

> Knowing that his color would be a barrier to him in reaching the
> coveted goal of his ambition, if he performed too brilliantly,
> hence he fought his battles systematically. Johnson, being a past
> master of feints and guards, his exceptional cleverness, great

speed and almost impenetrable defense, enabled him to wage
battle the full limit of schedule[d] rounds, winning by a narrow
margin, whereas a quick victory over his opponents would have
put his future interests in jeopardy.[9]

In order to appear less threatening to white boxing fans, Johnson employed a defensive boxing style, sometimes carrying his opponent to make the fight seem more evenly matched: "The ring, like the world, was assumed to be the white man's territory, and the black fighter's object was to yield it without suffering physical punishment, allowing his opponent to defeat himself."[10] As a result of this defensive style, most of the successful black boxers of Johnson's era had significantly lower knockout percentages than did their white counterparts.[11]

Still, it took several years—during which time he followed the champion from the United States to England and finally to Australia—for Johnson to convince Burns to agree to fight him for the title. Even then, Johnson received only $5,000 of the $35,000 purse and was forced to allow the fight promoter, who was Burns's good friend, to referee the fight. Despite those handicaps, Johnson beat the White man easily, subjecting him to a first-round knockdown and fourteen punishing rounds before the police intervened to stop the fight. Johnson later joked that "Burns had something coming to him, and I proposed to extend his punishment over a considerable length of time. I certainly wished to give him his $35,000 worth."[12] Just one generation away from slavery, the myth of black biological inferiority had been publicly embarrassed.

In Johnson's mind, his defeat of Burns was a personal achievement: "I did not gloat over the fact that a white man had fallen. My satisfaction was only in the fact that one man had conquered another, and that I had been the conqueror. To me it was not a racial triumph."[13] But the black community took the outcome of the fight as a victory for the entire race. Black newspapers proclaimed that "no event in forty years has given more genuine satisfaction to the colored people of this country than has the single victory of Jack Johnson."[14] In contrast, while white Americans were stunned by Johnson's victory, they were also quick to deny its importance. They argued that Johnson's claim to the heavyweight championship was illegitimate because Burns had never defeated Jim Jeffries, the former title holder; he had merely won the title from the man Jeffries tapped as his successor when he retired.

Even if Johnson's claim to the championship was disputable, the fact that a black man had been crowned heavyweight champion of the world gnawed at white Americans. It was simply inconsistent with the myth of black biological inferiority for Johnson to excel in a sport requiring physical endurance and mental agility. For the next two years white Americans clamored for an opportunity to reclaim the heavyweight title—and the ability to once again assert unquestioned racial supremacy. By the time Jeffries was lured out of retirement in 1910, Johnson had already successfully defended his title against white opponents on at least five occasions. However, Jeffries still boasted that "one punch to the belly will knock Johnson out,"[15] and the unflagging faith of white Americans in the myth of racial difference kept the odds on the fight at better than two to one in favor of the white man.[16]

The Johnson-Jeffries fight was also eagerly anticipated by black Americans. Black churches held prayer vigils for the champion, and individual blacks journeyed long distances to visit his training camp. Whether Johnson liked it or not, in the eyes of black Americans his fight against Jeffries was more than a contest between two individuals. A cartoon in the *Chicago Defender*, at the time the most prominent black newspaper in the country, portrayed the contest as Johnson fighting Negro persecution, race hatred, prejudice, and public sentiment—in addition to Jeffries.[17]

Considering the tremendous pre-fight excitement, the fight itself was anticlimactic. The *New York Times* reported that

perhaps never before was a championship so easily won as Johnson's victory to-day. He never showed the slightest concern during the fifteen rounds and from the fourth round on his confidence was the most glaring thing I ever saw in any fighter. . . . Jeffries didn't miss so many blows, because he hardly started any. Johnson was on top of him all the time, and he scarcely attempted a blow that didn't land.[18]

Still, the crowd of 20,000 that watched as Johnson knocked Jeffries down three times in the course of the fight was surprised when the referee declared the black man the victor. "There was very little cheering, Jeff had been such a decided favorite they could hardly believe that he was beaten and that there wouldn't still be a chance for him to reclaim his lost laurels."[19] The search for "The Great White Hope," a white man who could vindicate the myths supporting the American racial hierarchy by defeating Johnson in the boxing ring, had been a failure. Jack Johnson, "a Texas negro, the son of an American slave, [was] the undisputed heavyweight champion of the world."[20]

Johnson was characteristically race-neutral after the fight: "Whatever possible doubt may have existed and did exist as to my claim to the championship was wiped out. I had demonstrated the material of which I was made and I had conclusively vanquished one of the world's greatest boxers."[21] White Americans responded to his victory with violence directed at the entire black community. Riots and lynchings occurred all across the United States in the days after the fight: Two blacks were killed by a group of whites in an argument about the fight in Little Rock, Arkansas; six blacks were beaten by a white mob in Roanoke, Virginia; a gang of white sailors injured dozens of blacks in Norfolk, Virginia; three blacks were killed by white assailants in Shreveport, Louisiana; and in New York City, one black person was beaten to death and many others were injured by angry whites.[22] Perhaps the members of the lynch mobs hoped that the black community would be intimidated into remaining in a subordinated position even if white supremacy could not be vindicated in the boxing ring.

Black Americans also understood that Johnson's boxing success had ramifications for American race relations. The *Chicago Defender* wrote that "we shall not conceal the fact of our satisfaction at having these homilies and editorials [written by white newspaper editors in anticipation of a Jeffries victory] all knocked into the waste basket by the big fist of Jack Johnson. In this he did missionary work."[23] Because they saw Johnson's boxing successes in this light, black Americans were willing to endure the white reprisals that followed his victory. Indeed, the *Chicago Defender* declared that

> it was a good deal better for Johnson to win and a few Negroes to have been killed in body for it, than for Johnson to have lost and all Negroes to have been killed in spirit by the preachments of inferiority from the combined white press. The fact of this fight will outdo a mountain peak of theory about the Negro as a physical man,—and as a man of self-control and courage.[24]

Each generation of black Americans has paid a price to bring the next generation a step closer to experiencing full equality in the United States. By that measure, the human and political cost to the black community of Jack Johnson's victory over Jim Jeffries was seen as well worth it.

The black community's response to Johnson's personal life was far more ambivalent than was its response to his boxing career. Although Johnson's accomplishments deeply challenged the myths upon which the American racial hierarchy was based, he was hardly the "Race Man" that the black community wanted him to be. Race Men, like Johnson's contemporaries Booker T. Washington and W. E. B. Du Bois, were well-educated people with genteel manners and an unflagging commitment to uplifting their race. In contrast, Johnson owned a popular nightclub in Chicago, drove expensive cars recklessly, kept the company of a bevy of prostitutes, and was always willing to "take a chance on [his] pleasures."[25] His hedonistic lifestyle conflicted with the Victorian moralities of the black middle class, and his excesses earned him their scorn. Fearful that Johnson's behavior would be taken as representative of the entire black community, the Conference of Representative Chicago Colored Citizens issued a resolution, "pledg[ing themselves] to use [their] highest endeavors to blot out any negro or set of negroes whose immoral conduct tends to lower the moral standard or bring into disrepute the entire negro race."[26] Johnson was also publicly denounced by other prominent black Americans, including Booker T. Washington, who said that

it is unfortunate that a man with money should use it in a way to injure his own people in the eyes of those who are seeking to uplift his race and improve its conditions. . . . In misrepresenting the colored people of the country this man is harming himself the least. I wish to say emphatically that his actions do not meet my personal approval, and I am sure that they do not meet with the approval of the colored race.[27]

Those few members of the black community who defended Johnson's lifestyle only argued weakly that his behavior was to be expected of a "sport" and was no worse than that of white boxers.[28]

Johnson also distinguished himself from the Race Men by staunchly maintaining his independence from the black community. In contrast to men like Du Bois, who wrote that "the history of the world is the history, not of individuals, but of groups, not of nations, but of races, and he who ignores or seeks to override the race idea in human history ignores and overrides the central thought of all history,"[29] Johnson thought of himself as an individual unconstrained by race. Indeed, Johnson showed little loyalty to other blacks and "had neither faith, confidence nor respect for colored professional men."[30] After winning the heavyweight title, he refused to fight any of the other black men who had been denied the chance to contend for the championship because of the color line, saying "I won't box any of these colored boys now. . . . I'll retire still the only colored heavyweight champ."[31] Even after he retired, he resented the success of Joe Louis and other black boxers.[32] The black press criticized the fact that most of Johnson's friends and boxing associates were white men, commenting that "when [Johnson] turned away from his own people to seek associates among whites, and found them frequently among the most disreputable, there was a natural revulsion on the part of colored men."[33] Johnson simply found his need to express his individuality to be incompatible with the demands of racial solidarity.

However, it was Johnson's relationships with white women that most deeply troubled the black community. Johnson saw his choice of sexual partners as a matter of asserting and satisfying his individual desires completely divorced from racial politics. When his marriage to Lucille Cameron, a white woman, was questioned by both blacks and whites, he defended his decision in race-neutral terms:

> I am not a slave and . . . I have the right to choose who my mate shall be without the dictation of any man. I have eyes and I have a heart, and when they fail to tell me who I shall have for mine I want to be put away in a lunatic asylum. So long as I do not interfere with any other man's wife I shall claim the right to select the woman of my own choice. Nobody else can do that for me. That is where the whole trouble lies.[34]

However, Johnson was hardly raceblind in his relationships with women. Not only did he express a strong *preference* for white women as romantic and sexual partners, he also explicitly *renounced* black women. Early in his boxing career, Johnson chose to "forswear colored women and to determine that [his] lot henceforth would be cast only with white women."[35] Johnson attempted to justify his decision by claiming that the black women with whom he had been involved had been unfaithful to him.[36] But, since many of Johnson's white girlfriends worked as prostitutes, the black community did not accept Johnson's explanation that he preferred white women because they were more likely to be monogamous. Nor did it appear to the black community that Johnson's interest in white women was driven by romantic love. While genuine affection and friendship undoubtedly motivated him to keep company with some of the white women with whom he was sexually involved, Johnson's choice to seek loving relationships among women whom he paid to serve him and to whom he owed no reciprocal duty was more consistent with self-absorption than romantic devotion. Accordingly, Johnson's affirmative decision to renounce all black women was difficult to interpret as anything other than an attempt to distance himself from the black community and to partake of white racial privilege. This angered black Americans.[37]

Of course, some members of the black community defended Johnson's interest in white women by arguing that his preferences were unexceptional: "Most men like fair women, if you don't believe it just go into the best Negro homes amid the blackest of the most prosperous Negro families and you will find a yellow or almost white woman occupying the leading place of wife."[38] Others refused to ascribe any political meaning to his choice of romantic interests, characterizing "his marriage to a white woman as a mere chance affair and not a thing studied out by the champion in the sense of a demand, owing to his superior position, and apparently meaning the inferiority of his own race women."[39] However, for many others, Johnson's choice to value white women more highly than black women validated the white supremacy that his boxing success called into question.

The response of most of the black press was to denounce him. The *Newport News Star* declared that

> no Negro, who has any spark of manhood, and who prayed and
> hoped that Jack Johnson would win his battle with Jim Jeffries,
> and clearly establish his title to the championship of pugilists, in
> his class, now feels that he did himself the slightest tinge of
> honor. They would gladly recall that prayer and that hope, when
> they read of his fool infatuation for white women.[40]

The *New York Amsterdam News* argued that Johnson's choice of white partners indicated that he had forsaken his race and decried the fact that "white men of standing . . . conceitedly point to the example as an evidence of the black man's lack of race pride, his desire to be white and the general unworthiness of his race."[41] The Reverend Adam Clayton Powell, Sr., pastor of the Abyssinian Baptist Church in Harlem, confirmed that "the overwhelming majority of colored people have no sympathy whatever with Johnson in his inordinate and persistent desire to seek female companionship with the whites."[42]

Given that black men were routinely terrorized and lynched on the strength of any hint that they had intimate associations with white women, the black community was correct in assuming that Johnson's unapologetic romantic and sexual interest in women of that race would be taken as an audacious act of rebellion against the constraints of the

American racial caste system. White Americans feared the threat that interracial sex posed to the racial hierarchy for several reasons. First, intimate interracial relationships could undermine the myth of biological racial difference by affording people of different races greater opportunity to recognize their equal humanity and to forge bonds of trust and understanding. Second, mixed-race children could challenge the established hierarchy by complicating the line drawing necessary to maintain racial segregation and by weakening the familial boundaries that kept social and economic capital within the white community from one generation to the next.[43] And, perhaps most immediately, there were matters of ego—white men feared competition from black men for the attention of women.[44]

Thus, although interracial pairings have always been a part of the American scene, the white majority has consistently discouraged them— by social pressure, legal restrictions, and violence. For example, in colonial Virginia the legislature tried to prevent marriage between white indentured servants and enslaved blacks by declaring that the white party would be banished from the colony.[45] And in spite of the fact that white plantation owners took advantage of their unimpeded sexual access to enslaved black women frequently enough that it was said that "[the] men [lived] all in one house with their wives and their concubines; and the mulattoes one sees in every family partly resemble the white children,"[46] there were strong social sanctions against interracial sex in the antebellum South. After the Civil War, deprived of the mechanisms of social control that slavery provided,[47] southern whites were forced to find other means to shore up the American racial hierarchy. Antimiscegenation laws were revived as a symbol of white resistance to social equality with newly emancipated African Americans. Those rules both policed interracial sexual desires and defined white households as "racially impregnable institutions."[48] Moreover, the threat of violence always lurked behind those legal restrictions. Although the incidence of lynching peaked in 1892, the practice—which was often directed at black men who expressed sexual interest in white women—continued well into the twentieth century.[49]

Thus, perhaps it is not surprising that few black Americans applauded Johnson's open defiance of the taboos against interracial love and sex. Johnson's choice of sexual partners had negative ramifications for many members of the black community. Black Americans were punished physically and economically as a result of white anger over Johnson's liaisons with white women. "Many colored waiters, porters, in white barbershops, and colored men employed in various capacities were dismissed from their employment. Even Black professional men suffered reprisals as a result of the bitter agitation stemming from the . . . controversy."[50] Indeed, the black press was consumed with the fear that Johnson's behavior would result in retaliation by white Americans against the entire black community. The *Indianapolis Freeman* wrote that

> the persistent pursuing of this course will cause a wide-spread feeling of opposition to Negroes. He has no right to anything that promises so much mischief. He's free and all that, as he says, but there are "invisible" laws to which he must subscribe—the agreements of society—if he would enjoy a large measure of that freedom of which he boasts.[51]

Unlike his victory in the fight against Jeffries, Johnson's freedom to pursue his sexual and romantic interests was not seen as worth the sacrifice of human and political capital by black Americans. While Johnson incited the wrath of white Americans by challenging the American racial hierarchy in both situations, his relationships with white women were taken as a rejection of his own race and as an affront to the social and political cohesiveness of the black community.[52]

Thus, despite his success in challenging the myths of racial difference that maintained and perpetuated the subordination of all black Americans, Jack Johnson did not enjoy an unproblematic relationship with the black community. As the strength of that community lay in group solidarity, black Americans did not appreciate what Johnson would probably have described as his individualistic color-blind approach to life. Johnson contended that "[he had] found no better way of avoiding racial prejudice than to act in [his] relations with people of other races as if prejudice did not exist."[53] However, in acting as if racial prejudice did not exist, Johnson both flouted the conventions of the American racial caste system and ignored the fact that race has been affirmatively used by black Americans to forge a sense of common identity, to carve out a zone of safety from the violence of white Americans, and to fashion an agenda for unified action.

Just as surely as Johnson's boxing successes disproved the myth of black inferiority, the federal government's decision to aggressively prosecute him for having consensual sexual relationships with white women and the black community's response to his prosecution highlighted the social and political significance of race. The primary functions of law are to protect social order and to control those who would disturb that order. Because the assertion of strong black individuality has been incompatible with a social order premised on white supremacy, law in the United States has also functioned to control black Americans who exhibit that trait. This bias has been evident both in the government's failure to protect members of the black community from violence and intimidation and in the government's zealous prosecution of members of the black community for real and imagined infractions of the law.[54] Unable to find a Great White Hope to defeat him, white Americans turned to the law to punish Johnson for his flagrant violations of the American racial caste system. Black Americans rallied to Johnson's defense.

On October 18, 1912, Johnson was arrested and charged with the abduction of Lucille Cameron, an eighteen-year-old white woman. His arrest was cause for celebration among whites. "Effigies of Johnson were burned in white sections of Chicago, and crowds followed him when he was released on bail, shouting 'Lynch him! Lynch the nigger!'"[55] Johnson was arrested on a warrant sworn by Mrs. Cameron-Falconet, Cameron's mother, who disapproved of the sexual relationship between her daughter and the black boxer. Johnson claimed that Lucille Cameron worked as a secretary in his nightclub, the Café de Champion, and that "her association with [him] was purely of a business nature and devoid of undue intimacy."[56] However, Mrs. Cameron-Falconet was correct in her assessment that her daughter was romantically interested in the champion. When the young woman was taken into custody by police, she told them that "she loved Johnson and expected to become his wife."[57] Neither her mother nor federal officials could understand Cameron's expressed desires as anything but lunacy.[58] Any sexual involvement between Johnson and Cameron had to be nonconsensual in order to be consistent with the popular narrative of black male rape of white women. Accordingly, the government charged Johnson with violating the Mann Act (also known as the White Slave Traffic Act), a federal statute enacted in 1910 to combat the sexual exploitation of white women.[59]

The Mann Act was the product of the moral panic that swept the nation at the turn of the century. Americans were troubled by the challenge that increased immigration, greater migration to urban areas, and the early suffragist movement posed to traditional sexual mores.[60] In addition, movies, newspapers, and novels repeated and exaggerated claims that large numbers of young white women were being lured to big cities from Europe and small towns in the United States, held captive, and forced into "white slavery." Congress responded by making it a felony to knowingly transport or cause to be transported, or aid or assist in obtaining transportation for, or in transporting, in interstate or foreign commerce, any woman or girl for the purpose of prostitution or debauchery or any other immoral purpose.[61]

The primary objective of the statute was to allow for the prosecution of those who profited from the exchange of sex for money or who coerced women into sexual activity. Indeed, the vast majority of prosecutions brought under the Mann Act between 1910 and 1914 involved women involved in commercial prostitution.[62] However, the broad wording of the statute—neither "debauchery" nor "immoral purpose" was defined—left room for it to be used in cases involving consensual sex in the context of romantic relationships.[63] Given Johnson's fast-paced, nomadic lifestyle and the number of women with whom he was sexually involved, the assistant U.S. attorney prosecuting his case was certain that Johnson had violated the letter, if not the spirit, of the statute.

The only difficulty was Cameron. Despite the fact that federal prosecutors held her in jail to intimidate her and to prevent her from communicating with Johnson, she was uncooperative when brought before the grand jury to testify. Cameron refused to substantiate the allegation that Johnson operated an interstate prostitution ring and denied that he had lured her to Chicago to work as a prostitute. Not only was the government forced to dismiss the abduction charges, but as soon as Cameron was released from police custody, she and Johnson were married. At the time, "some writers speculated that Johnson wished to marry Lucille to prevent her from testifying against him. Others held that Lucille used the threat of her testimony to force the champion to wed her. Few journalists considered that love might actually be involved."[64] Whatever their motivations, the marriage of Jack Johnson and Lucille Cameron scandalized the country.

The response of most white Americans to the Johnson-Cameron wedding was swift and hostile.[65] Many of the officials attending the Annual Governors' Conference that took place the same week as the wedding agreed that interracial marriage should be legally prohibited:

"That Johnson wedding," spoke Governor John Dix of New York, "is a blot on our civilization. Such desecration of the marriage tie should never be allowed." Governor John Tener of Pennsylvania commented that "any law to prevent the mixture of bloods of different colors" had his hearty approval. Stating remorsefully that his state had no law to prohibit such alliances, Governor Hudson Harmon of Ohio placed his sympathies with those who agitated for an anti-intermarriage law.[66]

In the year after Johnson and Cameron were married, antimiscegenation bills were introduced in ten of the twenty states that allowed interracial marriages, and at least twenty-one such bills were introduced in Congress.[67] Indeed, the thought of "a brutal African prizefighter [joining] to his name that of even a fallen American woman" so enraged Congressman Seaborn Roddenberry of Georgia that he proposed a constitutional amendment prohibiting interracial marriages.[68] Roddenberry styled his proposed amendment as necessary to protect white women because "no more voracious parasite ever sucked at the heart of pure society, innocent girlhood, or Caucasian motherhood than the one which welcomes and recognizes the sacred ties of wedlock between Africa and America."[69] However, as the amendment would have prohibited voluntary interracial relationships as well as coercive ones, its actual effect would have been to constrain white women's free choice of sexual partners, thus protecting white men's exclusive right of access to them. The fact that Roddenberry did not express any concern about relationships between white men and black women also supports the notion that his intent was to control the sexual expression of white women and that of their black male lovers, not to prohibit all interracial sex or to protect all women from the real threat of male violence.[70] Indeed, by arguing that his proposed amendment would show that "government and the administration of law properly belong to the white people . . . and [the black man] has acquiesced,"[71] the congressman made plain that his primary objective was to reinforce the American racial hierarchy under which black Americans were not permitted to assert any individual desires that conflicted with that hierarchy, sexual or otherwise.

Black Americans may have had ambivalent feelings about interracial marriage in general, and about Johnson's involvement with white women in particular, but they were united in their opposition to laws prohibiting such unions. This position is not as inconsistent as it seems at first blush. At the same time as black Americans feared that mixed-race marriages would weaken the racial solidarity that bound their community together and gave it some safety and political clout, they also wanted to be free to express their individual sexual and romantic desires. In addition, they abhorred any laws that implied the inferiority of people of their race. The response of the editor of the *Washington Bee* was typical: "We are unalterably opposed to intermarriages, but we are just as unalterably opposed to the enactment of any statute, state or national, to prohibit them."[72] The *Chicago Defender* took a similar position, arguing that "it is not that we care to intermarry, but we demand the privileges accorded any other citizen, and we propose to fight to the bitter end any infringement of our rights."[73]

Black women opposed antimiscegenation legislation on the grounds that by making it impossible to legitimate interracial unions, such laws made them more vulnerable to sexual exploitation by white men.[74] Those laws would provide an excuse to white men who were reluctant to legitimate their sexual relationships with black women through marriage by denying that option to the couple. The black press was more concerned that any law prohibiting interracial marriage equally inhibit the sexual expression of men of both races. An open letter to Congressman Roddenberry suggested that "by all means let us have your resolution, but amend it so that if it is a crime for Negro men to marry white women legally in the north, it be a misdemeanor for white men to mate with Negro women illegally in the south."[75] Summarizing the opinions of the black community, W. E. B. Du Bois wrote that antimiscegenation legislation should be opposed, not because race had no significance, but because such laws treated blackness as if it were a physical taint, because sex out of wedlock was morally repugnant, and because such laws "leave the colored girl absolutely helpless before the lust of white men."[76] Due to the lack of enthusiasm of white Americans and the opposition of black Americans, none of the bills that were proposed that year to ban interracial marriage were enacted into law.[77]

Embarrassed by the failure of their first effort to prosecute Johnson, federal investigators redoubled their efforts "to secure evidence as to illegal transportation by Johnson of any other women for an immoral purpose."[78] Their exhaustive investigation located Belle Schreiber, a white prostitute who was one of Johnson's former girlfriends. In the years immediately after Johnson won the heavyweight championship, Schreiber had been one of a number of white women who traveled with him when he was on the road. Based on her testimony about their relationship, the government was finally able to obtain an indictment against Johnson for violations of the Mann Act. Johnson was charged with the crimes of transporting Schreiber across state lines for his personal sexual use, for the purpose of engaging her in prostitution and with sexual perversions (that is, physical abuse). And although he correctly argued that "there [were] thousands of others who could be prosecuted on similar reasons" and twice offered to plea bargain, the government refused to negotiate with him for fear of disappointing the white American public that wanted to see him behind bars.[79]

The government faced a difficult burden of proof at trial. In order to prevail, the prosecution had to show beyond a reasonable doubt not only that Johnson had sex with Schreiber but that he had transported her across state lines *for the express purpose of doing so*—a charge that Johnson adamantly denied. When the case went to trial on May 7, 1913, the government only had circumstantial evidence to support its case. It was undisputed that Johnson had wired $75 to Schreiber in Pittsburgh in response to her request for money. Witnesses also testified that Schreiber had worked as a prostitute and had provided sexual services to Johnson in the past. However, Johnson denied that he told her to use the money he sent to travel to Chicago and claimed that the additional $1,500 that he gave to her upon her arrival in that city was to help her furnish an apartment for herself, her sister, and her mother.[80] The prosecution countered that Johnson's intent to have sex with Schreiber upon her arrival in Chicago was clear from the fact that they had had sex on previous occasions. Although the government was aware that the relationship between Johnson and Schreiber "was emotional and sexual—not commercial,"[81] the prosecution argued that Johnson gave Schreiber the additional $1,500 to open a brothel.[82]

The all-white, all-male jury convicted Johnson after deliberating for an hour and a half. They found him guilty on both the sexual intercourse and prostitution counts. The government had been forced to drop the sexual perversion charges for lack of evidence. After the verdict was announced, the federal prosecutor bragged that the charges against Johnson had, in fact, been motivated by racial politics and a desire to control the sexual expression of black Americans.

> This verdict will go around the world. It is the forerunner of laws to be passed in the United States . . . forbidding miscegenation. This Negro, in the eyes of many, has been persecuted. Perhaps as an individual he was. But his misfortune is to be the foremost example of the evil in permitting the intermarriage of whites and blacks. He has violated the law. Now it is his function to teach others the law must be respected.[83]

U.S. District Court judge George Carpenter sentenced Johnson to one year and a day in prison.[84]

On appeal, the Seventh Circuit criticized the prosecution for failing to withdraw the sexual perversion charges in a timely fashion despite knowing that they could not be substantiated; for introducing testimony that Johnson had assaulted his first wife despite the fact that the testimony lacked relevance to the Mann Act charges against him; for repeating insinuating questions "with the obvious object of having . . . innuendoes taken in preference to the sworn answer"; and for generally creating an "atmosphere of prejudice."[85] Further, the Court of Appeals reversed Johnson's conviction on the prostitution counts on the grounds that there was "no proof that [Johnson] had ever been connected with or interested in brothels, or that prior to the act in Chicago he had ever aided this or any girl to engage in prostitution."[86] However, by the time his case was remanded for resentencing on the remaining charge of transporting Schreiber across state lines to have sex with her, Johnson had already fled the country.

Black Americans rallied to Johnson's side when they came to see his prosecution as racially motivated. Whether or not Johnson saw himself as part of the black community, that community understood that his prosecution was intended to reinforce the racial hierarchy that oppressed all black Americans. The *Chicago Defender* was among the early papers to portray the charges against Johnson as "an out-burst of race prejudice."[87] In October 1912, one week after he was first arrested, the *Defender* took the position that Johnson was not guilty of abducting Cameron or of claiming that he could "get any white woman [he] wanted" and accused the white press of sensationalizing the story in an attempt to inflame passions against black Americans.[88] The *Defender* also characterized the reluctance of the district court to release Johnson on bail, despite the bonds offered by his lawyers, as an indication that the U.S. legal system discriminated on the basis of race[89] and urged that "it is high time the race throughout the United States should raise their voices in unison and protest the treatment that is accorded Jack Johnson."[90]

Soon other black newspapers joined the *Defender* in condemning what was described as an effort "to persecute, rather than to prosecute, and beneath it all courses the vein of animus against the Negro himself and against his association with white women."[91] The editors of the *Indianapolis Freeman* confessed that they had "opposed and abused Jack Johnson quite as much as anyone else as it concerns his relation with white women. But at that we have not forgotten that the baffled and beaten champion has some rights; not more than other men, but as many."[92] The *Afro-American Ledger* was more forthright about the racial bias inherent in the prosecution, reporting that Johnson was a victim of "Race Prejudice," because "such reprehensible doings as are charged against him are of frequent occurrence, and excite but passing notice."[93] Similarly, the *New York Amsterdam News* wrote:

> The relentless persecution of Jack Johnson in Chicago by the State and Federal authorities is nothing less than a reproach to the American people and nothing more than a bald revelation of the prejudice regnant in American jurisprudence. The legal inquisitioners of the State of Illinois and of the nation are madly bent upon making a scapegoat of Johnson thus venting the vengeance of the Caucasian upon the black race because one of its members happens to be pugilism's champion.[94]

Despite his unpopularity, most of the black community agreed with Johnson's assessment that his trial "was a rank frame-up" by the time he was sentenced to jail.[95] The *Chicago Defender* confirmed that "public sentiment is largely in favor of the champion, many persons believing that he had not received a 'square deal.'"[96]

Despite the threat that many black Americans believed Johnson's transgressive behavior posed to the political strength of their community, they championed his cause. Indeed, because they believed that the fate of the entire black community was significantly linked to that of Jack Johnson, they understood group solidarity to be a matter of political necessity. To remain silent as white Americans enforced the boundaries of the racial hierarchy against any individual black person—even one who had intentionally distanced himself from other blacks—would be to tacitly validate that hierarchy. Although the black community consistently rejected the notion of black biological difference or inferiority, it embraced the political salience of shared racial identity and used race as a catalyst for unified opposition to the bias in the criminal justice system.

After his conviction, Johnson remained in self-imposed exile, traveling with his wife throughout Europe and South America, for seven years. During this time, he lost the heavyweight title to Jess Willard in a fight in Cuba.[97] Johnson later said that he threw the Willard fight in an effort "to wipe out prejudices against [him] and to still criticism of [his] conduct."[98] However, even after voluntarily surrendering himself to U.S. authorities in July 1920, he was resentenced to serve his original term of one year and a day in Leavenworth.

Upon his release from prison in 1921, Johnson was almost as warmly received by black Americans as he had been after his victory in the heavyweight championship fight against Jeffries.

> In Chicago a large crowd of blacks greeted Johnson and welcomed him home. But this was only the beginning. When the Twentieth Century Limited carrying Johnson arrived in New York, it was met by a small contingent of admirers. Then at 125th Street the real festivities began. Thousands of residents of Harlem celebrated his release and treated him like a "conquering hero." There was even a parade, with Johnson leading the way in a flashy black suit with broad white stripes.[99]

Black Americans welcomed Johnson as a member of their community because, like them, he had suffered injustice on account of his race. Indeed, they celebrated him despite his reluctance to embrace them in return because of his ability to persevere in the face of American racial politics. However, the significance of the black community's response to him seems to have been lost on Johnson. Even after his release from jail, he continued to hold himself apart from that community and exempt from the demands of race politics. In addition to marrying a third white woman after Lucille Cameron divorced him in 1924, "His mannerisms became not only more white, but absolutely European. In later years he always wore a beret, carried a cane, and spoke with a rich British accent."[100] The life of Jack Johnson and the consistent choice of the black community to rally around even its most reluctant heroes show that although "color is not a human or personal reality; it is a political reality."[101]

NOTES

Thanks to Eric Wold, Jim Walker, and Rebecca Zietlow for reading earlier drafts.

1. See Jennifer Wriggins, "Rape, Racism, and the Law," *Harvard Women's Law Journal* 6 (1983): 103, 118–21; Paula Giddings, *When and Where I Enter: The Impact of Black Women on Race and Sex in America* (New York: Bantam, 1984), 26–31, 43–44; Emily Field Van Tassel, "'Only the Law Would Rule between Us': Anti-Miscegenation, the Economy of Dependency, and the Debate over Rights after the Civil War," *Chicago-Kent Law Review* 70 (1995):

873, 914–18; Barbara Holden-Smith, "Lynching, Federalism, and the Intersection of Race and Gender in the Progressive Era," *Yale Journal of Law and Feminism* 8 (1996): 31, 35–38.

2. See, generally, Herbert Shapiro, *White Violence and Black Response: From Reconstruction to Montgomery* (Amherst: University of Massachusetts Press, 1988); Robert J. Kaczorowski, "Federal Enforcement of Civil Rights during the First Reconstruction," *Fordham Urban Law Journal* 22 (1995): 155, 157.

3. In the first decade of the nineteenth century, two black Americans, Bill Richmond and Tom Molineaux, had successful boxing careers in England. Each man fought but was beaten by Tom Cribb, the white British boxing champion. Nat Fleischer and Sam Andre, *An Illustrated History of Boxing*, 5th ed. (New York: Citadel, 1997), 26–27; Arthur Krystal, "Requiem for a Heavyweight," *New Yorker*, 20 July 1998, 74. Peter Jackson, a black boxer from St. Croix, became the heavyweight champion of England and Australia in 1892, but the white American champion, John L. Sullivan, refused to fight him. Jackson J. Stovall, "Jack Johnson and James Jeffries," *Chicago Defender*, 2 July 1910, 1. Three other contemporaries of Jack Johnson—Sam Langford, Joe Jeannette, and Sam McVey—were also denied the opportunity to fight for the U.S. heavyweight title because of the color line.

4. Audrey Smedley, *Race in North America: Origin and Evolution of a Worldview* (Boulder, Colo.: Worldview, 1993), 262.

5. Stephen Jay Gould, *The Mismeasure of Man* (New York: Norton, 1996), 109–12. (Bean's data, which also showed that within each race men had larger frontal lobes than did women, were subsequently disproved.)

6. See Finis Farr, *Black Champion: The Life and Times of Jack Johnson* (New York: Scribner, 1964), 26.

7. Randy Roberts, *Papa Jack: Jack Johnson and the Era of White Hopes* (New York: Free Press, 1983), 62.

8. "Burns Favorite over Negro Fighter," *New York Times*, 25 December 1908, 5.

9. Stovall, "Jack Johnson and James Jeffries," 1.

10. Roberts, *Papa Jack*, 26.

11. "Three of the great white heavyweights of the late nineteenth and early twentieth centuries were Sullivan, Sharkey, and Jeffries. Sullivan's knockout percentage was 71 percent, Sharkey's 68, and Jeffries's 71. For the same period the best Black heavyweights were Jack Johnson, Sam Langford, Peter Jackson, Joe Jeannette, and Sam McVey. Johnson's knockout percentage was 40 percent, Langford's 39, Jackson's 44, Jeannette's 36, and McVey's 41." Ibid.

12. Jack Johnson, *The Autobiography of Jack Johnson—In the Ring and Out* (New York: Citadel, 1992), 165.

13. Ibid., 58. See also Jeffrey T. Sammons, *Beyond the Ring: The Role of Boxing in American Society* (Urbana: University of Illinois Press, 1990), 37.

14. Roberts, *Papa Jack*, 55 (quoting the *Richmond Planet*). But see John Hoberman, *Darwin's Athletes: How Sport Has Damaged Black America and Preserved the Myth of Race* (New York: Houghton Mifflin, 1997), xiv.

15. "Former Champ Dixie Auto Victim," *Chicago Defender*, 15 June 1946, 1.

16. Johnson, *Autobiography*, 184; Farr, *Black Champion*, 81.

17. "The Fourth of July, 1910–1776," *Chicago Defender*, 2 July 1910, 1.

18. John L. Sullivan, "Johnson Wins in 15 Rounds; Jeffries Weak," *New York Times*, 5 July 1910, 1.

19. Ibid.

20. "Sad Crowd at Ringside," *New York Times*, 5 July 1910, 2.

21. Johnson, *Autobiography*, 63.

22. Roberts, *Papa Jack*, 109; Farr, *Black Champion*, 93–94.

23. William Pickens, "Talladega College Professor Speaks on Reno Fight," *Chicago Defender*, 30 July 1910, 1.

24. Ibid.

25. Roberts, *Papa Jack*, 81.

26. "Jack Johnson Meeting," *Chicago Defender*, 26 October 1912, 6.

27. *Afro-American Ledger*, 26 October 1912, 4.

28. Billy Lewis, "He Said He Would Do It," *The Freeman*, 14 December 1912, 7; Luna M. Scott, "Justice for Jack Johnson," *Chicago Defender*, 16 November 1912, 4.

29. W. E. B. Du Bois, "The Conservation of Races," in *W. E. B. Du Bois, a Reader*, ed. David Levering Lewis (New York: Holt, 1995), 21.

30. Cary B. Lewis, "Johnson Is Liberated," *The Freeman*, 23 November 1912, 1.

31. Johnson, *Autobiography*, 13.

32. Roberts, *Papa Jack*, 223–24.

33. "Negro Repudiation of Johnson," *Afro-American Ledger*, 2 November 1912, 4.

34. "Champion Jack Johnson Denies Charges against Him in the Daily Newspapers," *Chicago Defender*, 26 October 1912, 1. Cameron, Johnson's second white wife, similarly defended her marriage: "I am a free woman and have a perfect right to marry whom I please." "Jack Johnson Bridal Party," *Chicago Defender*, 14 December 1912, 1.

35. Johnson, *Autobiography*, 76.

36. Farr, *Black Champion*, 107; Roberts, *Papa Jack*, 75.

37. See Sammons, *Beyond the Ring*, 42. Indeed, the response of the black community to Johnson's relationships with white women was sufficiently hostile that the day after Etta Duryea, Johnson's first white

wife, committed suicide, the headline of the *Chicago Defender* defensively proclaimed: "Mrs. Johnson Was Not Hated by Negros [*sic*]," *Chicago Defender*, 14 September 1912, 1. Duryea disagreed. As she told her maid shortly before she shot herself, "I am a white woman and tired of being a social outcast. All misery comes through marrying a black man. Even the negroes don't respect me. They hate me." Roberts, *Papa Jack*, 141.

38. "Opposes Negro Press Criticisms of Jack Johnson," *The Freeman*, 23 November 1912, 6.

39. "Jack Johnson in Bad," *The Freeman*, 26 October 1912, 4.

40. Reprinted in *The Crisis*, December 1912, 72–73.

41. Reprinted in *The Freeman*, 9 November 1912, 7.

42. Al-Tony Gilmore, "Jack Johnson and White Women: The National Impact, 1912–1913," *Journal of Negro History* 58 (1973): 18, 23.

43. Of course, the mere existence of mixed-race people does not automatically dismantle racial hierarchy because "the advantages of being white were so obvious that race prejudice against Negroes permeated the minds of the Mulattoes who so bitterly resented the same thing from the whites." C. L. R. James, *The Black Jacobins: Toussaint L'Ouverture and the San Domingo Revolution*, 2d ed. (New York: Vintage, 1989), 42–43. Indeed, "history demonstrates that . . . those who are mixed-race will . . . assert their White ancestry, while downplaying their African ancestry, in order to further themselves in the social structure and flee repression." Tanya Kateri Hernandez, "'Multiracial' Discourse: Racial Classifications in an Era of Colorblind Jurisprudence," *Maryland Law Review* 57 (1998): 97, 119.

44. W. E. B. Du Bois contended that for most white men "the race question at bottom is simply a matter of ownership of women; white men want the right to use all women, colored and white, and they resent the intrusion of colored men in this domain." Giddings, *When and Where I Enter*, 61 (quoting Irene Diggs, "DuBois and Women: A Short Story of Black Women, 1910–34," *Current Bibliography of African Affairs* 7 [Summer 1974]: 260); Barbara K. Kopytoff and Leon Higginbotham, "Racial Purity and Interracial Sex in the Law of Colonial and Antebellum Virginia," *Georgetown Law Journal* 77 (1989): 1967, 1997; Charles Herbert Stember, *Sexual Racism: The Emotional Barrier to an Integrated Society* (New York: Elsevier Scientific, 1976).

45. Paul Finkelman, "The Crime of Color," *Tulane Law Review* 67 (1993): 2063, 2085.

46. Gerda Lerner, *Black Women in White America: A Documentary History* (New York: Vintage, 1973), 51–52.

47. After the Civil War, sexual relationships between black men and poorer white women became more common as a result of the shortage of

white men in the South. See Joel Williamson, *New People: Miscegenation and Mulattoes in the United States* (Baton Rouge: Louisiana State University Press, 1995), 89–90. The interpersonal politics of romantic relationships between white women and black men were also complicated by the American racial hierarchy. "Everybody knew that if a Black man refused a white woman's advances, it was quite likely that she would accuse him of rape and he would be lynched. If he didn't refuse, and an affair began, and it was found out, an accusation of rape followed by a lynching was, again, the likely result. The woman could hardly afford to admit the truth, because if she did she would be banished from the community." Nicholas Lemann, *The Promised Land: The Great Black Migration and How It Changed America* (New York: Vintage, 1992), 35.

48. Emily Field Van Tassel, "'Only the Law Would Rule between Us,'" 873, 896. Laws prohibiting interracial marriage remained in effect until 1967, when the Supreme Court held that they violated the Fourteenth Amendment of the U.S. Constitution. *Loving v. Virginia*, 388 U.S. 1 (1967). Peter Wallenstein, "Race, Marriage and the Law of Freedom: Alabama and Virginia, 1860s–1960s," *Chicago-Kent Law Review* 70 (1994): 371; Peggy Pascoe, "Miscegenation Law, Court Cases and Ideologies of 'Race' in Twentieth Century America," *Journal of American History* 83 (June 1996): 44. The states that had antimiscegenation laws as recently as 1967 include Alabama, Arkansas, Delaware, Florida, Georgia, Kentucky, Louisiana, Maryland, Mississippi, Missouri, North Carolina, Oklahoma, South Carolina, Tennessee, Texas, Virginia and West Virginia. Wallenstein, "Race, Marriage and the Law of Freedom," 436 n. 318.

49. Martha Hodes, "The Sexuality of Reconstruction Politics: White Women and Black Men in the South after the Civil War," *Journal of the History of Sexuality* 3 (1993): 402, 415.

50. Gilmore, "Jack Johnson and White Women," 23.

51. "Jack Johnson in Bad," 4.

52. It makes intuitive sense that interracial relationships might weaken the political cohesiveness of the black community because appeals to racial solidarity would be less persuasive when directed at blacks who have familial ties to both black and white people. However, historically it has been more common for the white partner in such relationships to be adopted into the black community than for the black partner to be accepted by his or her white relatives or to abandon the black community. See Lisa Jones, *Bulletproof Diva: Tales of Race, Sex, and Hair* (New York: Anchor, 1994), 31–32; Jane Lazarre, *Beyond the Whiteness of Whiteness: Memoir of a White Mother of Black Sons* (Durham, N.C.: Duke University Press, 1996), 2; James McBride, *The Color of Water: A Black Man's Tribute to His White Mother* (New York: Riverhead, 1996), 23.

53. Johnson, *Autobiography*, 239.

54. See, generally, Eric Foner, *Reconstruction: America's Unfinished Revolution, 1863–1877* (New York: Harper & Row, 1988); Shapiro, *White Violence and Black Response*; Ward Churchill and Jim Vander Wall, *Agents of Repression: The FBI's Secret Wars against the Black Panther Party and the American Indian Movement* (Boston: South End, 1990).

55. David J. Langum, *Crossing over the Line: Legislating Morality and the Mann Act* (Chicago: University of Chicago Press, 1994), 181.

56. Johnson, *Autobiography*, 80–81.

57. *The Freeman*, 26 October 1912, 7.

58. Mrs. Cameron-Falconet claimed that "Jack Johnson has hypnotic powers . . . and he has exercised them on my little girl." Farr, *Black Champion*, 122.

59. The White Slave Traffic Act of 1910, 18 U.S.C. §397, 398, 401, 404 (1910) (current version at 18 U.S.C. §2421–24 [West 1970]).

60. Langum, *Crossing over the Line*, 15–34.

61. 18 U.S.C. §397.

62. Langum, *Crossing over the Line*, 42, 75.

63. The Supreme Court subsequently upheld the constitutionality of the statute as applied in such cases. *Caminetti v. United States*, 242 U.S. 470, 485 (1917) ("While immoral purpose [transporting a woman across state lines to have sex with her] would be more culpable in morals and attributed to baser motives if accompanied with the expectation of pecuniary gain, such considerations do not prevent the lesser offense against morals of furnishing transportation in order that a woman may be debauched, or become a mistress or a concubine, from being the execution of purposes within the meaning of this law").

In recent years the Mann Act has been rewritten to be sex neutral and to strip federal authorities of the power to define what constitutes an immoral sexual purpose. In 1978, the act was amended to prohibit the transportation of any minor—either male or female—across state lines "with the intent that such minor engage in, any sexually explicit conduct for the purpose of producing any visual depiction of such conduct." Protection of Children against Sexual Exploitation Act of 1977, 18 U.S.C. §2251. Revisions enacted in 1986 prohibit the transportation of adults or children of either sex in interstate or foreign commerce "with intent that such individual engage in prostitution, or in any sexual activity for which any person can be charged with a criminal offense." Child Sexual Abuse and Pornography Act of 1986, 18 U.S.C. §2421. This amendment gives states the authority to define what sexual conduct can trigger a violation of the Mann Act because there are no federal laws criminalizing sexual activity.

64. Roberts, *Papa Jack*, 158.

65. Johnson's first marriage to a white woman, Etta Duryea, which took place on 18 January 1911, was not widely publicized and did not generate much white backlash. In contrast, his second interracial marriage, following closely on the heels of the suicide of his first wife and his arrest on charges of violating the Mann Act, was born in controversy.

66. Gilmore, "Jack Johnson and White Women," 30–32.

67. Roberts, *Papa Jack*, 159.

68. Congressional Record, 62d Cong., 12 December 1912, at 503 (statement of Rep. Roddenberry) (the proposed amendment provided "that intermarriage between negroes or persons of color and Caucasians or any other character of persons within the United States or any territory under their jurisdiction, is forever prohibited; and the term 'negro or person of color,' as here employed, shall be held to mean any and all persons of African descent or having any trace of African or negro blood").

69. Congressional Record, 62d Cong., 12 December 1912, at 504 (statement of Rep. Roddenberry).

70. "Since tolerance of coerced sex has been the rule rather than the exception, it is clear that the rape of White women by Black men has been treated seriously not because it is coerced sex and thus damaging to women, but because it is threatening to White men's power over both 'their' women and Black men." Wriggins, "Rape, Racism, and the Law," 116.

71. Congressional Record, 62d Cong., 12 December 1912, at 503 (statement of Rep. Roddenberry).

72. Roberts, *Papa Jack*, 160.

73. "Miscegenation," *Chicago Defender*, 24 May 1913, 4.

74. Giddings, *When and Where I Enter*, 105.

75. Bob Teatowles, "'Bob' Teatowles after Congressman," *Chicago Defender*, 21 December 1912, 1.

76. *The Crisis*, February 1913, 180.

77. Roberts, *Papa Jack*, 159. See also David H. Fowler, *Northern Attitudes towards Interracial Marriage: Legislation and Public Opinion in the Middle Atlantic and the States of the Old Northwest, 1780–1930* (New York: Garland, 1987), 302–14.

78. Roberts, *Papa Jack*, 148.

79. Ibid., 157, 167.

80. "Johnson Convicted as a White Slaver," *New York Times*, 14 May 1913, 1.

81. Roberts, *Papa Jack*, 151.

82. *Johnson v. U.S.*, 215 F. 679, 682 (7th Cir. 1914).

83. Billy Lewis, "Champ Jack Struck below the Belt," *The Freeman*, 24 May 1913, 7.

84. "Champion Jack Johnson Is Sentenced to Year in Prison," *Chicago Defender*, 7 June 1913, 1.

85. *Johnson v. U.S.*, 215 F. 679, 685–86 (7th Cir. 1914).

86. *Johnson v. U.S.*, 215 F. 679, 682 (7th Cir. 1914).

87. "Champion Jack Johnson Denies Charges against Him in the Daily Newspapers," 6.

88. Ibid., 1 (the headline read: "Daily Newspapers Try to Incite Riot").

89. *Chicago Defender*, 16 November 1912, 1 (the headline read: "All White People Up, All Black People Down, Policy of U.S. Government"). Johnson was represented by both white and black lawyers. The *Chicago Defender* proudly noted that his black attorneys, W. G. Anderson and Edward H. Wright, were able to get Johnson released on bail even though his white attorney, Benjamin C. Bachrach, had previously failed to do so. "Jack Johnson Wins Abduction Suit—L. Cameron Would Not Appear against Him," *Chicago Defender*, 23 November 1912, 1.

90. Scott, "Justice for Jack Johnson," 4.

91. "Slavery—Black and White," *Chicago Defender*, 14 December 1912, 3.

92. "Jack Johnson and the Courts," *The Freeman*, 16 November 1912, 4.

93. "A Victim of Race Prejudice," *Afro-American Ledger*, 2 November 1912, 4. See also "No Evidence against Jack Johnson," *Afro-American Ledger*, 30 November 1912, 1 ("there is not a scintilla of evidence upon which to base the prosecution much less the persecution of Jack Johnson, except that he has committed certain offences against established codes of morality—for which half of the men in New York or Chicago or elsewhere could just as well be indicted and railroaded to the penitentiary").

94. *New York Amsterdam News*, reprinted in Billy Lewis, "The Jack Johnson Case," *The Freedman*, 30 November 1912, 7.

95. Johnson, *Autobiography*, 83.

96. "Jack Johnson on Trial; Great Interest," *Chicago Defender*, 10 May 1913, 1.

97. "Willard Victor; Johnson Retires from Prize Ring," *New York Times*, 6 April 1915, 1.

98. Johnson, *Autobiography*, 24, 197–203.

99. Roberts, *Papa Jack*, 218–219.

100. Ibid., 224.

101. James Baldwin, *The Fire Next Time* (New York: Dell, 1962), 139.

6

TWENTY YEARS ON TRIAL

Takuji Yamashita's Struggle for Citizenship

Gabriel J. Chin

Attorney Takuji Yamashita did not earn a dime practicing law, never won a single case, and, while he finished law school, could not even manage to get admitted to the bar. Unable to join the legal profession, Yamashita, like many of his fellow immigrants, lived a humble and anonymous life as a restaurant worker, farmer, and housekeeper. Yet his twenty-year legal fight to gain recognition as a citizen of the United States made him one of the great Asian American lawyers of his generation. When, because of his race, the law denied him the right to become a naturalized U.S. citizen, he pursued his claims to the highest courts in the land. Although the Washington State Supreme Court and later the U.S. Supreme Court ultimately determined that Japanese Americans such as he had no right to become citizens, and therefore no right to practice law or enjoy other privileges of citizenship, his struggle left an indelible mark on the history of the law that, decades later, reminds Americans of the way those perceived to belong to undesirable races or nationalities were treated in the past.

Takuji Yamashita was born in Ehime Prefecture, Japan, in October 1874. In the late 1880s, a handful of Japanese, many from Ehime, immigrated to Tacoma, Washington, to escape high taxes and limited vocational choices.[1] Tacoma offered many opportunities; the immigrants found success operating or working in restaurants, laundries, and shops. The comparative good fortune of the first intrepid Asian immigrants encouraged more, and by the early 1890s, Tacoma had a growing Japanese immigrant community.

Some of the young immigrants did not limit their activities exclusively to elevating pursuits. Tacoma's "Opera Alley" neighborhood became known for its gambling dens and brothels that served customers of all races. To combat the temptations of Opera Alley, members of the First Baptist Church set up a mission modeled on the successful settlement houses of eastern cities. It was intended to provide a place for newcomers to stay where they could learn to speak English, find gainful employment, and adjust to their new surroundings. The mission also sponsored the immigration of promising youth from Ehime Prefecture. In 1892, the mission brought over its first two students, Yoshitaro Nakamura and Takuji Yamashita.

Yamashita and Nakamura adjusted brilliantly to Tacoma, completing the four-year course at Tacoma High School in just two years with near-perfect grades. Both then went on to the law school at the University of Washington. Yamashita was committed to living in the United States and to practicing law.[2] He went though the procedures necessary to become a naturalized citizen of the United States, receiving naturalization papers from the Pierce County Superior Court on May 14, 1902. Also in 1902, he passed the Washington bar examination. Yamashita satisfied all of the requirements, so admission to practice and enjoying the legal status of an attorney appeared to be a mere formality.

On the day Yamashita learned that he had passed the bar exam, he must have thought that he was living the American dream. The melting pot worked for him. People with different colored skins made him one of their own, invited him to the United States, helped him get established, and gave him the opportunity to rise as far as his talents could take him. Yamashita's attachment to life in America was typical of Japanese immigrants in Tacoma, many of whom attempted to integrate themselves into their adopted society, wore western clothing, spoke English, and used American furniture. Many Japanese were more than mere sojourners, coming to the United States as families and establishing permanent homes. A handful of intermarriages between Japanese men and Caucasian women signaled commitment to the United States and successful adjustment to American life, but perhaps the most symbolically meaningful evidence of Americanization was the establishment of the Mikados, the Columbias, the Union Laundry, and other Japanese-American baseball clubs.

The welcome Yamashita and others received was not the only reaction to Asian immigrants in Tacoma. In Washington, as well as throughout the rest of the West and the nation, Asian immigrants were subject to a political movement that opposed their coming. Although immigration

was not numerically limited at the national level, special rules were created for Asian immigrants, even though they represented only a tiny fraction of total immigration. By the time Yamashita arrived in the United
States, immigration of his fellow "Mongolians" of Chinese ancestry had
been almost entirely stopped by the Chinese Exclusion Act, passed by
Congress in 1882.[3] California, Nevada, Oregon, Idaho, and other states
had also taken action against immigrants of racially undesirable backgrounds, limiting their rights to own property or work in desirable
businesses and professions.[4] Private citizens also caused trouble for the immigrants. In 1900, in Pierce County, while Yamashita was in school, un-
armed Japanese hop pickers were run out of their homes by a gang of
armed whites. The next year, a Washington legislator proposed a bill that
would prohibit employment of all aliens, except in the capacity of domestic servants. In 1908, the International Exclusion League, a group
opposed to Japanese immigration, held its first convention in nearby
Seattle; the keynote speaker said, "We are loyal to the flag that floats over
our country, and I never want to see the time when that flag has a yellow
streak in it."[5]

Yamashita may have thought that he was protected to some extent from
the wave of anti-Asian sentiment because he was a citizen of the U.S. by
virtue of his naturalization certificate. Although a Washington statute
limited admission to the bar to U.S. citizens, he had a judgment stating
that he was a citizen. There was a problem, however. Yamashita faced one
of the oldest racially discriminatory provisions of the laws of the United
States. A 1790 law permitted naturalization only of an alien who was a
"free white person." After the Civil War, Congress extended naturalization rights to aliens of African nativity or descent, as well as to free white
persons.[6] In 1922, the Supreme Court praised the principle of racial limi-
tation as "a rule in force from the beginning of the government, a part of
our history as well as our law, welded into the structure of our national
polity by a century of legislative acts and judicial decisions. . . ."[7] As a
person of Japanese ancestry, Yamashita clearly was not of African nativity or descent. In the views of some, Japanese were not "white," although
the question was debatable under the pseudoscientific rules of racial eth-
nography in vogue at the time. Perhaps, then, his naturalization certificate was invalid. The Washington Supreme Court acknowledged that
Yamashita met the other qualifications for admission to the bar, in that
he was "over 21 years of age, has been a resident of the state for more
than 1 year, and that he has the requisite learning and ability qualifying
him for admission."[8] Yet the court did not immediately rule on the ap-

plication for admission, instead issuing an order expressing "doubt whether a native of Japan is entitled under the naturalization laws to admission to citizenship."[9]

Yamashita responded as any well-trained American lawyer would when faced with injustice: he litigated. He filed a brief in the Washington Supreme Court arguing that he was indeed a U.S. citizen and therefore had the right to practice law.[10] In its use of the legal system, its idealism, and its appeal to individual rights, this remarkable document itself provides powerful evidence for Yamashita's argument that he was an American. The eloquent and careful language of the brief offered no hint of the author's foreign origins.

The brief is a surprisingly solid piece of legal analysis, especially for a lawyer just starting out. Yamashita drew on legislative history and case law and even appealed to "the spirit which pervades [the C]onstitution" in support of a series of interesting technical arguments.[11] He observed that Washington admitted lawyers from other states without the necessity of a bar examination, including states that did not require citizenship as a prerequisite to admission. Thus, he argued, "the proposition that all applicants for admission to the bar in this state must be citizens of the United States becomes absurd."[12] He made the reasonable claim that when Congress limited naturalization to "free white persons" in 1790, it could not have specifically intended to exclude Asians, for "at that time there was not a Chinese or Japanese person on this continent."[13] He also made a point that seems to have eluded even modern scholars of U.S. immigration law: When Congress allowed natives of Africa or those of African descent to naturalize, it extended the privilege in principle to Asians, stating that "any person born in Africa, no matter what his color or race, whether Indian, Negro or Chinaman, is capable of becoming a citizen of this country since any such person is an alien of African ancestry."[14]

Yamashita's legal points were interesting, but to the modern ear, Yamashita's strongest claim was his final appeal to justice and to American principles:

> Your applicant desires to express the hope that this court will not
> take the position that members of a race which has shown itself
> in a brief period of years capable of taking its place in the front
> rank among the most highly civilized and enlightened nations of
> the world, as has the Japanese, are not fitted to become citizens
> of this, the most enlightened and liberty-loving nation of them
> all one whose government and institutions are founded on the

fundamental principles of freedom and equality, a government and institutions made possible by the blood of men who consecrated their lives to the establishment of a country in which all men are equal in rights and opportunities.[15]

The attorney general of Washington was not moved by Yamashita's plea. Mocking "the worn out star spangled banner orations, based on the Declaration of Independence that all men are created equal," the state's brief insisted that courts could not "disregard the plain language and intent of congress and admit members of one branch of a race of people because they are more enlightened than the great body of people belonging to the same race who are excluded."[16] Yamashita responded, "Your applicant has no apologies to make for the so-called 'worn-out star-spangled banner argument.' He knows of no tribunal to which an argument based upon the Declaration of Independence and the spirit of American institutions could be more appropriately addressed than to the Supreme Court of a free American state."[17]

In one respect, Yamashita's brief fell short of an entirely modern analysis of the race issue. Arguing that Japanese were not subject to the laws aimed at Chinese, he wrote, "Surely the Japanese are not to be denied from mere accident of birth and without regard to fitness the right to become citizens of the United States because of a strict and narrow construction of a statute which was intended only to exclude from citizenship an ignorant and servile class of coolies."[18] This could be read as arguing that the anti-Chinese legislation was aimed not at all Chinese immigrants, but only at those among them who some opponents of immigration claimed were virtually slaves. Alternatively, it could be understood as accepting a broader stereotypical view of the Chinese. But even if it were the latter, the lawyer Yamashita has to be granted some leeway. Yamashita undoubtedly recognized that in *Plessy v. Ferguson*, 163 U.S. 537 (1896), the Supreme Court had rejected the idea that the Constitution prohibited discriminatory laws and, moreover, that the Supreme Court had upheld special restrictions on Chinese immigrants.[19] Because he was acting in a legal forum, he had little choice but to acknowledge, at least, even odious rules of law as expressed by authoritative courts.

On October 22, 1902, the justices of the Washington Supreme Court unanimously rejected Yamashita's petition for admission to the bar. The court explained that only whites and persons of African descent were eligible to naturalize and that therefore a person of Japanese ancestry like Yamashita could not be naturalized. Yamashita's naturalization certificate was declared void. The court made no pretense of regret; indeed, it explained that "from its existence coextensively with the formation of the American republic, [racial restriction on naturalization] must be taken to express a settled national will."[20]

Yamashita's legal career, for which he was so well suited and so well prepared, had ended before it had begun. For the next twenty years, instead of trying cases and arguing causes, Yamashita lived in the Seattle-Bremerton area, managing restaurants and hotels and raising strawberries and oysters. Later, Yamashita, who married and had five children, also offered informal legal assistance to members of the community and worked for the Baptist Church. Yamashita must have been disappointed, but he told a fellow restaurant worker, "Life is too short to be bitter."[21]

After Yamashita's failed effort to gain admission to the bar, the lot of Asian immigrants in the United States continued to decline. In 1902 and 1904, the Chinese Exclusion Act was renewed by Congress on a permanent basis. In 1907–1908, the United States and Japan concluded the so-called "Gentlemen's Agreement" whereby Japan promised to reduce the number of travel documents available to Japanese desiring to enter the United States. Thus, like those of Chinese ancestry, who were banned by the Chinese Exclusion Act, the flow of Japanese immigrants to the United States was cut back by law.[22]

World War I brought another set of ironies to residents of Tacoma's Japantown as well as other Asian American communities. In 1917, a number of young Japanese Americans, including some "aliens ineligible to citizenship," registered for the draft; many entered military service and performed this fundamental patriotic duty with honor.[23] At the same time, distrust of aliens and Asians in particular was on the rise. In 1917, Congress created the "Asiatic Barred Zone," covering most of continental Asia, which, with very limited exceptions, prohibited any person whose racial ancestry was traceable to that region from entering the United States.[24]

At the Paris Peace Conference, which established the League of Nations, Japan fought vigorously for a simple provision in the covenant that would have stated that all races were equal. Although a majority of countries supported this effort, the chair of the conference, U.S. president Woodrow Wilson, prevented its inclusion. Wilson, who introduced segregation into the federal civil service, had written on the question of Asian immigration to the United States, "I stand for the national policy of exclusion. We cannot make a homogeneous population out of a people who do not blend with the Caucasian race. . . . Oriental coolieism will give us another race problem to solve and surely we have had our lesson."[25] Clearly, tolerance for Asian immigrants had just about expired.

After the war, politicians in Washington State felt that the time had come to address the "Japanese question." Should Japanese immigrants be allowed to compete with American shopkeepers, farmers, and workers? Some white Americans rejected the idea that Japanese immigrants should be cut out of the economy; one Tacoma resident insisted that "the Japanese in this state have been good citizens." This view did not carry the day. Far more influential were people like Major Bert Ross, a leader in the Veterans of Foreign Wars, American Legion, and Washington Anti-Japanese League, who supported exclusion of Japanese and other Asians from the United States. "Do we want the day to come when the people of the yellow race are considered our social equals?" he asked, testifying before the Washington House of Representatives. "Do you want your daughter or your sister to marry a Japanese?"[26]

In 1921, Washington legislators answered the "Japanese Question" by introducing a series of anti-Japanese bills. Only one major law actually passed. As of June 9, 1921, aliens "ineligible for citizenship" also became ineligible to purchase, lease, or inherit land.[27] This law applied primarily to Asians, because aliens of most other races were eligible for citizenship.

The effect of even this harsh measure was mitigated to some degree by the behavior of some who opposed the law. Certain government officials did not enforce the alien land law; compliant whites also sometimes helped Japanese farmers evade the law. After the law was passed, for example, Pierce County landlord John McAleer did not renew the lease of his Japanese tenants but allowed them to farm the property and provided in his will that the land would go to his tenants' child; the child was a U.S. citizen by birth. When the law was enforced, however, it had tremendous practical consequences. A person unable to purchase or lease land is unable to farm or to operate a restaurant or other business.[28] The law was enforced through criminal prosecution, as well as through governmental capture of land held by aliens in violation of the law.[29] Through the doctrine of "escheat," such property became the property of the state.[30]

In 1922, Takuji Yamashita demonstrated for a second time that he was a formidable legal strategist. Direct constitutional challenges to the Alien Land Law had failed.[31] Yamashita devised another approach to defeat the law. The law prohibited aliens ineligible for citizenship from owning land, but perhaps a domestic corporation could hold land free of restrictions. Accordingly, Yamashita proposed to establish a Washington corporation, the Japanese Real Estate Holding Company, which might hold land in full compliance with the law. However, Washington secretary of state J. Grant Hinkle refused to accept the articles of incorporation; just as bar admission was restricted to citizens, so to was the privilege of establishing corporations. Yamashita, Hinkle declared, was not a citizen. The stage was set for another judicial test of Yamashita's citizenship.

This time Yamashita did not litigate the case on his own. He had the help of Washington attorneys, as well as the assistance of George W. Wickersham, a leader of the New York Bar who, as President William Howard Taft's attorney general, helped draft the Sixteenth Amendment, which allowed direct federal taxation of incomes. Yamashita first appealed to the Washington Supreme Court, but given its treatment of his bar admission case, it was clear there could be no relief there. When that court refused to order the secretary of state to accept the articles of incorporation, Yamashita petitioned for and received a writ of certiorari, which would take the case before the highest court in the land.

In the U.S. Supreme Court, Yamashita and his team faced the Washington attorney general, Lindsey L. Thompson. Much of their debate was devoted to close technical analysis of the naturalization statutes and exploration of the nuances of contemporary pseudoscientific racial ethnology and classification. The heart of the controversy was set out in the concluding argument of each brief. Yamashita's brief baldly claimed that "the Japanese are Assimilable."[32] Washington responded with an argument entitled, "The Japanese are Not Assimilable."[33] Yamashita's brief pointed out that "the dignity of manhood is held up by the Declaration of Independence as the highest ideal of Americanism."[34] It concluded with an argument about the treatment of Japanese in general that could well have drawn from Yamashita's own life: the Supreme Court should not conclude that "the United States, after extending a hand to welcome to its civilization a great and then well-contented people, did not coldly withdraw that hand, on the ground that they were among the undesirable and outcast of the earth."[35]

The state responded with an un–self-conscious defense of racism that is almost refreshing in its candor. "The assimilability of a foreign race," the attorney general explained, "is not established by demonstrating their theoretical fitness for citizenship because the problem is a practical one which cannot be solved by applying rules of morality."[36] "There can be no real assimilation of an alien race," he continued, "unless it is accompanied by a social assimilation which destroys the marked physical characteristics which differentiate races. . . . The judicial knowledge of the court with respect to the problem of the Negro, of the Indian and the Chinaman in the United States will sufficiently demonstrate this fact."[37] The Japanese, Thompson insisted, like other colored races, were incapable of social assimilation. Therefore, offering political or legal equality would only make a difficult situation worse.

> In the final analysis, the problem is a practical one which cannot be answered by assuming all men to be perfect. The granting of political equality, while desirable in a race capable of assimilation, in the case of a race not so capable, simply intensifies the problem. The history of the South after the right of suffrage was conferred upon the negro is ample proof of this fact. Facts are stubborn and unescapable, and they are not met by showing that from the standpoint of morality they should not exist. . . . If the decision of this case should turn on the possibility of the successful assimilation of the Japanese, the writ should be denied, because the Japanese will never be assimilated in this country, at least in our generation.[38]

The Supreme Court made short work of Yamashita's arguments, affirming the Washington Supreme Court in a brief opinion holding that Japanese were not eligible for naturalization under federal law.[39] Adding insult to injury, the Supreme Court cited as authority the twenty-year-old decision of the Washington Supreme Court denying Takuji Yamashita admission to the bar.[40] The main opinion on the question of Japanese eligibility for naturalization was issued the same day in *Ozawa v. United States*,[41] another case in which George Wickersham was counsel and one directly presenting the issue of whether Japanese were eligible to naturalize. In holding that Japanese were racially disqualified by law from naturalizing, the Court emphasized that "of course there is not implied—either in the legislation or in our interpretation of it—any suggestion of individual unworthiness or racial inferiority. These considerations are in no manner involved."[42] This was cold comfort to the Japanese, who could never become naturalized American citizens, no matter how long they lived in the United States, nor how faithful they were to their adopted homeland.

Yamashita's failed effort to outflank Washington's Alien Land Law was not his last interaction with American law. Yamashita's wife and children returned to Japan in 1927. The Gentlemen's Agreement, coupled with a 1924 federal statute banning the immigration of virtually all aliens ineligible to citizenship,[43] meant that the trip could permanently exile the

Yamashitas from the United States. However, after a couple of months, they returned, successfully relying on a provision permitting previous residents to come back.

World War II brought a final reminder of Yamashita's precarious welcome in the United States. After the Japanese attack on Pearl Harbor, he and other Japanese in the United States were incarcerated in camps. During the war, he was held in the Manzanar and Tule Lake camps in California and then in Minidoka, Idaho. At last Yamashita was not made to suffer for his lack of American citizenship, for U.S. citizens of Japanese ancestry and aliens alike were incarcerated. The rationale for internment was the myth that Japanese were eternally loyal to Japan and ineradicably Japanese, that is, that Japanese believed that race and citizenship were inseparable. Yamashita's fight to become an American citizen showed that opponents of Asian immigration pointed the finger of accusation in the wrong direction. Supporters of internment, not the immigrants, believed that race was destiny; opponents of Asian immigration, not the immigrants, doubted the attraction of American virtues and institutions.

After being released from Minidoka, Yamashita, who had lost his home and businesses, moved to Seattle, where he became a housekeeper for a widow. In 1957, he returned to Japan, where he died two years later, at age eighty-four. His law degree hung on the wall.

From one point of view, Yamashita's story is one of heartache and disappointment. He fought nobly and ably, but he never became an American citizen or even a lawyer—in the eyes of the law, at least. Moreover, the battle he lost was critical. The California Supreme Court reported in 1933 that all of the states imposed "an invariable requirement [for admission to the bar] . . . that the applicant shall be a citizen of the United States or eligible to naturalization."[44] Because Asian immigrants were neither citizens nor eligible for naturalization, these rules delayed the development of a corps of Asian American lawyers until there were significant numbers who were both educated and citizens by virtue of native birth. Asian Americans were hardly the only group in this situation—women and African Americans, for example, often had also been denied the privilege of practicing law.[45] But physical exclusion from the United States coupled with exclusion from the bar meant that any judicial campaign for the rights of Asian Americans would be put off and therefore that there would be no Asian American Lincolns or Darrows or Marshalls, at least until well into the second half of the twentieth century.

Yet history has vindicated Yamashita's views.[46] Virtually every legal position he advocated is now the law of the nation. The Alien Land Laws targeting Asians were held unconstitutional or repealed.[47] In *Takahashi v. Fish and Game Commission*, the Supreme Court struck down state laws discriminating against "aliens ineligible for citizenship" as a class, recognizing that such laws were intended to disadvantage "certain racial and color groups."[48] In 1952, Congress abolished the last remaining racial limitations on naturalization, so any eligible alien may become a citizen without regard to race, religion, national origin, or sex;[49] today, Yamashita's naturalization would be valid. In 1965, Congress eliminated the last vestiges of anti-Asian policy from America's immigration law.[50] Finally, in 1973, the Supreme Court held in *In re Griffiths* that exclusion of resident aliens from admission to state bars violated the Equal Protection Clause of the Fourteenth Amendment.[51] Today, even as an alien, Yamashita could not be denied the right to practice law.[52]

On balance, Yamashita's legal career must be regarded as a remarkable achievement. Although he did not win his cases, he won a significant point, proving that the ability to be a good lawyer and a devoted citizen was not the monopoly of any particular race. His record of taking two cases to the highest court is unmatched by many successful lawyers after a lifetime of practice. He left an enduring legacy; every detail of his twenty-year struggle for justice is indelibly recorded in the files and opinions of the Washington Supreme Court and the U.S. Supreme Court and therefore in law libraries in every courthouse and law school in the United States. More important, his work reflected an honorable, idealistic, even touching hope for justice and faith in the principles of the system and of the Constitution. Although his dreams of a legal career were crushed, he still believed that justice could be achieved through law.

After this chapter was drafted, the renewed interest in and attention to Takuji Yamashita's life persuaded the Washington Supreme Court to reconsider his case. In March 2001, the Washington Supreme Court posthumously admitted Yamashita to the bar.[53]

NOTES

Thanks to Dominique Jinhong, Bert Lockwood, S. Elizabeth Malloy, Donna Nagy, Wendy Parker, and Davis G. Yee for their comments and suggestions, which improved this essay immensely; to Dr. Tazuko Kobayashi, great-grandchild of Takuji Yamashita, for providing information about the Yamashita family; to Dr. Ronald Magden for graciously sharing his expert knowledge of the facts and history of Washington's Japanese community; to the University of Cincinnati College of Law for research support; and especially to my friend Paul Finkelman for inviting me to participate in this project.

1. Most of the details about the Japanese in Tacoma and about Takuji Yamashita's life are taken from Ronald E. Magden, *Furusato: Tacoma-Pierce County Japanese, 1888–1977* (Tacoma, Wash.: Tacoma Longshore Book & Research Committee, 1998); Steven Goldsmith, "A Civil Action," *Columns Magazine*, December 2000 (available on the Internet, <http://www.washington.edu/alumni/columns/dec00/civil1.html>); and personal communications with Magden and Tazuko Kobayashi, great-grandchild of Takuji Yamashita.

2. After law school, Magden reports, Yoshitaro Nakamura's history is unknown.

3. For a discussion of the Chinese Exclusion Act and other anti-Asian laws, see Bill Ong Hing, *Making and Remaking Asian America through Immigration Policy, 1850–1990* (Palo Alto, Calif.: Stanford University Press, 1993); Lucy Salyer, *Laws Harsh as Tigers: Chinese Immigrants and the Shaping of Modern Immigration Law* (Chapel Hill: University of North Carolina Press, 1995); Gabriel J. Chin, "Segregation's Last Stronghold: Race Discrimination and the Constitutional Law of Immigration," *UCLA Law Review* 46 (1998): 1–74, reprinted in *Immigration and Nationality Law Review* 19 (1999): 3–76; Gabriel J. Chin, "The Civil Rights Revolution Comes to Immigration Law: A New Look at the Immigration and Nationality Act of 1965," *North Carolina Law Review* 75 (1996): 273–345, reprinted in *Immigration and Nationality Law Review* 17 (1995–1996): 87–159.

4. See, generally, Milton R. Konvitz, *The Alien and the Asiatic in American Law* (Ithaca, N.Y.: Cornell University Press, 1946), 1–4; Charles McClain, ed., *Asian Americans and the Law* (New York: Garland, 1994).

5. Magden, Furusato, 25.

6. Chin, "Civil Rights Revolution," 281.

7. *Ozawa v. United States*, 260 U.S. 178, 194 (1922).

8. *In re Takuji Yamashita*, 70 P. 482, 482 (Wash. 1902).

9. Applicant's Brief at 2, id.

10. Id.

11. Id. at 17.

12. Id. at 9.

13. Id. at 18.

14. Id. at 18–19.

15. Id. at 27.

16. Brief of Attorney General at 48, *In re Takuji Yamashita*, 70 P. 482 (Wash. 1902).

17. Applicant's Reply Brief at 7, *In re Takuji Yamashita*, 70 P. 482 (Wash. 1902).

18. Id. at 27-28.

19. See *Fong Yue Ting v. United States*, 149 U.S. 698 (1893) (upholding requirement that Chinese aliens register, under pain of deportation); *Chae Chan Ping v. United States* (The Chinese Exclusion Case), 130 U.S. 581 (1889) (upholding Chinese Exclusion Act and holding that Chinese residents of the United States could be prohibited from returning from an overseas visit).

20. *In re Takuji Yamashita*, 70 P. 482, 483 (Wash. 1902).

21. Reported in telephone interview between Fred Ohno and Ronald Magden, 15 June 1998. E-mail received 4 March 2002 from Ronald Magden to Gabriel J. Chin.

22. Chin, "Civil Rights Revolution," 281 and n. 30.

23. Magden, *Furusato*, 53–54. The Supreme Court "rewarded" the service of Japanese veterans of the U.S. armed forces by holding that they were ineligible for a special naturalization benefit offered to "any person of foreign birth who served in the military or naval forces of the United States during [World War I]." *Toyota v. United States*, 268 U.S. 402, 407, 412 (1925).

24. Chin, "Civil Rights Revolution," 281.

25. Paul Gordon Lauren, *Power and Prejudice: The Politics and Diplomacy of Racial Discrimination*, 2d ed. (Boulder, Colo.: Westview, 1996), 89 (citing Roger Daniels, *The Politics of Prejudice* [Berkeley: University of California Press, 1977], 55).

26. Magden, *Furusato*, 62.

27. The law made an exception for land used for residential purposes. See *State v. McGonigle*, 258 P. 16, 18 (Wash. 1927). Other states had similar laws. See Dudley O. McGovney, "The Anti-Japanese Land Laws of California and Ten Other States," *California Law Review* 35 (1947): 7–60, reprinted in Charles McClain, ed., *Asian Americans and the Law: Japanese Immigrants and American Law*, vol. 2 (New York: Garland, 1994).

28. Cf. *In re Fujimoto's Guardianship*, 226 P. 505 (Wash. 1924).

29. See, for example, *McGonigle*, 258 P. at 17 (discussing criminal prosecution for violation of law).

30. See *State v. Hirabayashi*, 233 P. 948 (Wash. 1925) (affirming judgment that alien property belonged to the state), *aff'd per curiam en banc*, 246 P. 577 (Wash. 1926), *aff'd per curiam sub nom. White River Gardens v. Washington*, 277 U.S. 572 (1928).

31. See *Terrace v. Thompson*, 263 U.S. 197 (1923); *State v. O'Connell*, 209 P. 865 (Wash. 1922).

32. Supplemental Brief for Petitioners at 67, *Yamashita v. Hinkle*, 260 U.S. 199 (1922) (No. 22-177).

33. Brief for Respondent at 77, id.

34. Supplemental Brief for Petitioners at 68, id.

35. Id. at 73.

36. Brief for Respondent at 78, id.

37. Id. at 80–81.

38. Id. at 84.

39. *Yamashita v. Hinkle*, 260 U.S. 199, 200 (1922).

40. Id. at 201.

41. 260 U.S. 178 (1922).

42. Id. at 198.

43. Chin, "Segregation's Last Stronghold," 14.

44. *Large v. State Bar of California*, 23 P.2d 288, 288 (Cal. 1933) (citation omitted), overruled, *Raffaelli v. Committee of Bar Examiners*, 496 P.2d 1264 (Cal. 1972); see also *In re Hong Yen Chang*, 24 P. 156 (Cal. 1890) (person of Chinese ancestry not eligible for admission to the bar); Kiyoko Kamio Knapp, "Disdain of Alien Lawyers: History of Exclusion," *Seton Hall Constitutional Law Journal* 7 (1996): 103–48. Establishment of a citizenship requirement for bar admission coincided with the diversification of the immigration stream around the turn of the century.

45. See, for example, *In re Lockwood*, 154 U.S. 116 (1894) (denying women bar admission); *In re Taylor*, 48 Md. 28, 33-34 (1877) (notwithstanding the Equal Protection Clause of the Fourteenth Amendment, African American citizens could be disqualified from admission to the bar on the basis of race). See generally Paul Finkelman, "Not Only the Judges' Robes Were Black: African-American Lawyers as Social Engineers," *Stanford Law Review* 47 (1994): 161–209.

46. History has also blessed the Yamashita family. The four of his children who were born in the United States left no issue, but a daughter, Haruko, born in Japan, had ten children and twenty grandchildren. Several of Yamashita's descendants studied or worked in the United States; his grandson and namesake was an executive at Matsushita responsible for the joint venture that held Rockefeller Center. Those who were concerned that a treasured cultural landmark was in the hands of "foreigners" (see, for example, James Barron, "Huge Japanese Realty Deals Breeding Jokes and Anger," *New York Times*, 18 December 1989, B1) need not have worried, because the center was under the care of the descendant of an American.

47. See, for example, *Sei Fujii v. State*, 242 P.2d 617 (Cal. 1952) (holding California's Alien Land Law unconstitutional); see also *Oyama v. California*, 332 U.S. 633, 647 (1948) (Black, J., concurring).

48. 334 U.S. 410, 420 (1948).

49. Chin, "Civil Rights Revolution," 287.

50. Id. at 298.

51. 413 U.S. 717 (1973).

52. Indeed, courts have even struck down limits on aliens serving as incorporators of businesses, the issue in *Yamashita v. Hinkle*. See, for example, *Haight v. District of Columbia Alcoholic Bev. Control Bd.*, 439 A.2d 487, 491 n.7 (D.C. App. 1981).

53. Heath Foster, "Victim of Racism Will Gain Posthumous Bar Membership," *Seattle Post-Intelligencer*, 5 February 2001.

7

A WHITE WOMAN'S WORD

The Scottsboro Case

P. J. Ling

The case hinged on the word of two women against that of nine youths. The women were white, the defendants black, and the charge was rape. To a succession of Alabama juries between 1931 and 1937, race was the crux. Even when one of the women admitted that she had lied, even when the medical evidence was clearly inconsistent with the allegations of gang rape, even though two of the accused were barely thirteen, another was virtually blind, and a fourth was so infected with venereal disease that any intercourse would have been acutely painful, the verdict was always guilty.

It had to be because the southern credo of white supremacy was enmeshed in sexual panic. "The Negro is a great big manchild," wrote a leading white citizen to the *Birmingham News* about the case. He added, "Sex is the dominant quality of his makeup and he can no more help it than can a monkey or an African Gorilla."[1] Small wonder that, except for a few liberals, most white Alabamians congratulated themselves in April 1931 that such an incident, occurring near the northern Alabama community of Scottsboro, had actually been referred to the courts rather than settled by a lynching.

Such feelings proved misplaced. The Scottsboro case haunted Alabama, revealing that its racism included a virulent anti-Semitism. The case produced not one but two landmark U.S. Supreme Court decisions and a mass protest campaign orchestrated by the Communist party, both in America and around the world. Returning from Europe in 1932, Atlanta lawyer Earl Sims felt compelled by Scottsboro demonstrations in Switzerland, France,

Germany, and Spain to write to Alabama governor Benjamin Miller. Sims assured Miller that he was "neither a nigger lover nor a communist" but asked, "Was it true that a barbarous penalty was to be applied to children?" While understanding the governor's exasperation at the out-of-state chorus of criticism, Sims hoped that Miller would demonstrate that, in his state, at least, civilization "was in the ascendancy."[2]

On arrest, the accused were indeed young, but they would all be men by the time they were out of custody. Roy Wright, age twelve, and his friend Eugene Williams, age thirteen, were mere boys; Roy's brother Andy and his friend Haywood Patterson were nineteen. They first encountered their five codefendants on a Chattanooga to Memphis freight train on March 25, 1931. Charles Weems was just twenty and Ozie Powell and Clarence Norris were nineteen. Norris had boarded the freight with sixteen-year-old Willie Roberson, whom he had met in Chattanooga. None of them knew the near-blind Olen Montgomery until he was arrested with the rest of them in northern Alabama.

A posse surrounded the train following reports that black youths had forced some whites off the train. Although their initial testimony was garbled by panic, most of the Scottsboro boys admitted that there had been a fight. In their version, the white youths had provoked it but had then jumped from the train when their opponents proved too strong. As the train picked up speed, the black youths had saved one white youth, Orville Gilley, by helping him to scramble back aboard. Several of the boys insisted that they had not seen any women until the train was boarded.

Their accusers, Mrs. Victoria Price, a twice-married Huntsville mill-worker, and her younger coworker, seventeen-year-old Ruby Bates, told a different story of violence and rape. The latter charge so immediately incensed the local white populace that, at the sheriff's request, Governor Miller sent a detachment of militia to guard the Scottsboro jail. Given the mood, it was generally believed that a speedy trial would be prudent. Jackson County judge Alfred E. Hawkins convened a grand jury for March 30 and assigned all seven members of the Scottsboro bar to defend the boys. However, three of the attorneys were hired to assist the prosecution under circuit solicitor H. G. Bailey, and three others were excused. This left only the elderly Milo C. Moody, described by one contemporary as a "doddering, extremely unreliable, senile individual who is losing whatever ability he once had."[3] Since four of the boys came from Chattanooga, the black ministers there raised $50 for an attorney, but this sum could only secure the services of Stephen Roddy, a white attorney with an alcohol problem.

When the trials opened on April 6, 1931, national guardsmen manned machine-gun nests in front of the Scottsboro courthouse. Understandably intimidated, attorney Roddy had fortified himself with drink. He attempted initially to claim that he was there as an observer rather than as defense counsel. Nonetheless, with the elderly Moody to assist the out-of-state lawyer, proceedings began. With no preparation, having conferred collectively with their lawyers for less than thirty minutes, the Scottsboro boys went on trial for their lives.

Despite the hostile, packed courtroom and the attendance of crowds sufficiently threatening to require a military presence, Judge Hawkins brusquely denied defense attorney Roddy's application for a change of venue. To the relief of prosecutor Bailey, Roddy failed to insist on separate trials for each of his nine clients but rather objected only to the grouping of Roy Wright, a juvenile, on the same docket as Clarence Norris and Charlie Weems. Setting Wright's case aside, the court selected twelve white males from the county list of jurors for the trial of Norris and Weems. Shortly after 2:30 P.M., the prosecution called its first witness, Mrs. Victoria Price.

Mrs. Price's testimony was vivid enough to leave a lasting impression on any audience. In the context of the early depression era, it was striking that this young woman was prepared to speak so frankly about the most sordid aspects of her alleged ordeal. She reported that she and Ruby Bates had gone to Chattanooga in search of work on March 24th, staying overnight at Mrs. Callie Brochie's boardinghouse. They had tried the mills for work the next morning, but, disappointed, they had jumped a freight train home to Huntsville. They had boarded a gondola (an open topped car, whose high sides, intended to hold in loose loads, offered protection from the cold crosswinds). The car was carrying chert, and upon this flinty cargo the two women settled down for the ride with seven white male youths. In the midst of their journey, Price testified, the gondola was stormed by twelve armed African Americans, yelling "Unload, you sons-of-bitches." According to her testimony, the blacks drove all the white males except for Orville Gilley off the gondola and then demanded sex of Price. When she refused, they took her by force.

In a strong voice and without a hint of embarrassment, Price gave the virtually all-male courtroom a graphic account of the sexual assault. She told how one of the boys held her legs open, another kept a knife at her throat, and a third wrenched down her clothes. Six of the defendants— Montgomery, Norris, Patterson, Weems, and both Andy and Roy Wright— raped her in succession. Throughout the ordeal, she never stopped fighting and begging them to quit, she said. As the train slowed for Paint Rock station, the rape had finished and she was able to pull on her clothes. As the sheriff's posse rounded up the hoboes off the freight, the shock of the assault made her lose consciousness. She awoke to discover herself in a car en route to Scottsboro.

Roddy's cross-examination of Price was brief. He attempted to establish that she was a woman of low character. Price admitted that she had separated from the second of her two husbands, but Judge Hawkins sustained prosecution objections to Roddy's attempts to imply that Price was actually a convicted prostitute. Deterred, Roddy ended his interrogation, and the state called R. R. Bridges, a well-known local physician, to give his evidence. He boosted the prosecution's case only by stating that his examination of the two women had revealed evidence of sexual intercourse. Less expected were his additional comments. There were no signs of violent assault, and the semen found was nonmotile, a technical term signaling the absence of active sperm.

The doctor's specialist vocabulary may explain why the defense failed to note that he was implying that the semen was not of recent origin. Solicitor Bailey extracted from Bridges that it was just "possible" that six men could have had intercourse with Price without leaving lacerations or contusions. Woefully, neither of the two defense attorneys spotted the significance of Bridges's testimony, and they similarly failed to realize the importance of evidence provided by a second medical witness, Dr. Marvin Lynch. He commented that it had been hard to get enough semen from Price's vagina to conduct a lab test. If Price had recently been raped by six men, this should not have been so. Both Bridges and Lynch remarked that neither woman showed any sign of shock.

When Ruby Bates gave evidence the next day, Roddy was again ineffectual. Far less confident in her account than Price, Bates described the rape tersely. One youth had held a knife and another a gun, while a third had raped her. She let slip that when the lawmen first arrived, she had told them solely about the fight. Only later had she mentioned the assault on Price and herself. The defense failed to press her on this or other discrepancies between her account and Price's.

It is probably true that even a skillful defense would have failed to overturn the prejudice against the defendants, but what confirmed that prejudice was the contradictory testimony of the frightened boys themselves. Panicking under cross-examination, Clarence Norris tried to save his own skin by accusing the other eight. Roy Wright, he alleged, had held the knife while the other seven had raped Price. He alone had not assaulted her, and Weems had been the instigator. Such testimony gained Norris little sympathy. A member of the posse testified that he had taken a knife off of Norris, and, recalled to the stand, Price identified the knife as the one that Norris had taken from her. Declining his own opportunity to address the jury, Roddy heard the prosecution urge the death penalty for both Norris and Weems. Judge Hawkins then explained the law and the range of sentences that could be given.

Even before the jury had properly withdrawn, the preliminaries for the trial of Hayward Patterson began. Testifying for a second time, Price recalled further details. Patterson had carried a .38-caliber pistol, and his accomplice, Charlie Weems, had packed a .45. As they stormed the car, they both fired into the air. Price was certain that Patterson was one of the six "whose private parts penetrated my private parts." Bates was conversely vaguer the second time, admitting that she couldn't be sure which of the defendants raped Price. As Bates stepped down, word came that the first jury had reached a verdict. Hawkins ordered that the Patterson jury retire while the Norris/Weems one filed back inside. Then the foreman handed a piece of paper to the clerk. He read the words, "We find the defendants guilty of rape and fix their sentence at death in . . ."[4] His remaining words were drowned out by cheers and yells of delight as spectators hurried to tell their friends outside. As the news spread, the 1,500-strong crowd outside the courthouse voiced its uproarious approval.

Judge Hawkins pounded his gavel in vain. Finally, he had eight spectators ejected from the courtroom. But the damage was done. For once, Roddy was alert. He called to the stand Major Starnes, who had been assigned to attend the Patterson jury in the adjoining room. He testified that the jury had clearly heard the reaction to the guilty verdict against Norris and Weems. Roddy asked for a mistrial in the Patterson case on the basis of this evidence of mob influence, citing the precedent of *Moore v. Dempsey* (1923). In *Moore v. Dempsey*, the U.S. Supreme Court overturned the sentences imposed on seventy-nine African Americans in the aftermath of the 1919 riots in Elaine, Arkansas. Despite this precedent, Judge Hawkins denied the motion.

Resuming its case against Patterson, the prosecution had Bridges restate that his examination of Price found signs of intercourse. Again, Roddy had no questions. A new prosecution witness, Ory Dobbins, claimed to have seen a colored man grab one of the women and throw her down as the train hurried past his rural home. Declining to question Dobbins, Roddy opened the defense by calling Patterson to the stand. Like Norris, Patterson tried to save his own skin by blaming others. While he and his three friends from Chattanooga had not touched Price, he initially said that he had seen Weems and the four other defendants rape her. Later, however, he insisted that he hadn't seen either woman until the train stopped at Paint Rock. The next witness—thirteen-year-old Roy Wright—was similarly panic-stricken. Having initially stated that after the fight with the white youths, the defendants had scattered along the train, he then testified that he had seen nine black youths having sex with Price and Bates but that neither he nor his friends were among them. Roy's older brother testified the next day. Andy, like young Eugene Williams who followed him onto the witness stand, admitted that there had been a fight but claimed that no guns were involved, and neither youth had seen any white women on the train. Finally, Ozie Powell claimed that he, too, had not seen the women on the train, and Olen Montgomery told how he had spent the entire journey alone. In summation, prosecutor Bailey urged the death penalty, and with instructions from Judge Hawkins, the second jury withdrew.

A third jury was selected swiftly for the trial of Olen Montgomery, Ozie Powell, Willie Roberson, Eugene Williams, and Andy Wright. In what was her final performance at Scottsboro, Price was at her most dramatic. Montgomery, the one with the sleepy eyes, she declared, was the first to violate her. She was equally sure that Powell and Roberson raped her friend Ruby. Roberson also held her legs while six of the prisoners, including Andy Wright and Eugene Williams, raped her. Those not directly engaged in the assault prowled the car waving open knives and urging the others on, shouting, "Pour it to her, pour it to her." Even the initial fight with the white youths became more dramatic in this re-telling. Price recalled that the black assailants fired seven shots as they stormed the car.[5] She depicted a scene of savagery that powerfully evoked for white southerners the evils of Reconstruction after the Civil War. Historian Frank Owsley warned the annual meeting of the American Historical Association in 1933 that the outcry against the Scottsboro verdicts was the "third crusade, the sequel to Abolition and Reconstruction."[6]

When informed that the Patterson jury had reached a verdict, Judge Hawkins ensured that there was no repetition of the previous day's up-roar. Warning that he would jail anyone who became demonstrative, he explained that such conduct "is liable to make the case have to be tried over." When the clerk read the guilty verdict and the sentence of death against Patterson, the court remained still and silent.[7] After lunch, the third trial resumed, and Ruby Bates testified that she was unable to iden-tify her assailants or those of Price. Returning to the stand, Bridges confirmed that the defendant Willie Roberson had syphilis but conceded under pressure from the prosecution that intercourse, while painful, was not impossible for him. The first of the defendants to testify was Ozie Powell, who admitted hearing the fight from an adjoining car but denied seeing the women. Next came the sad figure of Willie Roberson, who told the jury that his main concern on the train had been to lie as still as possible because "there was something the matter with my privates down there; it was sore and swelled up." Andy Wright then testified that he had seen the fight and had helped Orville Gilley scramble back on board. Accused by Bailey of taunting Price as he raped her with the words "you will have a baby after this," Wright fervently denied it, saying "I never had any talk like you stated, none at all. I will stand on a stack of Bibles and say it."[8]

The near-blind Olen Montgomery explained that, like Roberson, he had not been with the others. Given his condition, he had seen nothing. Eugene Williams repeated his testimony from Patterson's trial. Under cross-examination, he acknowledged that a knife shown to him was the one taken from him in Paint Rock. But he insisted that he had kept it in his pocket throughout the journey. As soon as the defense rested, Price was recalled and swore that she had seen the same knife in the hands of both Williams and Weems as they held it over her during the rape. To counter the defendants' claims that they were in other parts of the train, Bailey had members of the posse testify that the defendants had been arrested together and that all the boxcar doors were closed. Finally, Orville Gilley, the white man left in the gondola after the fight, testified for the first time that he had seen all five defendants in the car. Although Gilley should have been a key witness, he was ambiguous about whether or not the women were even in the car with him. Roddy made no attempt to cross-examine him and declined his opportunity to address the jury.

To try to expedite the case of Roy Wright, who should have been tried in a juvenile court, Bailey privately offered to recommend a sentence of life imprisonment if Wright pleaded guilty. However, a guilty plea would end young Wright's chances of an appeal, so Roddy declined. The ensuing hearing lasted less than an hour before the jury retired to consider its verdict. The following morning, a finding of guilty was returned against Montgomery, Powell, Roberson, Williams, and Andy Wright. By noon, however, the fate of Roy Wright was undecided; the jury was irreconcilably split, not over his guilt but over the severity of the penalty. Judge Hawkins reluctantly ruled a mistrial. Later that afternoon, and for the first time in his five years on the bench, a tearful Hawkins sentenced the other eight youths to death.

Reaction to the verdict in Alabama varied along class as well as color lines. Booker T. Washington's successor at Tuskegee Institute, Robert M. Moton, wrote to Governor Miller to express relief at the averted lynching but added that he hoped that the governor would ensure that the full protection of the courts extended even "to the humblest, the poorest, and the blackest member of our commonwealth."[9] The middle-class white members of the Commission on Interracial Cooperation (CIC) asked their state representative, James D. Burton, to investigate the case, particularly the background of the two women. Burton visited Huntsville immediately after the trial and talked to Price (once, he noted with distaste, she had spat out her tobacco). Although he could not find Ruby Bates, the comments he heard about both women left him convinced that they were unreliable witnesses. When the hearing to consider a request for a new trial was held in early June 1931, Judge Hawkins was presented with several affidavits testifying that Victoria Price and Ruby Bates were prostitutes who had black as well as white clients. These allegations had already reached the local press which, like the prosecution, dismissed them as shameful lies.

By this stage, however, the entire case was inextricably linked to the issue of communism. While the more moderate National Association for the Advancement of Colored People (NAACP) hesitated, the Communist Party of the United States of America (CP) authorized its legal wing, the International Labor Defense (ILD), to organize an appeal. The ILD organized mass telegram and petition campaigns in the North and staged rallies at which it denounced the judgment as typifying the wickedness of the southern ruling class. As the cases moved on appeal toward the U.S. Supreme Court, the CP organized a six-month European tour for Ada Wright, Roy and Andy's mother. Chaperoned by ILD leaders, Ada Wright was induced to link her sons's fate to the "war preparations of the American boss class" and the perfidy of Social Democrats who were "fawning at the feet of the lynchers and their spokesmen."[10]

Southern white moderates were appalled. The CIC's leader, Will Alexander, warned that protests only "complicated the case" and made it more difficult for moderates in the South to act.[11] When not attacking the southern judicial system, the ILD was equally vehement in its criticisms of the NAACP. Black newspapers tended to share this disdain toward what Boston journalist Eugene Gordon dubbed the "Nicest Association for the Advancement of Certain People."[12] The NAACP's hesitant defense of the boys and its obsessive anticommunism aroused particular anger in July 1931 when it reacted to news of a police assault on a sharecroppers' meeting at Camp Hill, Alabama, by blaming the incidents on Communist *agent provocateurs*. With a reporter at the scene, the *Baltimore Afro-American* carried the headline, "The Only Reds Involved Were Rednecks."

Goaded into pursuing the Scottsboro case, the NAACP further damaged its reputation with its condescension to the defendants and their families. Unable to persuade them to break permanently with the ILD, it declared that the Communists were taking advantage of "humble folk" who had had "few opportunities for knowledge." In response, Eugene Williams's mother, Mamie, declared that they were "not too ignorant to know that if we let the NAACP look after our boys, that they will die." In the late spring of 1931, ILD attorneys won a stay of execution, pending the outcome of their appeal to the Alabama Supreme Court. A year later, they saved the boys from execution, pending appeals to the U.S. Supreme Court. The ILD continually protested mistreatment of the boys by sheriffs and prison guards, and they were more willing than the NAACP to extend practical help to the parents: food, clothes, rent money, and sometimes bus or train fare to visit the boys in Alabama's Kilby Prison. "I don't care whether they are Reds, Greens or Blues," Janie Patterson would say, "they are the only ones who put up a fight to save these boys and I am with them to the end."[13]

But what was the end to be? To the ILD's critics, this was the crucial question. The ILD accompanied its legal fight with a constant propaganda campaign that used the case to publicize the CP and to denounce its enemies in both the established social order and among liberal groups. This last step was in line with current Comintern policy, which held that liberal reformers deflected the anger of the masses at injustice away from revolutionary action. To the NAACP, however, the propaganda campaign that deluged public officials in Alabama with hostile telegrams and endless petitions was profoundly damaging to the Scottsboro boys' chances. At the end of 1931, after months of bickering, the NAACP's team of attorneys, led by Clarence Darrow and Arthur Garfield Hays, explained why cooperation with the ILD team of George Chamlee and Joseph Brodsky had proved impossible. "I have no objection to any man's politics," declared Darrow, "but you can't mix politics with law." The cases, he added, would have to be won in Alabama, "not in Russia or New York."[14]

Given the case's explosive combination of race and sex, the Communists complicated what was already a difficult case. When the Alabama

Supreme Court opened its session on January 21, 1932, Chief Justice John Anderson denounced the "highly improper, inflammatory and revolutionary" mail he and his colleagues had received "with the evident intent to bulldoze this court." On March 24, the court upheld seven convictions but granted Eugene Williams a new trial on the grounds that he, like Roy Wright, was a juvenile at the time of his trial.[15] Moderate Alabamians blamed the verdict on the Communist-inspired mail campaign.

Despite its open mistrust of the legal system, the CP hailed the U.S. Supreme Court's decision on May 27, 1932, to hear the boys' appeal as a "tremendous partial victory for the revolutionary working class."[16] A greater success followed on November 7, 1932, when Justice George Sutherland read the majority opinion in *Powell v. Alabama*. The court had confined itself to the issue of whether the Scottsboro defendants had been denied proper legal counsel. The Sixth Amendment guaranteed the right to counsel in the federal courts. To extend this right to the state system, the majority opinion argued that proper legal counsel was implicit in the "due process" guarantees of the Fourteenth Amendment. Sutherland declared that the widespread acceptance of the right to counsel in state courts had made the practice an integral part of due process. In the Scottsboro case, the majority of justices felt that the hasty appointment of Roddy and Moody by the court, and especially the limited time allowed for them to consult with their clients and prepare a proper defense, amounted to a denial of the right to counsel. Accordingly, the Scottsboro verdicts were reversed and the cases remanded to the lower court.

The narrow basis of the judgment dismayed some. Socialist Morris Ernst complained that the opinion had disregarded the equally key issues of an impartial trial and of the exclusion of African Americans from southern juries. Harvard law professor Felix Frankfurter agreed that "upon the question of guilt or innocence it bears not even remotely; the Supreme Court has declared only that the determination must be made with due observance of the decencies of civilized procedure." The CP similarly castigated the decision as a guidebook for legal lynchings. Despite his misgivings, Frankfurter recognized that the decision was an important application of the Fourteenth Amendment and one that added a further safeguard to *Moore v. Dempsey's* requirement that no court should be dominated by a mob. As well as the absence of intimidation, a fair trial now required that the accused have the proper means to present his defense, most basically adequate counsel and time. This was a significant step, since as Supreme Court Justice Brandeis had declared in an earlier ruling, "The history of liberty cannot be disassociated from the history of procedural observances."[17]

If the right to counsel had been strengthened because of the Scottsboro case, securing the right counsel was the vital next step for the young defendants as they faced fresh trials in 1933. Acquittal would require a superb defense. After some hesitation, William Patterson of the ILD secured the services of Samuel Leibowitz, a flamboyant New York lawyer. "Your organization and I are not in agreement in our political and economic views," Leibowitz wrote to Patterson, but the ebullient Jewish defense attorney would take the case because, he explained, it involved no "controversial theory of economy or government" but simply "the basic rights of man."[18]

The new trials were moved to Decatur, fifty miles west of Scottsboro, because of the strong prejudice against the defendants in Scottsboro itself. The defense made clear from the outset that it intended to raise broad procedural issues as well as case-specific arguments by asking for the original indictments to be quashed because of the exclusion of African Americans from the jury rolls of Jackson County. Witnesses such as James S. Benson, editor of the *Scottsboro Progressive Age*, readily testified that they had never seen nor heard of a Negro juror but calmly explained that this was due not to exclusion, but selection. Jury service required citizens of good character; in Benson's view, this ruled out all the local African Americans. As soon as it became apparent that Alabama's jury system would be challenged, state attorney general Thomas G. Knight, Jr., announced that he would lead the prosecution. The principle of states' rights, he told the court in March 1933, required that the selection of jurors be left entirely to the discretion of local commissioners.

When Judge James Horton denied the defense motion to quash, Leibowitz secured a one-day recess during which he and the ILD lawyers gathered evidence of a similar pattern of exclusion of African Americans in juries in Morgan County, where Decatur was located. The next day, Leibowitz demonstrated that black doctors, businessmen, and ministers, men of property and education, had been omitted from the rolls. Horton denied the motion but ruled that the defense had established a *prima facie* case; in other words, he conceded that there was evidence to support their claims. This assured Leibowitz that he could appeal any conviction successfully before a higher court. However, in other respects, Leibowitz's tactics threatened the boys' chances. By challenging local customs in various ways, the defense team antagonized local people. Raymond Daniell of the *New York Times* reported that Leibowitz's insistent use of the courtesy title "Mr." for black witnesses and his questioning the integrity of local officials had caused "row upon row of rough-faced unshaven countrymen in blue denim overalls" to set their faces in "hard, unsympathetic lines."[19]

This communal antipathy to the Jewish attorney sharpened following his cross-examination of Victoria Price. Although the jury was instructed to disregard the information, Leibowitz offered evidence that Price had been jailed in Huntsville for fornication and adultery. He induced her to state that after the assault she was bleeding from the vagina and managed to imply that before taking the train she had had intercourse recently with another man. In his cross-examination of Bridges, Leibowitz carefully established that less than ninety minutes after the alleged rape, the women appeared calm. He had Bridges explain that spermatozoa normally live for a period of from twelve hours to two days in the vagina but that the small sample of semen found in Price was completely nonmotile, and he had the doctor directly contradict Price's claim that she was bleeding.

Having cast doubt on the boys' principal accuser and shown how the medical evidence supported the defense rather than the prosecution, Leibowitz tried to use the defendants' testimony selectively to add further doubts as to their collective guilt. He decided to put five of the nine boys on the stand, beginning with the two most pathetic: Willie Roberson and Olen Montgomery. Roberson explained in court that his syphilitic condition was so painful that he had to walk with a stick. Montgomery, in turn, testified how he only had enough vision in his right eye to "not get hurt, that is all." Roberson also stated that he had ridden toward the rear while Montgomery claimed that he had stayed on a tanker car for the entire journey.[20] If these two seemed unlikely sexual assailants and had not been together on the train, what credence could be given to Price's accusations? However, if Leibowitz offered a far more compelling defense for the accused than they had received during their first trial, his efforts were countered by the skills and local popularity of the new prosecuting counsel, Thomas J. Knight, Jr.

At age thirty-four, Knight was a very young state attorney general who had a well-honed courtroom manner of quick-fire questioning designed to confuse. Ozie Powell almost immediately contradicted himself under Knight's interrogation. However, although Knight questioned Patterson for over an hour, he was unable to unsettle him or Andy Wright or Eugene Williams. They all told the same story of a fight begun by white youths and insisted that they had not even seen the two women until the train was boarded.

Leibowitz tried to bolster the medical evidence for the defense by calling a Chattanooga gynecologist as an expert witness to establish that the women's medical examinations were inconsistent with their stories of gang rape. On the fourth day of the trial, the defense called Lester Carter to further undermine the credibility of Price's testimony. Resplendent in new clothes, the former hobo explained how he and Jack Tiller had sex with Ruby Bates and Victoria Price, respectively, in Huntsville and later in Chattanooga as well. Carter said that he had jumped off the train when the fight began. When taken by police to Scottsboro, he admitted no knowledge of either woman and had even overheard Orville Gilley refuse Price's demands that he back up her accusations. Unable to shake Carter's story, Knight successfully established that the witness had benefited financially from the ILD, a deal symbolized by Carter's new suit.

Next came Leibowitz's star witness, Ruby Bates, who confirmed Carter's story and recanted her previous testimony of rape. Like Carter, Bates was well-dressed, prompting Knight to begin his cross-examination by asking her who had bought her the fine coat and dress she now wore. He aimed to show that she, like Carter, had been bribed by the ILD, at the same time appealing to the anti-Semitic connotations of New York money. The jeering laughter that greeted Bates's weak performance under Knight's sharp questioning suggested that the ploy was effective. Back in her hometown of Huntsville, residents spoke openly about riding both Bates and her "red" guardians out of town on a rail.[21]

The main summation for the prosecution came from Morgan County solicitor Wade Wright, who made anti-Semitic attacks on Leibowitz and Joseph Brodsky. He urged the jurors to show the world "that Alabama justice cannot be bought and sold with Jew money from New York." Angrily, Leibowitz moved for a mistrial, but Judge Horton denied the motion, although he rebuked Wright for his improper behavior. Leibowitz tried hard to turn the prosecution's intemperance to his own advantage. In his three-hour summation, he referred to the charges of "Jew money" and highlighted the doubts that had been cast on Price's testimony. He asked only that Patterson receive a "fair, square deal."[22] In his final argument for the prosecution, Knight appealed to the jurors' resentment of outside interference. The defense had "framed" its testimony, but this should not deter an Alabama jury from reaching a verdict of death in the electric chair.

Judge Horton, for his part, asked the jury to disregard the steady stream of telegrams of protest that had been delivered during the trial. He noted that the testimony of the two women was contradictory. Bates admitted that she had previously perjured herself, but the story told by her and Carter had not been contradicted by state evidence. The jury should concentrate on the central issue of whether there was reasonable doubt as to the guilt of Haywood Patterson.

The jury deliberated for twelve hours but not over Patterson's guilt, which they determined on their first ballot after five minutes. The delay was over the death penalty. Explaining the verdict, reporters stressed the damaging impression made by Bates and Carter, both fresh from New York with a new wardrobe in a time of acute economic depression. The continuing outside agitation and Leibowitz's attack on the broader tenets of white supremacy also jeopardized his clients' chances. Most basically, however, the verdict still rested on the phobia of miscegenation.

When Leibowitz returned to New York, more than 3,000 blacks filled Pennsylvania Station. Asked to explain the verdict, he vented his anger and fatigue. If they had seen "those bigots whose mouths are slits in their faces, whose eyes pop out like a frog's, whose chins drip tobacco juice, bewhiskered and filthy," he railed, "you would not ask how they could do it."[23] Such an outburst was a serious error because eight of his clients still had to face Morgan County juries. Barely a week later, on April 16, 1933, Judge Horton sentenced Patterson to die in the electric chair on June 16th. Brodsky moved for a retrial, and Horton suspended the sentence. Next, the judge postponed the other Scottsboro cases until local passions subsided.

The interval gave Judge Horton time for reflection. On June 22, 1933, he convened the court in his hometown of Athens, Alabama. However, instead of listening to defense motions, Horton read a prepared judgment setting aside the jury's verdict. He detailed the inconsistencies between the medical evidence and the rape allegations and the absence of effective corroboration of Price's claims. He concluded, "History, sacred and profane, and the common experience of mankind teach us that women of the character shown in this case are prone for selfish reasons to make false accusations both of rape and insult upon the slightest provocation for ulterior purposes." Price and Bates, in his patrician view, were culprits, not victims.

With hindsight, one can argue that fear induced Price's accusations. Confronted with a posse, she feared a multiplicity of charges. She and Bates were breaching vagrancy laws, and since Bates was only seventeen, Price might also be charged under a law prohibiting the transport of a minor across state lines for immoral purposes. As a married woman traveling with two men, Orville Gilley and Lester Carter, and en route to meet a third,

Jack Tiller, Price knew that she risked a charge of adultery. Fresh out of jail on the latter charge, Price seized upon the surest defense available to a white woman in the South: she cried rape by a black man. To save herself from a series of minor charges, she placed the Scottsboro boys on death row.

Bates, who went along with her older companion during the first trials, could not sustain the lying, especially when ILD attorneys offered her better treatment and more respect than she had ever known before. Addressing a crowd in Baltimore in May 1933, she advanced the CP's line that the boys had been "framed by the bosses of the south and two girls." As one of the girls, she was sorry for what she had done at the first trial but added, "I was forced to say it." Now, she declared, "I am willing to join hands with black and white to get them free."[24] When she returned to the witness room after testifying at the Decatur trial, Janie Patterson and Ada Wright smiled and took the hand of their sons' former accuser. Bates spoke alongside the defendants' mothers at ILD rallies. She corresponded with the women when they were apart and sent letters of congratulation to their sons when Judge Horton ordered a new trial in June 1933.

Bates's sensational recantation and Horton's overturning of the jury verdict, however, largely reinforced existing views of the case. Knight was adamant that Patterson be retried. He announced that Orville Gilley had filed an affidavit that corroborated Price's testimony in fine detail. The contrast between Knight's political fortunes and those of Judge Horton revealed the venom of local opinion. In Morgan County, Horton's supporters were unable to find any open support for the judge's reelection. Despite campaigning vigorously across the district, Horton lost a runoff election 9,416 votes to 6,856. It was the kind of result, lamented the *Birmingham Post*, "that made honorable men eschew politics."[25] The same racial resentment that ended Horton's career advanced Attorney General Knight to the lieutenant governorship. A Black Belt plantation district candidate, Knight unusually carried northern hill counties like Morgan by a handy margin.

Since Roy Wright and Eugene Williams had been adjudged juveniles, there were seven defendants scheduled for trial in late November 1933. The new judge was William Washington Callahan, who seemed set on avoiding Judge Horton's mistake of alienating local opinion. He was determined, in his words, "to debunk the Scottsboro case."[26] This meant minimizing the trial. There would be no National Guard, no time wasted on what Callahan regarded as peripheral technicalities or extraneous testimony, and no unnecessary delays: the whole thing should be over in three days. Such an approach deeply damaged the defense. Leibowitz continued to challenge the racial composition of local juries, and the jury lists for Jackson County were checked in court. Ten African Americans were named on the roll, but according to a defense handwriting expert, their names appeared to have been added after the closing date of registration had been marked by drawing red lines in the jury books. Callahan denied the defense's motion, claiming that experts always confused him and that he could not believe that his neighbors would commit fraud. Leibowitz believed that appellate courts would take a different view.

As the trial proceeded, Callahan sustained nearly all of the prosecution's objections during Leibowitz's cross-examination of Price. On his own initiative, the judge also interrupted Leibowitz's questioning with such remarks as "that's a waste of time," "that's enough of that," "that will do," and "treat the lady with more respect."[27] By not allowing the defense to ask Price about the thirty-six hours preceding the alleged assault, Callahan wrecked its whole strategy of giving the jury a more compelling explanation of why Bridges found semen in Price's vagina, but no other evidence of rape. When Leibowitz induced Gilley to acknowledge that he had been with Price in Chattanooga, Callahan preempted questions concerning their relationship there. When Leibowitz asked Carter, yes-or-no, if the two couples had intercourse in the presence of one another, Callahan called his question "vicious." Appalled, Leibowitz moved for a mistrial. The motion was denied. And when illness delayed the taking of a deposition from Bates, who was too fearful to return to Decatur, Callahan refused the defense a one-day adjournment.

In his summation, Knight demanded the death penalty in a manner that Leibowitz asserted "was an appeal to passion and prejudice." "It certainly is," responded Knight, "It's an appeal to passion!" Having overruled another motion for a mistrial, Callahan allowed Knight to insist on the death penalty as a deterrent to "protect the womanhood of the state of Alabama." In charging the jury, Callahan took it upon himself to refute the defense's case. As a final sign of prejudice, when instructing the jury as to the forms of verdict available, the judge neglected to provide the form for an acquittal. If the first two Scottsboro trials had shown signs of mob intimidation, the third displayed evidence of pressure from the bench. The guilty verdict against Haywood Patterson was entirely predictable and the same pattern prevailed in the retrial of Clarence Norris.

The appeals process continued to delay the scheduled executions, although with increasing difficulty. When the ILD filed a motion for a retrial in February 1934, it was ruled to be too late, despite Judge Callahan's prior approval. In June 1934, the Alabama Supreme Court denied Patterson's appeal on these technical grounds and rejected Norris's appeal on the basis of the exclusion of African American jurors. In October, a botched attempt by ILD representatives to "buy" Victoria Price's cooperation was exposed. This triggered a fight between the ILD and Leibowitz over who should represent the boys. After much bickering, Leibowitz agreed to lead Norris's appeal before the U.S. Supreme Court while ILD attorneys Osmund Fraenkel and Walter Pollak represented Patterson. Lieutenant Governor Thomas Knight represented Alabama.

The nine justices who considered the issue of racial exclusion raised by the cases in the spring of 1935 were well aware that Scottsboro had generated national indignation. The absence of African Americans from juries within living memory created a *prima facie* case for judicial review, and the questionable insertion of black names onto the Jackson County rolls added to the justices' misgivings. Chief Justice Hughes reversed the verdict and ordered the lower court to ensure that any future proceedings allow Clarence Norris equal protection under the law. Somewhat disingenuously, without commenting on the harsh technical grounds for the state's denying his appeal, the Supreme Court simply returned the Patterson case to the Alabama high court so that it could consider the case in the light of the *Norris v. Alabama* ruling.

Liberals outside of the South hoped that this second rebuff might open the way for the defendants' release. There was a new governor, Bibbs Graves, in Alabama, and his lieutenant, Knight, might decide that the case had taken his political career far enough. Inside Alabama, however, white public opinion remained obdurate, and so the defendants returned to Judge Callahan's courtroom. In November 1935, with one black member, a Jackson County grand jury reindicted the Scottsboro boys.

One hopeful sign was a new harmony among the boys' supporters now that the CP had urged its members to form a Popular Front. A by-product of the new policy was the decision to use a local attorney, Clarence Watts of Huntsville, as the main counsel. While this reduced Leibowitz's tendency to antagonize the South, the main problem for the defense remained Judge Callahan. When the fourth trial of Haywood Patterson began, it was clear that Callahan would be as hostile as ever. By keeping the court in session for twelve hours, the judge ensured that the defense rested its case on the afternoon of the second day. The local prosecutor urged the jury not to "quibble over the evidence. . . . Get it done quick and protect the womanhood of this great State."[28] Clarence Watts, in reply, hoped that they would have the courage to do the right thing in the face of a clamor for the wrong thing. Callahan's hostile summation extinguished defense hopes.

The jury's guilty verdict assigned Patterson a jail term of seventy-five years. Jury foreman John Burleson was largely responsible for this change. An abstemious Methodist, he believed that Patterson was guilty, but he knew that Negroes had "more animal in 'em than white folks. The beast in 'em rides 'em and they go temporarily insane and do things they swear they would never do."[29] This racist logic prompted Burleson to hold out against the death penalty calls of his fellow jurors. White belief in the innate savagery of the defendants was boosted the following day. As the prisoners were being returned to the Birmingham jail, Ozie Powell reacted violently to verbal and physical abuse and slashed a deputy sheriff's throat. The driver, Sheriff Sandlin, halted the car and shot Powell in the head, causing permanent brain damage. The long period in prison took its toll on the other defendants as well. Allan Chalmers of the Scottsboro Defense Committee began to fear that "we may yet free the boys only to discover that they have already been executed as far as practical living is concerned."[30]

The sudden death of Knight in July 1936 raised hopes that Governor Graves might agree to some life- and face-saving compromise over the now notorious case. Despite these hopes, 1937 began inauspiciously when the Alabama Supreme Court affirmed Patterson's conviction. In the summer of 1937, Clarence Norris was tried, convicted, and sentenced to death for a third time, and his codefendants, Andy Wright and Charlie Weems, received prison terms of ninety-nine and seventy-five years, respectively. On the separate matter of his assault on the deputy sheriff, Ozie Powell was sentenced to twenty years.

The pressure took its toll on counsel as well as defendants. Before the Weems trial, Watts withdrew from the defense team, broken by the ostracism of his Huntsville neighbors. For his part, Leibowitz could no longer disguise his anger at the sectionalism and anti-Semitism of the latest trials. At the end of the Weems trial, he shouted, "It isn't Charley Weems on trial in this case, it's a Jew lawyer and New York State put on trial here." It was "poppycock" for the state to claim that blacks and whites received equal justice in Alabama. Having interviewed a thousand potential jurors in Morgan County, he had not found one who would admit prejudice under oath, but on the street they rated a Negro's chance of a fair trial as less than one in a thousand.

Both sides were tiring. Alabama authorities decided to drop the rape charges against Powell, and shortly thereafter, they announced that no further charges would be brought against Williams, Montgomery, Roberson, and Roy Wright. The same evidence that released four defendants perversely kept four more in jail. However, this anomaly did not fall within the jurisdiction of the U.S. Supreme Court, which declined to review Haywood Patterson's conviction on October 27, 1937.

The only recourse left was an appeal for clemency to Governor Graves. Southern moderates pointed out that freeing the Scottsboro boys would be politic, since Congress was currently considering antilynching legislation. Graves, however, insisted that his hands were tied until the appeals process was exhausted. But, at the same time, the Scottsboro Defense Committee could not surrender the appeals without concrete guarantees from the governor. In mid-June 1938, the Alabama Supreme Court affirmed the death sentence of Clarence Norris and the prison sentences of Andrew Wright and Charley Weems. Graves immediately commuted Norris's sentence to life imprisonment. However, he went no further, and in August the state parole board unanimously denied pardons to all four.

Weighing the political costs of executive action, Governor Graves decided to interview Norris, Patterson, Powell, Weems, and Wright. First, he interviewed Patterson, who was carrying a concealed blade when he arrived at the governor's mansion. Graves doubted whether Patterson had planned an assassination but suspected he had hoped to escape. A sneering and uncooperative Ozie Powell was next. Wright and Weems spoke more sense, in the governor's opinion, but gave clearly coached answers to his questions. Moreover, immediately after his interview, Weems violated Kilby Prison's strictest rule by strutting into the white section to boast of his impending release.

Norris was interviewed last. Prison officials at the Atmore Prison Farm had warned Graves that Norris and Patterson were feuding over a homosexual lover they shared. After asking Norris about his alleged crime, Graves asked about his death threats to Patterson. The handcuffed prisoner looked the governor in the eye and snarled, "Yes, I'll kill him! I never furgits [sic]."[31] "They are anti-social, they are bestial, they are unbelievably stupid," a shaken Graves concluded, "and I do not believe they can be rehabilitated in freedom."

After Graves's refusal to pardon the remaining five defendants, the media seemed to lose interest in the case. After briefly and unsuccessfully trying to cash in on their notoriety, the four released youths mostly managed to adjust to the difficulties of an anonymous life. Roy Wright, described as near psychotic in prison in 1937, was happily married and had a steady job by 1939. Eugene Williams and Willie Roberson also settled eventually, but Olen Montgomery was frequently jailed for drunkenness. His every misdeed proved to Alabama authorities that the remaining prisoners were unworthy of parole. Montgomery's difficulties, which included a rape accusation in Detroit, haunted Allan Chalmers of the SDC. "I have a feeling that even though we get the rest of them out," he wrote in 1943, "they are probably already too ruined by this experience."[32]

The main process working in favor of the imprisoned "boys" was the passage of time, which pushed them further away from the headlines. In November 1943, the Alabama parole board quietly released Weems, and in January, Andy Wright and Clarence Norris were paroled. But being required to find work quickly, Wright and Norris had to work for low wages at an Alabama lumber company. Fleeing the state, they broke their parole and, when Chalmers persuaded them to surrender to state authorities, were returned to jail. In late 1946, Ozie Powell was released, and Norris was paroled once more. Wright was returned to jail again when local employers refused to hire a "Scottsboro Boy."

With little chance of parole, Haywood Patterson escaped from a work gang in the summer of 1948 and remarkably made it to his sister's home in Detroit. Assisted by the Civil Rights Congress, the ILD's successor, he stayed in hiding for two years before the Federal Bureau of Investigation caught up with him. Aware of the black vote's influence in Michigan, Governor Mennen Williams blocked his extradition. On June 9, 1950, nineteen years and two months after his first arrest, Andy Wright—the last of the Scottsboro Boys—walked through the gates of Kilby Prison. He told reporters he had no hard feelings and felt sorry for the girl who had lied, because she probably didn't sleep at night.

Like most of the defendants, Victoria Price and Ruby Bates lived their lives in penurious obscurity. Debilitated by tuberculosis, Bates lived with her mother in Huntsville, while Price eked out a living in neighboring Flintsville. Frightened of what might be done to her on account of her gender and her poverty, Price had wrapped herself in the one social identity that offered her the probability of privilege and protection, whiteness. Nearly a hundred white Alabamian jurors were blind to every other fact, but the more desperately they defended white supremacy, the more they railed against outside interference, the more vulnerable they made the southern way of life. Patrician southerners grew increasingly ashamed and liberals nationally grew ever more embarrassed as echoes of European anti-Semitism and authoritarian injustice reverberated around an American courtroom. The nation, rather than simply race, had been put on trial, and for nine young African Americans, it had failed.

NOTES

1. Quoted by James Goodman, *Stories of Scottsboro* (New York: Pantheon, 1994), 116.

2. Ibid., 59.

3. Dan T. Carter, *Scottsboro: A Tragedy of the American South* (Baton Rouge: Louisiana State University Press, 1969), 18. Unless otherwise indicated, all general details are taken from this study.

4. Ibid., 36, 37.

5. Ibid., 42–43.

6. Goodman, *Stories*, 113.

7. Carter, *Scottsboro*, 43.

8. Ibid., 45–46.

9. Goodman, *Stories*, 58.

10. Carter, *Scottsboro*, 172.

11. Goodman, *Stories*, 58.

12. Ibid., 68.

13. All quotations from Goodman, *Stories*, 84.

14. Carter, *Scottsboro*, 101–2.

15. Ibid., 156, 159.

16. Ibid., 160.

17. Goodman, *Stories*, 88–89.

18. Ibid., 104.

19. Carter, *Scottsboro*, 202.

20. Ibid., 221–22.

21. Ibid., 235.

22. Ibid., 235–37.

23. Ibid., 244.

24. Goodman, *Stories*, 198.

25. Ibid., 207.

26. Carter, *Scottsboro*, 275.

27. Goodman, *Stories*, 212.

28. Carter, *Scottsboro*, 345.

29. Ibid., 348.

30. Ibid., 361.

31. Ibid., 390; Goodman, *Stories*, 323.

32. Carter, *Scottsboro*, 402.

8

KOREMATSU V. UNITED STATES REVISITED

1944 and 1983

Roger Daniels

Be not afraid of greatness; some men are born great, some achieve greatness, and some have greatness thrust upon them.

Shakespeare, *Twelfth Night*

Fred Korematsu is a man whose greatness was thrust upon him. Each of the other litigants in the so-called *Japanese American Cases*—Minoru Yasui, Gordon Hirabayashi, and Mitsuye Endo—deliberately challenged the unjust government decrees that led to the incarceration of the West Coast Japanese American community.[1] Fred Korematsu just wanted to be left alone.

Fred Toyosaburo Korematsu was born in Oakland, California, in 1919, one of four sons of immigrants from Japan.[2] He graduated from Oakland High School in 1938, briefly attended college, and then completed a course in welding at a trade school. He found employment as a shipyard welder, which entailed membership in the Boilermakers Union.[3] In June 1941, perhaps anticipating a call from his draft board, Korematsu volunteered to join the U.S. Navy and was rejected; in July he was classified 4-F, unfit for military service, because of gastric ulcers. Sometime in the months before the United States entered the war, he began keeping company with

Ida Boitano, a second-generation Italian American woman whose parents objected to their romance. Thus, on the eve of the Pearl Harbor attack, Korematsu, who lived with his parents in San Leandro where they ran a nursery, was a 22-year-old U.S. citizen with a good job and reasonable prospects. The war cost him his job—the Boilermakers insisted that Japanese Americans be fired—but he found other welding jobs in the booming war economy. His biography was significantly different from most of his Nisei (American-born children of Japanese-born parents) contemporaries in at least three respects: he was employed in manufacturing and had been a member of a largely white trade union; he had an interracial romance; and, as near as we can tell, almost none of his associations outside of his family were in the ethnic community.

What Franklin Roosevelt called the date of infamy changed forever the lives of Japanese Americans, especially those who lived on the West Coast. The 1940 census had enumerated 126,948 mainland Japanese Americans, 88.5 percent of whom lived in the three West Coast states, chiefly—73.8 percent of the total—in California. The majority, 62.7 percent, were native-born U.S. citizens in early 1940. All foreign-born Japanese, except for a couple of dozen World War I veterans of the U.S. armed forces, were "aliens ineligible to citizenship" because of their race; their American-born children, of course, were citizens. To put these numbers into perspective, nine-tenths of one percent of the population of the continental United States was of Japanese birth or origin: the figure for the Pacific states was 1.2 percent, and that for California, 1.4 percent. Rarely in history have so few frightened so many.[4]

On December 7 and 8, 1941, Roosevelt signed proclamations that, under the authority of sections 21–24 of Title 50 of the U.S. Code, declared that Japan, Germany, and Italy were at war with the United States. Thus, in the language of the law, "all natives, citizens, denizens, or subjects of [those countries], being of the age of fourteen years and upward, who shall be in the United States and not actually naturalized, shall be liable to be apprehended, restrained, secured, and removed as alien enemies."[5] As a result of the Alien Registration Act of 1940, which had required all resident aliens to register at their local post offices, the government knew that there were some 1.1 million "alien enemies" in the continental United States: 695,363 Italians, 314,715 Germans, and 91,858 Japanese.[6] While, in theory, all of those persons over thirteen years of age were liable to internment, the Roosevelt administration never intended to intern any sizable percentage of them. Attorney General Francis Biddle, a civil libertarian of sorts, and his staff in the Department of Justice planned for a minimal program and were aware of the gross injustices suffered by German and Italian resident aliens in Winston Churchill's Great Britain.[7] In preparation for war, various federal security agencies, military and civilian, had prepared Custodial Detention Lists, better known as "ABC Lists," master indices of persons who were, allegedly, potentially dangerous subversives.[8] The "A" list consisted of persons identified as "known dangerous" aliens; the "B" list were "potentially dangerous" individuals; and the "C" list were people who merited surveillance due to pro-Axis sympathies. As is common for internal security lists, they were largely based on "guilt by association" rather than individual investigations; most of the names came from membership and subscription rolls of organizations and publications deemed subversive.

It is not yet—and may never be—possible to give precise figures for either the total number of persons interned or their breakdown by nationality. The best "guesstimate" of the total number of persons resident in the United States actually interned is something under 11,000, broken down as follows: Japanese, perhaps 8,000; Germans, perhaps 2,300; and only a few hundred Italians. Many more were arrested and held in custody for days and even weeks without being officially interned.

In addition, the U.S. government brought more than 2,000 Japanese, a few hundred Germans, and a few dozen Italians into the United States from several Latin American countries, chiefly Peru. These were persons who had originally been interned by Latin American governments at the request of the United States, which feared that such persons might be engaged in dreaded—and we now know chimerical—"fifth column" activities. If fanatical American officials, such as ambassador to Peru R. Henry Norweb, had had their way, the entire Japanese Peruvian population, some 25,000 persons, would have been brought to the United States, but Washington soon called a halt to this foolishness.[9] Thus only a small fraction of Japanese nationals were picked up, most of them during December 1941.

Although there were many hardships caused by the internment program, it was, all things considered, a relatively modest and traditional one.[10] There were, as 1942 began, more than a quarter of a million ethnic Japanese at liberty in the continental United States and Hawaii. But, as the war news became worse and worse, military and political leaders, abetted by journalists and pressure groups, campaigned for a program of incarceration for all ethnic Japanese, both alien and citizen. An intricate sequence of events resulted in the issuance of Executive Order 9066 by

President Roosevelt on February 19, 1942, the real date of infamy as far as the Constitution was concerned.[11]

EO 9066, invoking what came to be known as "military necessity" ("whereas the successful prosecution of the war requires every possible protection against espionage and against sabotage") authorized the secretary of war and military commanders he might designate to "prescribe military areas . . . from which any or all persons may be excluded" and "to provide for [excluded] residents . . . transportation, food, shelter, and other accommodations . . . until other arrangements are made." No ethnic group was specified, but government spokesmen, military and civilian, immediately made it clear that Japanese were the primary targets. The next day, a secret letter from Secretary of War Henry L. Stimson delegated that authority to the West Coast commander, Lieutenant General John L. DeWitt. A secret memorandum to DeWitt from Assistant Secretary of War John J. McCloy divided the affected population into six classes, as follows:

1. Japanese aliens
2. American citizens of Japanese lineage (whom DeWitt's headquarters soon began referring to as "Japanese non-aliens")
3. German aliens
4. Italian aliens
5. Any persons, whether citizens or aliens, who are suspected for any reason by you or your responsible subordinates, of being actually or potentially dangerous, either as saboteurs, espionage agents, fifth-columnists, or subversive persons
6. All other persons who are, or who may be, within the Western Defense Command[12]

No persons other than Japanese or persons of part-Japanese ancestry were incarcerated by DeWitt's headquarters, although a number of Italian and German nationals were forced to move from prohibited areas. DeWitt at one time planned to place European alien enemies in camps, but Washington quickly overruled him. In practice, the delegation of authority to DeWitt was pro forma: the civilians who ran the War Department, Stimson and McCloy, pulled the strings and eventually replaced DeWitt with a more politic general. DeWitt also intended to incarcerate all Japanese living in the Western Defense Command, which included Montana, Wyoming, Idaho, Nevada, and Utah, but his superiors restricted him to the state of California, the western regions of Washington and

Oregon, and the southern part of Arizona. There was even some talk of mass incarceration of European alien enemies elsewhere.[13]

Since the government defended the incarceration of some 70,000 citizens as "military necessity," it is instructive to note just how slowly it moved. EO 9066 was promulgated on the seventy-fourth day after Pearl Harbor; the first Japanese U.S. citizens to be sent to camps were moved on March 29, the one hundred and second day after Pearl Harbor; and the last group to be sent into exile entered camp on September 29, nearly ten months after the war began.

But the infringement of the rights of Japanese Americans by their own government began immediately after Pearl Harbor when Attorney General Biddle signed an order closing the Canadian and Mexican borders to enemy aliens and "all persons of Japanese ancestry, whether citizen or alien." By the end of the month, the attorney general had virtually nullified the Fourth Amendment by formally authorizing warrantless searches of any premises in which an enemy alien lived. Since most Nisei lived in multigenerational households, this covered most citizens. But it was the army, acting under Roosevelt's blanket delegation of authority, that was the chief violator of the rights of the Nisei. On March 2, DeWitt issued the first of a series of numbered proclamations. Proclamation No. 1 divided the three West Coast states into two military zones: a coastal area called Military Area No. 1, from which presumably enemy aliens and any Japanese person would eventually be excluded, and an interior Military Area No. 2, for which no "prohibition or regulation or restriction" was contemplated. It also provided that any enemy alien or "person of Japanese Ancestry" living in Military Area No. 1 had to execute a "Change of Residence Notice" at a post office one to five days before departure. Enemy aliens needed government travel permits, but citizens did not.[14] As a citizen, Fred Korematsu could have moved from the West Coast—as a few thousand Nikkei did—anytime before March 29. By that time what Justice Owen J. Roberts later described as "a cleverly designed trap" was closing around Korematsu and the other Japanese American citizens still in Military Area No. 1.

On Thursday, March 18, DeWitt's headquarters announced that the "evacuation" of Japanese aliens and American-born Japanese would begin the following week. But before that evacuation could be effective, it was necessary for a statute to be enacted making it a federal crime for anyone to disobey a military order given under authority of EO 9066. Secretary Stimson had sent a draft of such a bill to Congress on March 9; on March 13, a staff officer, Colonel B. M. Bryan, explained to a Senate committee that "the purpose of this bill is to provide for enforcement in the Federal courts of orders issued" by DeWitt's headquarters. On March 19, the War Department's draft was adopted by both houses by unanimous consent. One senator, Ohio Republican Robert A. Taft, did demur, briefly, calling it the "sloppiest" criminal law he had ever read. He predicted, accurately, that it would "be enforced in wartime" and argued that it would be held unconstitutional in peacetime. Taft, however, did not vote against it. The bill, which made it a misdemeanor for anyone to disobey an order applying to a military zone designated under an "executive order of the president . . . if it appears that he knew of or should have known of the . . . order" and punishable by a fine not to exceed $5,000 and/or a year in jail, became Public Law 503.[15] This cleared the way for DeWitt's Public Proclamation No. 3 of March 24, which established an 8 P.M. to 6 A.M. curfew in Military Area No. 1 for enemy aliens and "all other persons of Japanese ancestry."[16] Three days later, on March 27, DeWitt issued Public Proclamation No. 4, which froze all Japanese persons, regardless of citizenship, within Military Area No. 1, effective at midnight, March 29.[17] The last element of Justice Roberts's trap was now in place.

On that same day, March 29, the first of the army's cleansing operations under EO 9066 took place as the Japanese Americans of Bainbridge Island near Seattle were removed from their homes under Exclusion Order No. 1, issued March 24, 1942. There would follow 107 other exclusion orders, each covering a specified area in California or the western halves of Oregon and Washington. It was Exclusion Order No. 34 that affected Korematsu's home of San Leandro; under its provisions, 1,214 Japanese Americans were sent to "Assembly Centers," one of the government's euphemisms for concentration camp, on May 9.[18] There should have been 1,215, but Fred Korematsu did not report to the local assembly point.

A month or so earlier, Korematsu had left home, telling his parents that he was going to Nevada. He and his "girl," Ida Boitano, planned to go to the Midwest. He employed a plastic surgeon with a bad reputation to perform what turned out to be not very effective surgery to change his appearance on March 18. He apparently forged or acquired a draft card identifying himself as "Clyde Sarah" and told people that he had been born in Las Vegas and was of Spanish-Hawaiian origin.[19] He was a successful fugitive—a fugitive for whom no one was looking—for three weeks. On May 30, he was arrested, apparently on a citizen's complaint, by the San Leandro police, who quickly turned him over to the Federal Bureau of Investigation (FBI).

Korematsu was one of at least fifteen Japanese American persons in northern California who were apprehended by law enforcement officers after their areas had been cleared of Japanese. Ernest Besig, head of the San Francisco office of the American Civil Liberties Union (ACLU), visited several in jail, looking for someone who would make a test case.[20] Only Korematsu agreed. He was tried in the local federal district court, convicted, and placed on probation for five years on September 8, 1942. Immediately upon conviction, armed military police took him into custody and sent him to the assembly center at Tanforan.

Korematsu's attorney, Wayne M. Collins, appealed to the Circuit Court of Appeals, Ninth Circuit.[21] In that court, the government, which had been needlessly afraid of what the courts might do to the whole program of incarceration, even before its inception, delayed by moving to dismiss the appeal on the technical grounds that Korematsu's probationary sentence was not final and thus unappealable. The appeals court certified that procedural question to the Supreme Court, which ruled, on June 1, 1943, that the sentence was appealable and returned the case to the Ninth Circuit, which then heard it. Six months later, on December 2, 1943, the Ninth Circuit used the Supreme Court's decision in *Hirabayashi v. U.S.* (June 21, 1943) as a basis for rejecting Korematsu's appeal, even though that case only dealt with curfew violation and specifically eschewed any ruling on forced migration. Underlining the old adage that what seems like a stone wall to the layman can be a triumphal arch for the lawyer, the court majority baldly stated that although the "Supreme Court did not expressly pass on the validity of the evacuation order. . . . We are of the opinion that this principle, thus decided, so clearly sustains that validity of the proclamation for evacuation . . . that it is not necessary to labor the point." The Ninth Circuit refused to consider questions of "discrimination because of race and ancestry" since the Supreme Court had already decided them negatively. Interestingly, in an obvious attempt to emphasize Korematsu's race and to negate his Americanness, the court's docket suppressed Korematsu's first name, so that the case is officially *Toyosaburo Korematsu v. U.S.*[22]

One member of the court, however, Judge William Denman, did dissent, as he had dissented on March 28, 1943, when the Ninth Circuit denied Gordon Hirabayashi's appeal.[23] In both dissents Denman argued that the cases should have been heard in full by the Ninth Circuit, whose judges, as westerners, were the best qualified by their experience to understand the facts of the cases. He made it clear that he believed that a racism similar to that practiced by the Nazis had played a part in the government's actions regarding Japanese Americans, thus anticipating Justice Frank Murphy's famous caveat in his concurring opinion in *Hirabayashi*.

(Denman: "Descended from Eastern Asiatics, [Japanese Americans] have been imprisoned as the Germans imprisoned the Western Asiatic descended Jews," March 28, 1943.

Murphy: "[The result of DeWitt's order] bears a melancholy resemblance to the treatment accorded to members of the Jewish race in Germany and in other parts of Europe," June 21, 1943.

Denman: "Their treatment is not unlike that of Hitler in so confining the Jews in his stockades," December 2, 1943.)

Largely because of deliberate government stalling, Fred Korematsu's case was not argued before the Supreme Court until October 11 and 12, 1944, more than two years and four months after he had been arrested. The Court's decision in *Hirabayashi*, more than a year before, had left some doubt as to what the justices might do. Although that decision was unanimous, it had been decided on narrow grounds. Gordon Hirabayashi had intended to challenge the whole procedure that resulted in mass incarceration, but Chief Justice Harlan Fiske Stone's opinion ruled only on curfew violation, and three of the nine justices, William O. Douglas, Wiley B. Rutledge, and Murphy, had written concurring opinions.

Stone shrank "judicial review of the war powers almost to the vanishing point."[24] In a classic example of "blaming the victim," he argued that the history of discrimination against Japanese Americans in the United States intensified their solidarity and thus retarded their assimilation, making them more likely to be pro-Japanese as opposed to pro-American. This, and other aspects of Japanese American history, including the canard that "espionage by persons in sympathy with the Japanese Government" had been "particularly effective in the surprise attack on Pearl Harbor," were used by Stone as an excuse for racial discrimination, which according to Stone, was "odious to a free people."

Because racial discriminations are in most circumstances . . . prohibited. . . . We cannot close our eyes to the fact . . . That in time of war residents having ethnic affiliations with an invading enemy may be a greater source of danger than those of a different ancestry.

Justice Douglas, concurring, agreed that "we cannot override the military judgment that lay behind these orders" but stressed that "loyalty is a matter of mind and of heart not of race. . . . Detention for cause is one thing. Detention on account of ancestry is another." Justice Rutledge's concurrence said nothing about the case but insisted that there are "bounds beyond which [a military commander in wartime] cannot go, and, if he oversteps them, then the courts may not have the power to protect the civilian citizen."

Justice Murphy's concurring opinion was more than a caveat; in fact, we now know that it had been written as a dissent and that Murphy, a person with a strong streak of patriotism who itched to get into the war himself, slightly amended it under great pressure from his colleagues, particularly Justice Felix Frankfurter. He first wrote that the statute under which Hirabayashi was convicted was "unconstitutional in its broad aspects."[25] But what he did publish was a strong condemnation of his colleagues' action.

> The broad provisions of the Bill of Rights . . . are [not] suspended
> by the mere existence of a state of war. . . . Distinctions based on
> color and ancestry are utterly inconsistent with our traditions
> and ideals. . . . Today is the first time, so far as I am aware, that
> we have sustained a substantial[26] restriction of the personal
> liberty of citizens of the United States based on the accident of
> race or ancestry. . . . It bears a melancholy resemblance to the
> treatment accorded to members of the Jewish race in Germany.
> . . . This goes to the very brink of constitutional power. [Origi-
> nally, Murphy had written "over the brink of Constitutional
> power."]

Thus, in October 1944, when Fred Korematsu's case finally came before the Supreme Court, his attorneys, Collins and Charles M. Horsky, had reasonable hopes for a favorable decision. It seemed to them that the case was not only a matter of what Douglas had called "detention on account of ancestry," but it was also now clear that there could not be even the slightest threat of a Japanese attack on the West Coast, a danger stressed in Stone's *Hirabayashi* decision. Despite these circumstances, Justice Hugo L. Black, writing for a 6–3 majority, upheld Korematsu's conviction, arguing, in the first instance, that "in the light of the principles we announced in the *Hirabayashi* case, we are unable to conclude that it was beyond the war power . . . to exclude those of Japanese ancestry from the West Coast war area at the time they did."

This argument ignored the distinction Douglas had made in *Hirabayashi* between curfew and detention, but the justice, after initially circulating a dissent in *Korematsu*, eventually ignored that distinction and silently concurred with Black. Writing in 1980, Douglas expressed regret for his action and said that Black and Frankfurter had dissuaded him from issuing his opinion, which he now remembered as a concurrence "agreeing to the evacuation but not to evacuation *via* the concentration camps" rather than a dissent.[27]

Stung by the objections of three of his colleagues, Black denied that exclusion and detention were the same thing:

> It is said that we are dealing here with the case of imprisonment of a citizen in a concentration camp solely because of his ancestry. . . . Our task would be simple, our duty clear, were this a case involving the imprisonment of a citizen in a concentration camp because of racial prejudice. Regardless of the true nature of the assembly and relocation centers—and we deem it unjustifiable to call them concentration camps with all the ugly connotations that term implies—we are dealing specifically with nothing but an exclusion order. To cast this case into outlines of racial prejudice . . . merely confuses the issue.

Elsewhere in the opinion, Black called attention to the companion case, *Ex parte Endo*, handed down the same day, which is discussed later.

So spoke Justice Black in 1944. In a *New York Times* interview twenty-three years later, given with the understanding that it would not be published until after his death, Black was blunter and insisted that he would do the same thing again. "People were rightly fearful of the Japanese in Los Angeles, many loyal to the United States, many undoubtedly not. . . . They all look alike to a person not a Jap."[28]

Frankfurter's concurring opinion ignored race and focused on the war power.[29] Seemingly wishing to distance the Court from the act itself, he concluded that "to find that the Constitution does not forbid the military measures now complained of does not carry with it approval of that which Congress and the Executive did. That is their business, not ours."

Three justices, Owen J. Roberts, Robert H. Jackson, and Murphy, dissented; Rutledge, from whom a dissent might have been expected in view of his concurrence in *Hirabayashi*, silently concurred.[30] Roberts saw a difference between *Korematsu* and *Hirabayashi*, which only involved "keeping people off the streets at night." For Roberts, there was a chain of events under which Korematsu was first to be sent to an Assembly Center—which Roberts held was "a euphemism for a prison"—and then passed on to a

War Relocation Authority Relocation Center—which the justice said was a euphemism for concentration camp. All of this, he insisted, was "a clear violation of Constitutional rights."

Robert H. Jackson's dissent pointed out that Korematsu was indicted and convicted merely because he was "the son of parents as to whom he had no choice, and belongs to a race from which there is no way to resign." Appropriately for the future prosecutor at Nuremburg, he attacked the notion of accepting military judgment in a court of law. DeWitt's report, he insisted, was not evidence but an

> unsworn, self-serving statement, untested by any cross-examination, that what he did was reasonable. And thus it will always be when courts try to look into the reasonableness of a military order. . . . A judicial construction of the due process clause that will sustain this order is a far more subtle blow to liberty that the promulgation of the order itself.

He also regretted his concurrence in *Hirabayashi*, noting that the majority was now saying that, having agreed to curfew, the question of going to an assembly center was also settled. Jackson now believed that the courts may not "be asked to execute a military expedient that has no place in law under the Constitution."

Justice Murphy found that the exclusion of "all Japanese persons" from the Pacific Coast on a plea of military necessity "goes over 'the very brink of constitutional power' and falls into the ugly abyss of racism." He, alone of the justices, examined DeWitt's *Final Report* and other public documents to show that justification for military necessity was not based on reliable evidence but rested mainly "upon questionable racial and sociological grounds not ordinarily within the realm of expert military judgment." His dissent ended in a peroration not inappropriate for our own time:

> All residents of this nation are kin in some way by blood and culture to a foreign land. Yet they are primarily and necessarily a part of the new and distinct civilization of the United States. They must accordingly be treated at all times as the heirs of the American experiment and as entitled to all the rights and freedoms guaranteed by the Constitution.

The action of the majority in *Korematsu* cannot be understood without at least a glance at *Ex Parte Endo*, handed down the same day. Mitsuye

Endo was an admittedly loyal citizen of Japanese American ancestry who was ordered to leave her home in Sacramento by Civilian Exclusion Order No. 52, May 7, 1942. She was confined, first at the Sacramento Assembly Center and then in the War Relocation Authority (WRA) camps at Tule Lake, California, and Topaz, Utah. She and her attorney, James Purcell, applied for a writ of habeas corpus, which the federal district court denied, and on appeal the case was certified to the Supreme Court from the Ninth Circuit Court of Appeals. This was a route to freedom that Justice Douglas had previously mentioned, and his opinion ordered Endo's release by the WRA. But her release came only after more than two years and seven months of confinement. Douglas's opinion found no fault with either the president or the military, but with the civilian WRA, which had acted largely as an adjunct to the military.

There were no dissents, but two justices, Murphy and Roberts, felt that the opinion was deficient. Murphy argued that detention in Relocation Centers of admittedly loyal American citizens was "but another example of the unconstitutional resort to racism inherent in the entire evacuation program. . . . If, as I believe, the military orders excluding her from California were invalid at the time they were issued, they are increasingly objectionable at this late date, when the threat of sabotage and espionage have greatly diminished."

Roberts had three complaints. First, he thought it "inadmissible to suggest that some inferior public servant exceeded the authority granted by the executive order." Second, Douglas's opinion pretended that Congress was, somehow, innocent in regard to the confinement of Endo and other citizens. Roberts insisted, quite correctly, that Congress knew what was going on. In fact, he might have added that many in Congress complained that the WRA was "coddling" Japanese Americans. Third, Roberts insisted that the majority had avoided the serious constitutional question of whether or not Endo's detention was legal. Roberts had no doubts: "An admittedly loyal citizen has been deprived of her liberty for a period of years. Under the Constitution she should be free to come and go as she pleases."

But Roberts, Murphy, and Jackson were minority voices. The majority held that indefinite incarceration of innocent citizens of a certain ancestry on the basis of an executive order was constitutional, at least in a time of emergency. The scholarly reaction was largely negative. Eugene V. Rostow, then just beginning his career as a legal scholar, labeled the Japanese American cases "a disaster" and "our worst wartime mistake."[31] Even though the last appellation is incorrect—a mistake is an error of judgment, an aberration, and what happened to Japanese Americans was a rather logical culmination of more than a century of anti-Asian measures by the United States—Rostow's early denunciation was an important hallmark in the reputation of these cases.

Congress, however, used the vile precedent thus established in one of the most flagrant attacks on civil liberty ever put on the American statute books: the Emergency Detention Act of 1950, the quintessential Cold War statute.[32] Enacted over President Harry S. Truman's veto shortly after the beginning of the Korean War, the law was explicitly modeled after the "constitutional" procedures ratified by *Korematsu*. The law authorized "the detention of persons who there is reasonable ground to believe probably will commit or conspire with others to commit espionage or sabotage." All that was required to set this process in motion was the proclamation by the president of an "Internal Security Emergency" and for him to delegate authority to the attorney general. The government had several facilities on a standby basis. Ironically, one of them was Tule Lake, where Mitsuye Endo spent part of her captivity. Happily, in the nearly two decades the statute was on the books, no Internal Security Emergency was ever declared. Its repeal in 1971 followed a campaign spearheaded by two Japanese American legislators from Hawaii. When the Department of Justice recommended its repeal, Deputy Attorney General Richard G. Kleindeinst acknowledged the concerns of Japanese Americans and others and judged that "the repeal of this legislation will allay the fears and suspicions—unfounded as they may be—of many of our citizens. This benefit outweighs any potential advantage which the Act may provide in a time of internal security emergency."[33]

And, of course, even after repeal of the detention act, various government officials have used the Japanese American precedent as an excuse for other evil acts. In 1989, for example, the George H. W. Bush administration's ambassador to El Salvador, William Walker, tried to explain away the killing of civilians by Salvadorian soldiers by saying that "things like this happen" and likening it to the incarceration of Japanese Americans during World War II.[34]

By the time that the act was repealed, a few activists in the Japanese American community had begun what became a campaign for "redress," defined as an apology plus some kind of tangible if symbolic recognition that what was done to Japanese Americans during World War II was wrong.[35] During a decade of agitation, the relatively conservative national Japanese American Citizens League was persuaded to support redress. In

1980, Congress created the presidential Commission on Wartime Relocation and Internment of Civilians (CWRIC) to investigate whether injustice had been done to Japanese Americans and Aleuts as a result of EO
9066 and, if so, to recommend appropriate remedies to Congress.[36] The
CWRIC report, *Personal Justice Denied*, revealed little about the causes of
the injustice done to Japanese Americans that was not already known to
professional historians.[37] It concluded that the incarceration of Japanese
Americans

> was not justified by military necessity. . . . The broad historical
> causes . . . were race prejudice, war hysteria, and a failure of
> political leadership. Widespread ignorance of Japanese Americans
> contributed to a policy conceived in haste and executed in an
> atmosphere of fear and anger at Japan. A grave injustice was done
> to American citizens and resident aliens of Japanese ancestry
> who, without individual review or any probative evidence against
> them, were excluded, removed, and detained by the United States
> during World War II.[38]

The commission's powerfully phrased findings were the major factor in
the passage of the Civil Liberties Act of 1988, which eventually provided
not only an apology but also tax-free $20,000 payments to the Japanese
American survivors.

   In the course of the investigation, CWRIC researcher Aiko Herzig-
Yoshinaga discovered documents that made possible what had been
thought impossible: a way to reopen *Korematsu* and the other long-closed
Japanese American cases of World War II. Political scientist and attorney
Peter Irons used some of Herzig-Yoshinaga's discoveries plus his own considerable research to produce *Justice at War* (1983), which demonstrated
that, despite awareness within the Department of Justice that critical elements in the War Department's case justifying the evacuation of Japanese
Americans were simply fabricated, the Department of Justice's lawyers,
including Solicitor General Charles Fahey, presented briefs that misstated
facts to the Supreme Court.[39] Irons has recounted that, when he presented
some of his evidence at a CWRIC hearing, one of the commissioners, Judge
William Marutani, asked whether the wartime cases could be opened by
use of a writ of *coram nobis*. *Coram nobis*, which means "the error before
us," is a little used writ from English common law to redress prisoners
after they have been released.[40] Irons pursued this possibility in collabo-
ration with a remarkable group of Asian American attorneys, the Asian
Law Caucus. All worked, *pro bono*, "for free."

The non-profit Asian Law Caucus, founded in San Francisco in 1972, began as a storefront operation staffed by volunteers but grew to include a sizable staff and an annual budget of nearly $1 million. Its participation in the rehearings of *Korematsu* is perhaps its most illustrious accomplishment, as most of its cases involve local and administrative courts. (Other Asian American attorneys in Portland and Seattle handled the rehearings of Yasui and Hirabayashi.)

After a great deal of research, the legal team, led by Dale Minami, filed a "petition for writ of error coram nobis" on January 19, 1983, with the clerk of the U.S. District Court Northern District of California in San Francisco, the same court in which, more than forty years before, Korematsu had been convicted.[41] Minami remembers how delighted the attorneys were when the clerk told them that Judge Marilyn Hall Patel, a pronounced liberal recently appointed by Jimmy Carter, had been assigned to hear the case. After considerable delay, the government moved to vacate Korematsu's original conviction but did not admit previous government misconduct. After a good deal of filing and counterfiling, Judge Patel announced her decision on November 10, 1983. She ruled the government's motion out of order, accepted the petition, voided the original indictment, and reversed Korematsu's original conviction. Patel, however, warned that

> *Korematsu* remains on the pages of our legal and political history. As a legal precedent it is now recognized as having very limited application. As historical precedent it stands as a constant caution that in times of war or declared military necessity our institutions must be vigilant in protecting constitutional guarantees. It stands as a caution that in time of distress the government must not be used to protect governmental actions from close scrutiny and accountability. It stands as a caution that in times of international hostility and antagonisms our institutions, legislative, executive and judicial, must be prepared to exercise the authority to protect all citizens from the petty fears and prejudices that are so easily aroused.

The cases of Gordon Hirabayashi and Minoru Yasui were reheard with varying results in district courts in Seattle and Portland.[42] The *coram nobis* legal team hoped that at least one of the cases would reach the Supreme Court, which would then have an opportunity to comment on and perhaps formally overrule or void its wartime Japanese American decisions. The Ronald Reagan administration's Department of Justice refused to appeal the reversals of *Korematsu* and *Hirabayashi*, and Minoru Yasui's death in November 1986 made his case moot.

Despite that disappointment, the lawyers had accomplished a great deal. It is believed that this was the first time that a criminal conviction approved by the Supreme Court had been reversed. The cases provided a kind of vindication for not only their clients but for Japanese Americans generally. In addition, the court decision and the ensuing publicity was certainly a factor in the eventual approval of real redress, the passage of the Civil Liberties Act of 1988.

But perhaps the most important accomplishment of the *coram nobis* cases was in affirming American ideals. As the political scientist Morton Grodzins pointed out a half-century ago, the decisions in the Japanese American cases "betrayed all Americans."[43] Fred Korematsu clearly understood that. Allowed by Patel to address the court just before she handed down her ruling he commented that

> I still remember forty years ago when I was handcuffed . . . as a
> criminal here in San Francisco. . . . As long as my record stands in
> federal court, any American citizen can be held in prison and
> concentration camps without a trial or a hearing. . . . I would like
> to see the government admit that they were wrong and do
> something about it so this will never happen to any American
> citizen of any race, creed, or color.[44]

NOTES

1. The term, *Japanese American Cases,* now almost universally used by commentators, was popularized and perhaps coined by Eugene V. Rostow, "The Japanese American Cases—a Disaster," *Yale Law Journal* 54 (1945): 489–533. A popular version appeared in a magazine of general circulation: Rostow, "Our Worst Wartime Mistake," *Harper's* 191 (1945): 193–201. He did not include the *Yasui* case, which was all but ignored by commentators before 1971. The other key early treatment is Milton R. Konvitz, *The Alien and the Asiatic in American Law* (Ithaca, N.Y.: Cornell University Press, 1946). These cases are, in chronological order: *Yasui v. U.S.,* 320 U.S. 115 (1943), *Hirabayashi v. U.S.,* 320 U.S. 81 (1943), *Korematsu v. U.S.,* 323 U.S. 115 (1944), and *Ex Parte Mitsuye Endo,* 323 U.S. 283 (1944).

2. This and subsequent biographical information not otherwise attributed is from Peter Irons, *Justice at War* (New York: Oxford University Press, 1983), 93–99.

3. International Brotherhood of Boilermakers, Iron Shipbuilders, Blacksmiths, Forgers, and Helpers, American Federation of Labor.

4. The numbers for Hawaii were quite different. The 157,905 ethnic Japanese in the island territory were 37.4 percent of the population. For a sophisticated analysis of the Hawaiian situation, see Harry N. Scheiber and Jane L. Scheiber, "Bayonets in Paradise: A Half-Century Retrospect on Martial Law in Hawaii, 1941–1946," *University of Hawai'i Law Review* 19, no. 2 (1997): 478–648.

5. Roger Daniels, "L'Internamento di 'Alien Enemies' negli Stati Uniti durante la seconda guerra modiale," *Acoma: Revista Internazionale di Studi Nordamericani* (Rome) 11 (Estate autunno 1997): 39–49. The internments of Japanese, German, and Italian nationals were authorized by Proclamation No. 2525, 7 December 1941, and Proclamations No. 2526 and No. 2527, 8 December 1941. Similar control over Hungarian, Bulgarian, and Rumanian aliens was covered by Proclamation No. 2563 of 17 July 1942.

6. The act, also known as the Smith Act, is 54 *Stat.* 670.

7. One of Biddle's wartime speeches, for example, was titled, "Identification of Enemy Aliens: Let Us Not Persecute These People," *Vital Speeches of the Day* 8 (15 February 1942): 279–80. For Britain in World War II, see A. W. Brian Simpson, *In the Highest Degree Odious: Detention without Trial in Wartime Britain* (Oxford: Clarendon, 1992). For a historical survey, see Colin Holmes, *A Tolerant Country? Immigrants, Refugees and Minorities in Britain* (London: Faber, 1991).

8. The organizations creating the lists were, primarily, the Federal Bureau of Investigation (FBI), the Special Defense Unit of the Department of Justice, the Office of Naval Intelligence (ONI), and the Intelligence Branch (G-2) of the army. Obviously, the lists were only as good as the persons compiling them, and they were filled with errors of omission and commission, particularly with regard to Japanese aliens, as, to the best of my knowledge, only one American intelligence official, Lieutenant Commander Kenneth D. Ringle, could read Japanese. For his activities, see Roger Daniels, *Asian America: Chinese and Japanese in the United States since 1850* (Seattle: University of Washington Press, 1989), 183, 210–13. The best single work on the the U.S. intelligence apparatus in this era is Jeffrey M. Dorwart, *Conflict of Duty: The U.S. Navy's Intelligence Dilemma, 1919–1945* (Annapolis: Naval Institute Press, 1983).

9. C. Harvey Gardiner, "The Latin American Japanese and World War II," in *Japanese Americans: From Relocation to Redress*, ed. Roger Daniels, Sandra C. Taylor, and Harry H. L. Kitano (Seattle: University of Washington Press, 1991), 142–45 and Gardiner, *Pawns in a Triangle of Hate: The Peruvian Japanese and the United States* (Seattle: University of Washington Press,

1981). In 1998, the Department of Justice agreed to redress payments of $5,000 to each Latin American Japanese survivor.

10. For Minoru Yasui's account of his father's internment and subsequent hearing, see John Tateishi, *And Justice for All: An Oral History of the Japanese American Detention Camps* (New York: Random House, 1984), 62–93.

11. For a detailed account and the text, see Roger Daniels, *The Decision to Relocate the Japanese Americans* (Philadelphia: Lippincott, 1975; 2d ed., expanded, Malabar, Fla.: Krieger, 1986). Its initial appearance was in 7 *Fed. Reg.* 1407 (1942).

12. Record Group 107, National Archives, and printed in full in Roger Daniels, *American Concentration Camps: A Documentary History of the Relocation and Incarceration of Japanese Americans, 1941–1945*, vol. 3, *February 20, 1942–March 31, 1942* (New York: Garland, 1989).

13. On 28 March 1942, McCloy wrote the chief of the Army Field Forces: "As the war progresses it may become necessary to move aliens inland from the East and South Coasts in a manner similar to the way we are now moving Japs along the West Coast. Would it not be well to send an officer to the West Coast to study the method used out there for evacuation and to plan for similar action in their own areas. This will save a lot of time and avoid confusion and criticism if we are ever called on to remove aliens from other areas." A month and a half later, in the midst of a mild political storm about rumors that Germans and especially Italians were going to be moved, McCloy lied to his boss, Henry Stimson, writing that the reports did not stem from the War Department and that "we have persistently notified . . . everyone who has consulted us that we intend *no* mass evacuations on the East Coast." Memoranda, McCloy to General Joseph T. McNarney, 28 March 1942, and McCloy to Stimson, 15 May 1942, both RG 107, National Archives.

14. Public Proclamation No. 1 is printed in U.S. Congress, House, House Report No. 1911, 77th Cong., 2nd sess., 2722–26.

15. *Congressional Record*, 19 March 1942, 2722–26.

16. U.S. Department of War, *Final Report: Japanese Evacuation from the West Coast 1942* (Washington, D.C.: GPO, 1943), 297ff.

17. U.S. Department of War, *Final Report.* 105ff.

18. DeWitt's Exclusion Orders may be found in the *Federal Register.* No. 34 is at 7 *Fed. Reg.* 3967.

19. Irons, *Justice at War.* There are minor inconsistencies between Irons's interview with Korematsu and the material collected by the F.B.I. about him that Irons does not attempt to resolve.

20. At this time, the national ACLU refused to accept cases challenging the government, but some of its West Coast affiliates, including those in

Los Angeles, San Francisco, and Seattle, did support protesters. See Daniels, *Asian America*, 277, fn. 19.

21. Collins was a determined battler for Japanese American rights, defending such unpopular persons as Iva Toguri, the alleged "Tokyo Rose," and Japanese American renunciants. See Donald M. Collins, *Native American Aliens: Disloyalty and the Renunciation of Citizenship by Japanese Americans during World War II* (Westport, Conn.: Greenwood, 1985).

22. *Toyosaburo Korematsu v. U.S.*, 140 F. 2d at 289–90. On the day that I wrote this note, the Associated Press reported a diatribe by House majority leader Tom DeLay (R-Tex.), making fun of Asian American names. Called to account, DeLay apologized, in writing, insisting that: "In no way did I mean to suggest that Asian-Americans should not participate in democracy." *Cincinnati Enquirer*, 18 July 1998.

23. Denman's opinion was unreported, but he included it in his dissent in *Korematsu* at 300–304.

24. Alpheus T. Mason, *Harlan Fiske Stone: Pillar of the Law* (New York: Viking, 1956), 675.

25. For details of the original draft, see Sidney Fine, "Mr. Justice Murphy and the Hirabayashi Case," *Pacific Historical Review* 33 (1964): 201, and J. Woodford Howard, *Mr. Justice Murphy: A Political Biography* (Princeton: Princeton University Press, 1968), 300ff.

26. One assumes that Murphy did not regard the many restrictions placed on African American and Native American citizens as "substantial."

27. Howard Ball, "Judicial Parsimony and Military Necessity Disinterred: A Reexamination of the Japanese Exclusion Cases, 1943–44," 176–85 at 181 in Daniels et al. eds., *Japanese Americans: From Relocation to Redress*. William O. Douglas, *The Court Years, 1939–1975: The Autobiography of William O. Douglas* (New York: Random House, 1980), 280.

28. *New York Times*, 25 September 1971.

29. I believe that Frankfurter, who had regularly advised "Jack" McCloy on matters affecting enemy aliens, should have recused himself. Howard Ball, "Judicial Parsimony and Military Necessity Disinterred," at fn. 63, states that Black, Douglas, and Stone also should have recused themselves, the first two because of prior social contacts with DeWitt, the last because of his role in collaborating with the executive branch by providing information about the *Korematsu* and *Endo* decisions and delaying the announcement of them to suit the War Department and the White House.

30. In the judicial conference in which the justices debated the case, Rutledge explained to his brethren: "I had to swallow *Hirabayashi*. I didn't like it. I knew that if I went along with that order then I had to go along

with detention." Del Dickson, ed., *The Supreme Court in Conference* (*1940–1985*) (New York: Oxford University Press, 2001), conference of 16 October 1944, 690.

31. Rostow, "The Japanese American Cases."

32. 64 *Stat.* 1019; it is Title II of the Internal Security Act.

33. Kleindienst, letter to James O. Eastland, Chairman, Committee on the Judiciary, U.S. Senate, 2 December 1969. Copy furnished by Department of Justice.

34. *Hokubei Mainichi* (San Francisco), 22 December 1989.

35. Mitchell Maki, Harry H. L. Kitano, and S. Megan Berthold, *Achieving the Impossible Dream* (Urbana: University of Illinois Press, 1999), analyze the struggle for redress.

36. Aleuts had been evacuated in 1942 to get them out of harm's way, but they were resettled under abominable conditions in southern Alaska and suffered a high death rate. The term "internment" was, of course, inaccurate, as is the generally used phrase, "the internment of the Japanese Americans." Only the few thousand enemy aliens kept in custody by the Immigration and Naturalization Service were interned.

37. Commission on Wartime Relocation and Internment of Civilians, *Personal Justice Denied* (Washington, D.C.: GPO, December 1982). Despite the date, the report was not released until 24 February 1983. A scholarly reprint was published by the University of Washington Press in 1997.

38. Commission on Wartime Relocation and Interment of Civilians, *Personal Justice Denied*, 18.

39. Irons, *Justice at War*. See my review in *American Historical Review* 89 (1984): 871–72.

40. Peter Irons, ed., *Justice Delayed: The Record of the Japanese American Internment Cases* (Middletown, Conn.: Wesleyan University Press, 1989), 7–9. See also Eli Frank, *Coram Nobis: Common Law, Federal, Statutory: With Forms* (Albany, N.Y.: Newkirk, 1953). The best-known previous use of the writ in the United States was by Alger Hiss. See his *In the Court of Public Opinion* (New York: Knopf, 1957). The Supreme Court has held that *coram nobis* should be used "only under certain circumstances compelling such action to achieve justice" and to correct "errors of the most fundamental character." *U.S. v. Morgan*, 346 U.S. 502, 511–12 (1954).

41. The attorneys of record, in addition to Minami and Irons, were Dennis W. Hayashi, Donald K. Tamaki, Michael J. Wong, Robert K. Rusky, Karen N. Kai, Russell Matsumoto, and Lorraine K. Bannai. Other attorneys who made major contributions to the success of the effort were Eric Yamamoto, Leigh Ann Miyasato, Edward Chen, and Marjie Barrows. This and other information comes from documents, including briefs,

which were supplied by Minami and a number of conversations with him.

42. For details, see Irons, *Justice Delayed*, 250ff.

43. Morton Grodzins, *Americans Betrayed: Politics and the Japanese Evacuation* (Chicago: University of Chicago Press, 1949), 374.

44. As cited in Irons, *Justice Delayed*, 25–26.

9

BROWN V. BOARD OF EDUCATION

Mark Tushnet

Brown v. Board of Education (1954) shaped Americans' understanding of constitutional law for the rest of the twentieth century.[1] For nearly all of its history, the Supreme Court developed constitutional law in ways that preserved the status quo or obstructed legislative change sought by political liberals. *Brown* was different. Not incidentally, it provided an important ideological underpinning for the civil rights movement, which was already developing when the Court acted. President Harry S. Truman's order desegregating the armed forces placed one branch of government on the side of civil rights. *Brown* placed a second branch there, leaving Congress as the sole holdout. Even more important for advocates of civil rights, the decision confirmed that their cause was not only just but also that achieving its goals was compelled by the nation's most fundamental political commitments, as embodied in the Constitution. More broadly, it placed the Constitution on the side of liberal social change, providing a model for judicial activism in a liberal rather than a conservative direction. It was the basis for what came to be known as the "rights revolution." *Brown* prodded all sorts of groups and individuals to cast their political claims in constitutional terms, to the point that, by the end of the twentieth century, even conservatives found it worthwhile to insist that the government was trampling *their* rights.

Supreme Court decisions are not issued in a vacuum. They result from decisions made by earlier courts and, perhaps more important, by the ordinary people who decide to become litigants and by the lawyers they find to help them. The British philosopher Jeremy Bentham said that the law resulted from the actions of "Judge and Company." *Brown* shows how accurate Bentham's observation is.

The Civil War ended in 1865, but southerners did not treat their defeat in battle as a reason for transforming their social system. As soon as they regained control over their state legislatures, they enacted so-called Black Codes, whose provisions limited the legal rights of newly freed slaves. In response, Congress enacted the Civil Rights Act of 1866 and then, concerned about that statute's constitutionality, amended the Constitution to add the Fourteenth Amendment, which, among other provisions, provided that "no State . . . shall deny to any person within its jurisdiction the equal protection of the laws." The Supreme Court readily concluded that the Equal Protection Clause barred states from adopting statutes that expressly denied African Americans legal rights available to whites and in 1880 invalidated a West Virginia statute that denied African Americans the right to serve on juries.[2]

The Equal Protection Clause's implications for other statutes were less clear to the Court. Three years after the jury discrimination case, the Court upheld an Alabama statute penalizing interracial sexual relations more severely than other nonmarital sexual relations.[3] As the Court saw it, the statute did not violate ideas of racial equality because both African Americans and whites were punished equally for the same activity.

The Court continued to adhere to that analysis of the Equal Protection Clause in its most important race discrimination decision in the late nineteenth century, *Plessy v. Ferguson*.[4] *Plessy* upheld the constitutionality of a Louisiana statute requiring racial segregation on railroads in the state. Although the case itself involved discrimination in transportation, it relied on a pre–Civil War Massachusetts decision upholding school segregation in Boston, and *Plessy* came to be understood as a case allowing segregation of all sorts. The Supreme Court decided two cases involving segregated schools in the next three decades, and each time it assumed that *Plessy* provided the governing rule.[5] The Louisiana statute in *Plessy* provided that separate facilities for African Americans had to be equal in quality to those for whites, and although the Court's decision did not explicitly endorse that requirement, it soon came to be understood as one allowing segregation only if the separate facilities were equal. In another railroad case in 1914, the Court said that the requirement of equality had to be taken seriously.[6]

Providing separate but equal facilities would have been quite expensive, and in any event southern legislatures were unwilling to provide equality even on the terms the Court allowed. A sustained challenge by the National Association for the Advancement of Colored People (NAACP) led the Supreme Court to address the question of separate-but-equal in the years from 1938 to 1950. First, the Court held that a state that ran a law school for whites had to provide one for African Americans too,[7] forcing states to establish separate professional programs for African Americans, albeit quite reluctantly. After the end of World War II, increasing numbers of African Americans sought to obtain advanced degrees and discovered that these programs were inadequate. In one case, Oklahoma required a middle-aged African American student seeking a graduate degree in English to sit in an alcove apart from other students in his classes and in a separate area of the school's cafeteria.[8] The Court indicated that this sort of isolation ensured that the student would not get an educational experience equivalent to that provided to white students. In another case, Texas opened a law school for African Americans that operated in an office building across the street from the state capitol, was staffed by professors who also taught full-time at the state law school for whites, and used the state law library across the street as the law school's library. In 1950, the Court held that the Texas law school program did not satisfy the separate-but-equal requirement, in large measure because a separate school for African Americans could not provide a variety of intangible educational benefits, including the ability to establish professional contacts in law school that would prove useful as students entered the practice of law.[9]

Outside the Court, the landscape was changing as well. President Franklin Roosevelt's New Deal programs began to shift the allegiance of African Americans from the Republican party of Abraham Lincoln to the modern Democratic party. Urban Democratic party organizations in the North, to which many African Americans migrated, supported political action on behalf of their new constituents. The struggle against Nazism in World War II placed explicit racism as public policy under severe strain. In 1944, Gunnar Myrdal, a Swedish sociologist, published a massive study of what he called *The American Dilemma*, which was, as Myrdal analyzed it, the tension between the nation's ideological commitment to racial equality and its actual practice. The southern system of segregation was put under additional stress by the international military and ideological competition with the Soviet Union, which presented itself, particularly to people in Africa and Asia, as the true defender of real equality for all people and pointed to segregation as an illustration of the hypocrisy of the U.S. claim that its system of democratic governance should be emulated. Against this background, the lawsuits that became *Brown v. Board of Education* took shape.

The five lawsuits that ended up in the Supreme Court under the name of *Brown v. Board of Education* resulted from a combination of grassroots activism and top-down leadership. The NAACP had made litigation part of its program shortly after it was founded in 1909 by an interracial group of social reformers. The organization's involvement with litigation during its early years was largely reactive, responding to cases involving lynchings and mob violence. Starting in the mid-1920s, the NAACP began to consider a more systematic approach to litigation. Using a grant from the Garland Fund, a left-wing foundation created by the heir to a mining fortune, the NAACP hired Nathan Margold, a recent graduate of Harvard Law School, to develop a plan for strategic litigation that would ultimately lead to the end of segregation. Unfamiliar with the real world of litigation, Margold produced an ambitious and quite unrealistic proposal.

The Margold Report did, however, convince NAACP officials that they should support some sort of strategic litigation plan. After Margold left to assume a position in the Roosevelt administration, the NAACP hired Charles Hamilton Houston to implement Margold's plan. Houston joined his father's law practice in Washington after graduating from Harvard Law School, but more important, he became the chief academic officer at Howard Law School, which he transformed from an unaccredited and undistinguished institution into a school where students learned, in Houston's terms, to use law as a tool for social engineering. Upon becoming the NAACP's chief lawyer, Houston abandoned the proposals Margold made and instead began to attack the separate-but-equal doctrine along two tracks. Understanding that southern states were most vulnerable when they offered no programs whatever, Houston helped bring suits against university systems that provided no graduate or professional programs for African Americans. Understanding how to build an organization, Houston also brought suits against school districts, challenging their practice of paying African American teachers substantially less than they paid equally well-trained and experienced white teachers.

While at Howard, Houston trained a generation of civil rights lawyers. His favorite was Thurgood Marshall, a hardworking young man with an effusive personality that made him an extremely effective litigator. Houston rescued Marshall from a struggling depression-era private law practice and brought him to the NAACP's New York office to train as his successor. Marshall took over the litigation effort in 1939.

The NAACP's legal staff slowly increased in size. After World War II, Marshall hired Robert Carter, a New Yorker who pressed Marshall to move the challenge to segregation forward more quickly; Jack Greenberg, a white graduate of Columbia Law School; and Constance Baker Motley. The national staff was at the heart of a network of cooperating lawyers scattered around the country. The local lawyers were in closer touch with the African American communities and with local NAACP members and helped identify places where the practice of segregation created particularly bothersome problems for communities that could be persuaded to join in a broader attack on segregation. The lawyers in New York convened conferences to devise strategy, wrote briefs, and coordinated the local lawyers, who carried the bulk of the day-to-day work of conducting litigation.

The most important strategic decision involved timing. Houston had developed a program that took the separate-but-equal doctrine seriously and attempted to force the South to comply with the requirement of equal facilities. He nurtured the hope that truly enforcing equality under the separate-but-equal doctrine would make segregation too expensive for the South to maintain, although he also knew that southerners would accept extremely high costs to keep the races separate. Eventually, his successor, Marshall, understood that at some point the NAACP would have to pursue what the lawyers called a direct attack on segregation, a challenge to the core holding of *Plessy v. Ferguson*. The only real question was when.

By the late 1940s, NAACP officials had been publicizing the possibility of challenging segregation for over a decade. They kept pointing out that, while the law required that segregated schools for African Americans be equal to those for whites, everywhere segregation existed the schools for African Americans were grossly inadequate. They made it clear that they were ready to do what they could to help parents attack inadequate segregated education. Marshall was more cautious than some of his staff, particularly Carter. Marshall wanted to be sure that NAACP cases undermined *Plessy* so substantially that taking the next step and repudiating the 1896 decision would seem relatively easy. Carter, in contrast, thought that the social environment had changed so much by the late 1940s that the NAACP could begin the direct attack right away.

NAACP members in the South kept presenting the lawyers with problems that could have been handled within the framework of a strategy seeking to enforce the separate-but-equal doctrine; they wanted better facilities and better transportation to school and did not themselves think that their immediate problems would be solved by a direct attack on segregation. Marshall's caution combined with the membership's narrow interests in a way that let him delay a decision to institute the direct attack until he was ready. The Supreme Court's decision in the Texas law school case was all Marshall needed. Its emphasis on the intangible aspects of education provided what the NAACP called a "road map" for the challenge. With that decision in hand, the NAACP lawyers presented the organization's members with the direct attack, and the members willingly acceded. After several years of preparation in each case, the first desegregation case was filed in 1949, the others in 1951.

The preliminaries always took more time than impatient members and staff lawyers expected. Each of the lawsuits—from South Carolina, Virginia, Kansas, Delaware, and the District of Columbia—that the Supreme Court decided in 1954 developed in response to the conditions of local schools and the circumstances of the local African American communities. In 1947, James Hinton, president of the South Carolina NAACP, gave a speech in which he mentioned that the organization was interested in bringing lawsuits in districts where white children were bused to school while African American children had to walk. Joseph DeLaine, minister and schoolteacher from Clarendon County, took Hinton's message to heart. When he returned home, DeLaine began to organize his church members, who petitioned the school board for buses and then filed a lawsuit. The chosen plaintiff was Levi Pearson, whose children had to walk to school in Clarendon County. Unfortunately, it turned out that Pearson lived on the border between two tax districts and did not pay taxes to the board responsible for buses in Clarendon County, so his lawsuit was dismissed.

DeLaine persisted. In February 1949, Marshall met DeLaine during a trip to South Carolina to locate a good place to begin a lawsuit. He persuaded DeLaine to switch his focus from the buses to a broader attack on segregation itself. To ensure that the community supported the broader suit, Marshall insisted that DeLaine locate twenty potential plaintiffs from throughout the county, and the latter compiled a list of volunteers. Once the lawsuit was filed in the name of the twenty volunteers in 1951, whites in Clarendon County began to retaliate against the plaintiffs. DeLaine lost his teaching job, and Harry Briggs, whose name appeared first on the complaint, was fired from his job as an auto mechanic.

In Virginia, the lawsuit resulted from the efforts of Prince Edward County resident Barbara Johns. Johns came from an activist family: Her uncle Vernon was a prominent Baptist minister who was Martin Luther King, Jr.'s predecessor in Montgomery, Alabama. Johns was born in New York City in 1935, but after her parents moved to Washington, D.C., she moved to Prince Edward County to live with her grandparents. In April 1951, she was a student at Robert Russa Moton High School in Farmville, which was filled to nearly three times its capacity. The school board had responded to the overcrowding only by building three flimsy structures—called the tarpaper chicken shacks by critics—on the school grounds. Frustrated at the school's condition, Johns organized a student strike. She arranged for the school's principal to get a telephone call telling him, falsely, that two of his students were about to be arrested in the downtown bus terminal. Immediately after he left the building, Johns circulated notes to every classroom with the principal's forged signature, instructing teachers to discharge their students for a schoolwide assembly. The teenager addressed the students, describing in powerful rhetoric the school's inadequate facilities, saying, "I want you all out of here." In response, the students walked out and marched to the county courthouse.

The students met later that day with Reverend Leslie Francis Griffin, a Baptist minister who was as militant as Vernon Johns. Griffin, who was taken by surprise by the students' action, suggested that they contact Oliver Hill, a Richmond lawyer who was close to the NAACP's leadership. Hill was unhappy with the students' actions, believing that they might have jeopardized their academic studies without any real prospect that their strike would succeed. He also worried that Prince Edward County, in southern Virginia, was more committed to segregation than places like Norfolk or Richmond and that it would be harder to bring a case there than elsewhere in the state. Hill and his partner, Spottswood Robinson, however, were already thinking about bringing some sort of desegregation lawsuit in the general area of Farmville, and they agreed to meet Johns, Griffin, and other students a few days later. The students impressed Hill and Robinson, who agreed to take their case on the condition that the students change their focus from trying to get a new high school to trying to overturn Virginia's segregation laws. Eventually Griffin became the first named plaintiff in the lawsuit against Prince Edward County.

The legal situation in Kansas differed from that in South Carolina and Virginia, for Kansas law did not require segregation but allowed some larger cities to segregate their schools if they wanted to. Esther Brown, a thirty-year-old white woman who lived near Kansas City, was active in the leftist Progressive party, which was preparing to run former vice president Henry Wallace to challenge the reelection of President Harry S. Truman, a Democrat. Brown became concerned about the schools for African Americans in South Park, one of the city's suburbs, when she saw their condition while driving her maid home and decided to do something about it. In 1947, she lobbied the school board unsuccessfully before turning to Elisha Scott, an African American attorney in Topeka, to take legal action. Meanwhile, parents in South Park held their children out of school until Scott's lawsuit began. The South Park school board lost the case because the city was not authorized by state law to segregate its schools. African American civic leaders throughout Kansas, prodded in part by Esther Brown, saw opportunities for challenging segregation in their cities. When Wichita's African American teachers, concerned that they would lose their jobs if the schools were desegregated, mobilized against bringing a desegregation suit there, the NAACP branch in Topeka took the initiative. Starting in 1948 and lasting through early 1951, the Topeka branch tried to organize a lawsuit that would challenge segregation directly. Eventually they located a number of possible plaintiffs, including Oliver Brown, a welder in one of the city's railway shops and an assistant pastor in his church, whose daughter Linda had to walk across railroad tracks and a busy street to catch her school bus. Although safety concerns were part of the parents' complaints, they had become convinced that they should attack segregation itself.

Like Barbara Johns in Virginia, the daughter of Gardner Bishop, an irascible barber, attended an overcrowded junior high school for African Americans in Washington, D.C. The nearest school for whites had more space than students, but the school board made only feeble efforts to relieve the overcrowding in the black school by creating satellite facilities many blocks away. Bishop and other parents held their children out of school for several months during the 1947–1948 school year in protest, and he organized the parents into an alternative parent-teachers association, lobbying hard for change. During the strike, Bishop heard a talk by Houston. On returning to his private law practice in Washington after completing his service as the NAACP's chief lawyer, Houston had taken as his clients a number of African American labor unions, which helped allay Bishop's suspicions that an elite African American lawyer could not adequately support the causes Bishop cared about. Houston persuaded Bishop to challenge the district's education system. Initially, Houston tried to secure more funds for the segregated schools, but the lawsuit he filed was rejected in 1950. In a powerful dissent, however, Judge Henry Edgerton made clear that some federal judges were open to broader challenges to segregation. After Houston died prematurely a few months later, Bishop hired James Nabrit, who wanted to convert the lawsuit into a direct challenge to segregation.

Led by Bishop, eleven African American students attempted to enroll in a new junior high school for whites but were of course turned down. Among the applicants was Spottswood Bolling, Jr., whose mother worked for the government as a bookbinder. In 1951, Nabrit filed the lawsuit that reached the Supreme Court as *Bolling v. Sharpe*, which named the school board president as a defendant.

In Delaware, the challenges to segregation began with parents' concerns about transportation and school quality. Ethel Belton's children had to ride the bus for nearly an hour to attend the black high school in Wilmington rather than go to the local school for whites, and when they got there they had fewer curricular choices than were offered at the white school. Sarah Bulah's children watched the bus taking white children to school pass them as they walked to their school because the school board did not provide bus transportation to the African Americans school. Belton and Bulah went to Louis Redding, the local African American lawyer, with their complaints. He told them that he would not help "get a Jim Crow bus" but would bring a desegregation suit.

Three of the lawsuits challenging state segregation laws were filed in federal court, as was the District of Columbia case; the Delaware case went to the state courts because the lawyers hoped that they could find a more sympathetic judge there. In none of the cases did the lawyers really expect that the lower court would overturn *Plessy v. Ferguson*, a Supreme Court decision that had been on the books for more than fifty years, but they did hope to build records that would persuade the High Court to repudiate *Plessy*. Coordinated by Marshall and his staff, the lawyers made two important strategic decisions. They put in as much evidence as they could about the differences between the white schools and the ones available to African American children. In addition, prodded by Robert Carter, the second-in-command to Thurgood Marshall, they presented evidence that African American children were harmed psychologically by segregation. Kenneth Clark, a young African American psychologist, tested schoolchildren by showing them dark and light-colored dolls, asking them which was "nicer." As Clark interpreted the results, African American children attending segregated schools did indeed think that the light-colored dolls were nicer than the others, from which he concluded that segregation was damaging to black self-esteem. Although some of the NAACP lawyers were skeptical about Clark's analysis, Marshall thought the evidence was helpful.

The lower court in Kansas ruled against the NAACP in August 1951, but it made one factual finding that was quite beneficial. The three judges on the court agreed, in a passage the Supreme Court later quoted, that

> segregation of white and colored children in public schools has a
> detrimental effect upon the colored children. The impact is

greater when it has the sanction of law; for the policy of separating the races is usually interpreted as denoting the inferiority of the negro group. A sense of inferiority affects the motivation of a child to learn. Segregation with the sanction of law, therefore, has a tendency to [retard] the educational and mental development of negro children and to deprive them of some of the benefits they would receive in a racial[ly] integrated school system.

The South Carolina court, which upheld segregation, also had three judges on it. One, J. Waties Waring, was a scion of South Carolina society who had gradually become a racial liberal under the influence of his New York–reared second wife. Another was John J. Parker, whose nomination to the Supreme Court by President Herbert Hoover had been defeated by a lobbying campaign by labor unions and the NAACP. South Carolina governor James Byrnes, a former Supreme Court justice himself, understood that the nation's legal climate was changing. Responding to the changes, and to the threat of litigation, Byrnes sponsored a legislative program that would appropriate a significant amount of money to upgrade the state's schools for African Americans. Parker took the opportunity provided by Byrnes's program to hold that, although Clarendon County's schools were not yet equal, they would become equal once the new state money was spent on the African American schools.

Only in Delaware was the outcome something of a surprise. Based on earlier experience, the NAACP's lawyers filed the Delaware case in state court rather than in the federal courts, where all the other cases had been filed. Collins Seitz, the Delaware judge, took the separate-but-equal doctrine seriously and found that the schools were in fact not equal. He might have said, as Judge Parker did, that the state could take some time to equalize the schools. Instead, Judge Seitz held that the inequality had to be remedied immediately by desegregating Delaware's schools. Of course, he continued, if the state upgraded the schools for African Americans, it might then start segregating again. But no one thought that was a realistic prospect.

Having lost in all the lower courts except for Delaware, the NAACP's lawyers asked the Supreme Court to overturn *Plessy*, and Delaware's lawyers sought reversal of the judgment in their case. The justices actually invited an early appeal of the District of Columbia case after the others were on the Court's docket, so that they could consider the constitutionality of segregation in all its aspects.

The justices sitting on the Supreme Court when the desegregation cases arrived were a distinguished group. Several had served in the House and Senate, others in the Cabinet. Justices William O. Douglas and Felix Frankfurter were prominent legal academics who had been close advisers to Franklin D. Roosevelt. All were quite sensitive to the questions of public policy and partisan politics that their constitutional decisions implicated.

The justices' views about the Constitution had been shaped by Roosevelt's struggle against the Supreme Court in the mid-1930s, when the Court obstructed the implementation of important New Deal initiatives. Roosevelt's appointees, and then Truman's, reacted by becoming extremely skeptical about judicial review. Generally, they thought, legislative majorities should be able to pursue whatever policies the people thought wise. Yet many of the same justices were troubled by the authoritarianism they saw in some boss-dominated U.S. cities and, more important, abroad in Nazi Germany and Soviet Russia. Some justices began to argue that certain constitutional provisions, notably the First Amendment, had a "preferred position," meaning that courts could intervene to protect such liberties more readily than they could protect others. The Court itself suggested that the courts should be particularly alert when legislation harmed "discrete and insular minorities," of whom African Americans were the clearest example.

For the Court, the desegregation cases exposed tensions in the constitutional thought of liberals influenced by the New Deal. Confrontations between a conservative Court and Franklin Roosevelt taught the justices that judicial restraint was desirable. Attacks on Jehovah's Witnesses early in the 1940s and persistent problems of racial justice led them to believe that activism was sometimes appropriate. The justices knew that segregation was deeply embedded in the South's social order and, not incidentally, in the Democratic political coalition to which all the justices were sympathetic. Invalidating segregation might improve the Court's standing among northern liberals and African Americans but would damage it in the eyes of white southerners, particularly as the lower courts actually sought to bring about desegregated schools. Invalidating segregation would also contribute to splintering the Democratic party coalition. These tensions led the Court to delay decision in the cases. Argued first in 1952, they were argued again a year later, after Republican Dwight Eisenhower was elected president and Earl Warren was appointed chief justice. Then, after the Court decided that segregation was indeed unconstitutional, a third argument was held on the question of what remedy the Court should order.

Four justices, Hugo Black, Douglas, Harold Burton, and Sherman Minton, adhered to the view that segregation was unconstitutional throughout the Court's consideration of the cases. But, after hearing the first set of arguments, the Court did not take a vote. Chief Justice Fred Vinson, a Kentuckian, was reluctant to overrule *Plessy v. Ferguson.* Stanley Reed, also from Kentucky, was even firmer. The views of Tom Clark, a Texan who had been Truman's attorney general, were unclear, although he had written the decision invalidating segregation in Texas's law school. The key justices at this point were Frankfurter and Robert Jackson. Both believed that segregation was unwise as a matter of public policy, but they were concerned that the Court could not easily find a way of expressing that policy judgment as a matter of constitutional law, particularly in light of *Plessy.* Frankfurter also worried about how to get the South to comply with an order requiring desegregation. Had the Court been forced to decide the case in 1952, Frankfurter and Jackson undoubtedly would have voted to overrule *Plessy.* But no one was in a position to lead the Court, and Frankfurter prodded his colleagues to set the case for reargument, a course it only occasionally takes. Mostly to justify that course, the Court asked the advocates to address five questions, three dealing with the history of the Fourteenth Amendment and two addressing what the law would require as a remedy if segregation was found unconstitutional.

Several important developments occurred over the summer before the reargument. The advocates researched the history, attempting to find out whether the amendment's drafters thought that the amendment itself outlawed school segregation and whether it authorized a court in the future to find school segregation unconstitutional, even if the amendment did not make segregation unconstitutional immediately. John W. Davis, arguing for Virginia, was heartened by what the research disclosed, and Marshall was discouraged. Meanwhile, Frankfurter had his law clerk Alexander Bickel write a memorandum on the history. Bickel concluded that the history behind the Fourteenth Amendment was inconclusive with respect to the specific question of school segregation, freeing Frankfurter to follow his strong policy preference against segregation. And, most important of all, Vinson died and was replaced by Earl Warren. Warren, while governor of California, had been the Republican party's candidate for vice president in 1948 and was a serious candidate for the presidency in 1952 until he saw how effectively Eisenhower's supporters had organized to secure his nomination. He had no ambivalence whatever about striking segregation down.

Warren provided the leadership the Court needed, guaranteeing that there would be at least five or six votes to overrule *Plessy*. Once the outcome was clear, Frankfurter went along with the decision, especially because Bickel's memorandum gave him the cover he needed. Jackson was more of a problem. He continued to be concerned about whether overruling *Plessy* could be justified as a matter of law rather than policy. But in early 1954 he suffered a heart attack, which sapped his energy and made it difficult for him to pursue an independent course. When Warren visited Jackson in the hospital, he persuaded him to join the Court's opinion. That left only Reed as a potential dissenter, and Warren used all of his political skills to bring Reed along, appealing particularly to Reed's sense of patriotism and the importance of having a unanimous opinion to persuade the South to comply with the decision.

Warren deliberately wrote a short opinion, hoping that newspapers would publish the entire opinion for everyone to read. The tone was equally deliberately flat. The opinion did not castigate the South for having adopted an unconstitutional system and sought to appeal to common understandings about the importance of education in modern life. The opinion put the historical inquiry to one side, calling the record "inconclusive." It continued, "In approaching this problem, we cannot turn the clock back to 1868 when the [Fourteenth] Amendment was adopted, or even to 1896 when [*Plessy*] was written." According to the Court, it had to "consider public education in light of its full development and its present place in American life throughout the Nation."

Emphasizing the impact of segregation on young children, Warren wrote, "To separate them from others of similar age and qualifications solely because of their race generates a feeling of inferiority as to their status in the community that may affect their hearts and minds in a way unlikely ever to be undone." He cited the finding of fact made by the lower court in the Kansas case and then made his one mistake. The opinion stated that "this finding is amply supported by modern authority," and late in the drafting process he inserted a footnote referring to modern psychological studies, including Clark's, to support the otherwise unremarkable observation that segregation harmed African American children. The Court's critics seized on the footnote, saying that the decision rested on social science rather than law. Warren came to regret including the footnote, which he thought from the beginning was unimportant.

The opinion concluded that "in the field of public education the doctrine of 'separate but equal' has no place. Separate educational facilities are inherently unequal." The opinion received the attention Warren sought. The Court's opponents criticized the decision, but their vigor was weakened by the Court's decision not to require southern states to do anything immediately. Instead, the Court set the cases for yet another round of arguments, to be directed at the precise remedies that should be ordered.

The justices faced a dilemma. Implementing a decision that segregation was unconstitutional could be quite simple. According to the Court, segregation was wrong because school boards used race to assign students to schools. All they had to do to comply with the decision was to stop doing that. The obvious way to do so was to create neighborhood schools. Doing so would require a bit of tinkering with district lines, to ensure that each school had the right number of children, and assigning teachers to these neighborhood schools would also take a bit of work. But it was clear that these administrative problems were relatively small. Marshall pressed the justices to order desegregation forthwith, by which he meant within the six to eighteen months that, he estimated, it would take to work out the administrative details.

The fact that immediate desegregation could be accomplished through neighborhood schools with only minor administrative issues to be resolved masked the other horn of the Court's dilemma. They knew that many white southerners, particularly in the Deep South, would strenuously resist complying with any order requiring that their children attend schools with African American children. Yet, as defenders of the law, they could hardly acknowledge openly that there was a real risk that people would fail to comply with their decision. When Warren wrote the opinion on remedy, he included a sentence making that point: "It should go without saying that the vitality of these constitutional principles cannot be allowed to yield simply because of disagreement with them."[10]

Resistance there would be, though, and the Court had to do something about the risk. So Frankfurter proposed that school districts be given some unspecified period of time in which to adjust to the desegregation decision. Marshall had supported the argument for desegregation forthwith by pointing out that the Court had consistently said that constitutional rights were personal and present, giving the example that no one would say that a political dissident's right to make a public speech could be protected by giving the state a year or more to figure out when and where the speech should take place. Frankfurter discovered a phrase from some old cases in which the Court said that certain decrees could be carried out "with all deliberate speed." The opinion did say that school boards should "make a prompt and reasonable start toward full compliance." But it also emphasized the need for flexibility and for "adjusting and reconciling public and private needs." The Court's opinion summarized its holding in Frankfurter's favored phrase: The lower courts should enter orders that would "admit to public schools on a racially nondiscriminatory basis with all deliberate speed the parties to these cases."

The Court's opinion in *Brown* seemed to be confined to public education. Quickly, however, the Court showed that it meant the decision to undermine all forms of Jim Crow segregation, invoking the decision in cases involving city-owned parks and golf courses and, notably, city-owned transportation systems. The decision finding it unconstitutional to segregate buses in Montgomery, Alabama, was issued on the same day in November 1956 that a state court planned to hand down a ruling that would have effectively terminated the Montgomery bus boycott, which had attracted national attention and thrust Martin Luther King, Jr., into a position of national civil rights leadership.

In the field of education itself, however, *Brown*'s impact was limited. States in the Upper South moved in the direction of desegregation rather rapidly. Some districts adopted neighborhood schools, but the effects of doing so were limited because housing segregation meant that the neighborhoods that fed the schools were almost entirely white or black anyway. Some districts developed desegregation plans that forced African American students through a maze of regulations to determine to which schools they would be assigned, and to no one's surprise, the students who managed to comply with the regulations were assigned—on the basis of supposedly nonracial criteria—to schools that happened to be as segregated as they had been before 1955. Other districts took advantage of the "all deliberate speed" formulation to adopt plans that would desegregate one grade a year, sometimes starting with first grade and working up, sometimes starting with the senior year in high school moving down. The courts generally accepted these plans, which promised full desegregation in twelve years.

The Deep South resisted even more strenuously. Sporadic violence broke out when even modest desegregation efforts were made. Supported by editorials written by James Jackson Kilpatrick in his Richmond newspaper, the *News Leader*, southern legislatures enacted laws resting on a constitutional theory under which they were entitled to "interpose" their authority between their citizens and the national government. Eventually, some school systems, including the one in Prince Edward County, simply closed down rather than desegregate; white parents set up "private" schools that received significant funds from the government, and African American children attended schools in their communities' churches or in northern districts to which their parents sent them. Southern politicians engaged in systematic efforts to suppress the NAACP and its litigation program, which diverted the organization's limited resources from support for desegregation to self-defense against these attacks. Potential plaintiffs understood the risks they and their children faced in attempting to desegregate the schools, and few volunteered for the ordeal.

The Supreme Court refrained from addressing the problems associated with implementing its decision. Between 1955 and 1963, it addressed school segregation only once, when in 1958 it rebuked Arkansas governor Orval Faubus for provoking violent resistance to the gradual desegregation of Little Rock's schools.[11] Desegregation actually occurred generally throughout the South only when Congress intervened by providing in the Civil Rights Act of 1964 that segregated school systems would be ineligible for federal financial assistance, the amount of which was increasing substantially at around the same time.

Eventually, most rural school districts were nearly completely integrated. The situation in cities, both North and South, was different. Residential segregation, and deliberate decisions by many school boards, produced systems with large numbers of one-race schools. Many whites abandoned the cities for the suburbs, where the price of housing limited opportunities for African Americans.

In 1971, the Supreme Court endorsed efforts to desegregate some areas by busing students to desegregated schools, and two years later it ruled that northern school systems had to desegregate if they had taken deliberate actions in the past to create segregated schools.[12] Those, however, were the Court's last interventions in support of desegregation. Over the next decades, the Court regularly ruled against further steps. It rejected the argument that effective desegregation in metropolitan areas required that the city and its suburbs be included in any desegregation plan.[13] It allowed districts to remove themselves from judicial supervision once the courts found that they had taken substantial steps in the direction of desegregation, even if some areas of discrimination remained.[14] By the turn of the century, the experiment with court-ordered desegregation had effectively ended, largely a failure.

What remained were the cultural effects of the Court's action in *Brown*. The decision contributed to the civil rights movement, not necessarily by motivating actions that would not otherwise have been taken, but rather by giving important support to the movement's moral claims. It changed the Supreme Court's image from that of a conservative institution whose primary political function was to obstruct liberal change to one that could be relied on to intervene actively in matters of general political importance. Finally, it vindicated the civil rights movement's decision to cast its most urgent moral claims on the American political order as claims that the Constitution already treated as rights. In doing so, it helped Americans think that *all* of their moral claims might be expressed as legal arguments that the existing Constitution was being violated. *Brown* contributed to broader processes through which political contention took the form of arguments about law in the late twentieth century, from the abortion rights question to the disability rights movement and beyond.

NOTES

1. *Brown v. Board of Education*, 347 U.S. 483 (1954).
2. *Strauder v. West Virginia*, 100 U.S. 303 (1880).
3. *Pace v. Alabama*, 106 U.S. 583 (1883).
4. 163 U.S. 537 (1896).
5. *Cumming v. Richmond County Board of Education*, 175 U.S. 528 (1899); *Gong Lum v. Rice*, 275 U.S. 78 (1927).
6. *McCabe v. Atchison, Topeka & Santa Fe R.*, 235 U.S. 151 (1914).
7. *Missouri ex rel. Gaines v. Canada*, 305 U.S. 337 (1938).
8. *McLaurin v. Oklahoma State Board of Regents*, 339 U.S. 637 (1950).
9. *Sweatt v. Painter*, 339 U.S. 629 (1950).
10. *Brown v. Board of Education II*, 349 U.S. 294 (1955).
11. *Cooper v. Aaron*, 358 U.S. 1 (1958).
12. *Swann v. Charlotte-Mecklenburg Board of Education*, 402 U.S. 1 (1971); *Keyes v. School Dist. No. 1, Denver, Colo.*, 413 U.S. 189 (1973).
13. *Milliken v. Bradley*, 418 U.S. 717 (1974).
14. *Freeman v. Pitts*, 503 U.S. 467 (1992).

10

INTERRACIAL MARRIAGE ON TRIAL

Loving v. Virginia

Peter Wallenstein

One night in July 1958, two newlyweds suddenly awoke in their home in Caroline County, Virginia, startled by the sound of men in their room and the glare of flashlights on their faces. One of the three intruders demanded to know who they were and why they were together in bed. Mildred Loving murmured, "I'm his wife," and Richard Loving pointed to a marriage certificate hanging on the wall. "That's no good here," retorted the trio's leader, Sheriff R. Garnett Brooks. The young couple were arrested and taken to jail.[1]

Mildred Jeter and Richard Loving had been seeing each other for several years, and during the spring of 1958 they determined that the time had come for them to marry. It seemed to him that they could not have their wedding in Virginia, but he thought that, if they went to the District of Columbia, they would be all right. They drove a hundred miles north to the nation's capital, had their ceremony, and moved back to the community in which they had lived all their lives. They lived with Mildred Loving's parents.

The issue that had given him pause and led to their trip to the big city—and the problem that led to their arrest that summer night—was that, under Virginia law, Richard Loving was white, and Mildred Jeter was black. It was no crime in Virginia to be white or black, male or female. But it was a serious crime for two people to marry if one of them was white and the other was not. If convicted of marrying in violation of Virginia's law against interracial marriage, each person could be sent to the state penitentiary for at least one year and for as long as five years.

Other Virginians had spent years in prison for breaking that law, and now it looked like two more people would join their ranks. The Lovings were terrified of the prospect. They were free while awaiting their trial, but a trial nonetheless loomed. Not only was there no way to turn the clock back to May, but they also would not have wanted to. They wanted to marry and live together in peace in their rural community. Richard Loving had thought they could do both if they went out of state to marry, but they discovered that the same law banning their getting married in Virginia also outlawed their living together there as a black-white married couple no matter where their ceremony had taken place.

This essay tells the story of two people across nine years of their lives. The man and woman who wanted to be Mr. and Mrs. Loving were not unique in having their freedom threatened because of their racial identities under the law. For generations, other Virginians had encountered similar threats to their happiness, though the specific provisions changed over time. In 1691 colonial Virginia had enacted a law that banished the white partner in couples like the Lovings who crossed racial boundaries when they married. Virginia's five-year prison sentence for interracial marriage had been enacted in 1878.[2]

Nor was Virginia remotely unique, even as late as 1958. Most of the states in the United States, in the North and the West as well as in the South, had, at one time or another, banned interracial marriages. The term *miscegenation*—which was applied to laws that restricted interracial marriage—originated in the North during the Civil War, when Democrats had tried to worry voters there that the party of Abraham Lincoln favored interracial marriage. Massachusetts maintained such a law until 1843, shortly before the Civil War, and California did so until 1948, only ten years before the Lovings were arrested in Virginia.[3]

The threat of imprisonment was less universal than the restrictive laws themselves, which did not all specify the same racial boundaries between the groups that could not intermarry. For many years, California banned marriages between whites and either blacks or Asians; Oklahoma, which defined American Indians—indeed, anyone who had no African ancestry—as white, outlawed marriages between people who were defined as "white" and people who were "not." In California, interracial couples were for many years unable to obtain marriage licenses, but such people sometimes went out of state and, unlike the Lovings, moved back home with impunity. Oklahoma had rarely prosecuted anyone for interracial marriage, but inheritance of property had been tangled up in that state's miscegenation laws many times since statehood in 1907.[4]

The U.S. Supreme Court itself long treated miscegenation laws as constitutionally permissible. The Court upheld an Alabama miscegenation law in 1883. The decision in *Plessy v. Ferguson* (1896), which for half a century validated the concept of "separate but equal" in American life and law, dealt with segregated transportation but spoke, too, of laws requiring school segregation and laws against interracial marriage, which, it said, had been "universally recognized as within the police power of the State." In a 1917 case in which the Court dealt with segregated housing as mandated by city ordinances, both sides to the controversy agreed that the constitutional issue was settled in transportation, education, and marriage, but they differed as to whether property rights were violated by laws requiring segregated housing.[5]

Such matters concern students of race and the law in American history. The Lovings, however, focused on their own situation, Virginia's law on interracial marriage as it stood in 1958. For the next nine years, they lived with the consequences of, challenged, and eventually changed that law, not only for Virginians but for Americans everywhere. Time and again during those nine years, interracial marriage was on trial, as such marriages had often been in the American colonies and then in the American states. In those many times and places in U.S. history, when interracial marriage went on trial, partners to a marriage were indicted for a crime that arose for the sole reason that somebody with one racial identity was alleged to have married someone of another racial identity.

In June 1967, within days of their ninth wedding anniversary, the Lovings won a case in the U.S. Supreme Court that permitted them to live together in Virginia as husband and wife, as Mr. and Mrs. Loving, with their three children.[6] During those nine years, they lived as defendants, felons, exiles, fugitives, litigants, and even as prisoners—all for the crime of interracial marriage. Finally, the U.S. Supreme Court decided in their favor and declared all the laws against interracial marriage unconstitutional and no longer enforceable in any court.

Three cases from Virginia other than the Lovings', dating from the 1930s through the 1950s, illustrate the variety of ways in which two people could find themselves caught up in a court case over the state's miscegenation statute.

In 1937, in Fincastle, Virginia, Grace Mohler married Samuel Christian Branaham. Both were later indicted for violating the Virginia ban on interracial marriages. Grace Mohler escaped conviction when she testified that she had not known that Samuel Branaham was of African descent. Branaham testified that he was not, in fact, of mixed race, yet other testimony contradicted him. Judge Benjamin Haden declared Branaham to be black, not white, and imposed on him a one-year prison sentence, the shortest possible under the law. Then he suspended that sentence for thirty years, a period during which Branaham must not live with Grace Mohler or marry any other white woman. As a newspaper account put it, having been "adjudged a Negro," Samuel Branaham was ordered "never again to live with the pretty young white woman he married here a year ago under penalty of serving a year's suspended sentence."[7]

In 1952, Ham Say Naim, a Chinese sailor from Malaya, married a white woman from Virginia. For their wedding ceremony, they crossed into North Carolina, a state that, unlike Virginia, permitted marriages between Caucasians and Asians, though—like Virginia—not between whites and blacks. For some months, Mr. and Mrs. Naim made their home in Norfolk, Virginia. Then they separated. Ruby Elaine Naim filed a petition seeking annulment on grounds of adultery, and if that effort failed, she asked that an annulment be granted on the basis of Virginia's ban on interracial marriages. The judge knew an easy case when he saw one. Here was a marriage between a white person and a nonwhite, and the couple had gone to North Carolina in order to evade Virginia law. Of course the marriage was void, and he granted Ruby Naim the annulment she sought.[8]

It was Ham Say Naim's turn to go to court. On the basis of his marriage to an American citizen, he had applied for an immigrant visa, and unless he remained married to her he could not hope to be successful. He challenged the local court's decision on the basis that the Fourteenth Amendment overrode the Virginia statute, but a unanimous Virginia Supreme Court ruled against him. "Regulation of the marriage relation," insisted Justice Archibald Chapmen Buchanan, is "distinctly one of the rights guaranteed to the States." Refusing to give up, Naim appealed to the U.S. Supreme Court. Unhappily for Naim, the nation's High Court was not yet ready to address his concerns, and it evaded his case.[9] His marriage was over; under Virginia law, it had never begun. His hopes for American citizenship, to the extent that they depended on that marriage, were over as well. Interracial couples across America would have to await another opportunity to obtain a favorable hearing from the U.S. Supreme Court.

At about the same time the Lovings first encountered problems with Virginia's miscegenation laws, the Calma family was also living in Virginia. Rosina and Cezar Calma—she was white and he was Filipino—had married in New Jersey in 1954 but later relocated to Virginia under Cezar Calma's military orders. Virginia authorities did not arrest them, yet the law of interracial marriage nonetheless intruded. When they sought to end their marriage, Virginia courts refused to recognize its validity, and thus they could not terminate it through divorce in the state of their residence.[10]

Momentum was building toward a change in the policy that outlawed marriages between people of different racial identities. A 1948 court decision in *Perez v. Sharp* was one significant straw in the wind; by a 4–3 majority, the California Supreme Court overturned that state's miscegenation law. Between 1948 and 1965, many states—extending from Indiana to Arizona—repealed their laws. By the time the Lovings' case went to the Supreme Court, statutes banning interracial marriages had been eliminated everywhere except the eleven states of the former Confederacy, together with the six states of the Border South—Delaware, Maryland, West Virginia, Kentucky, Missouri, and Oklahoma. Maryland repealed its miscegenation law in early 1967, effective June 1, while the *Loving* decision was pending. A block of sixteen states, a third of the nation, retained such laws until the Supreme Court overturned them in June 1967.[11]

At the federal level, the situation was a bit ambiguous in the mid-1960s. The Supreme Court had evaded efforts to overturn miscegenation laws, and the Civil Rights Act of 1964 addressed such matters as public education and public accommodations but said nothing whatever about marriage. Nonetheless, in the late 1950s and early 1960s, the Supreme Court ruled in a variety of cases in ways that applied its central finding in *Brown v. Board of Education* (1954), that laws mandating racial separation violated the Fourteenth Amendment. In this context, a case arose in Virginia that eventually applied *Brown* to marriage and put an end to the enforcement of miscegenation laws throughout the nation.

Various changes in American law and culture took place during the twentieth century, especially in the 1960s, to make the 1967 *Loving* decision possible. Even today, the questions persist: How much control should people have over their lives? And how much power should government (whether federal or state and local) have to restrict people's freedom? What fundamental rights do people have—even if those rights are not explicitly protected in the U.S. Constitution?

Beginning in the 1920s, the U.S. Supreme Court declared that people had various rights upon which their state governments could not infringe. For example, parents had a right to teach their children a foreign language, despite state laws that said otherwise, and they had a right to send their children to private rather than public schools.[12]

In subsequent years, the Court built on these precedents to expand American liberties. In perhaps the leading privacy case before 1967, the

Supreme Court ruled in *Griswold v. Connecticut* (1965) that married people have the right to decide whether to use birth control information and devices to prevent pregnancy. Six years after *Loving*, in *Roe v. Wade* (1973), the Court further extended its rulings on privacy when it struck down statutes that prohibited women from obtaining abortions, especially in the first three months of pregnancy.[13] Thus, across a fifty-year period from 1923 to 1973, the Court determined that Americans have a zone of privacy—the right, at least under certain circumstances, to go about their lives without having state authorities intervene and tell them what they must and must not do.

Those cases had to do with marriage, sexuality, parenting, religion, and language—all vital dimensions of liberty, all vital components of American culture. They had nothing directly to do with race, but another series of cases reconfigured individual liberty and state power regarding race. The leading case was *Brown v. Board of Education*, decided in 1954, four years before the Lovings decided to marry.[14]

The decision in *Brown* expressly overruled the old rule from *Plessy v. Ferguson* of "separate but equal," at least as far as public education was concerned, and subsequent decisions applied the new rule more generally. Congress, too, acted against segregation and other racial discrimination. The Civil Rights Act of 1964 banned racial exclusion or segregation in motels and restaurants, on buses and trains, and from grade school to college.[15]

None of these laws or court cases said that Virginia could no longer enforce its miscegenation law, but, at about the same time, the Supreme Court began to apply the spirit of the decision in *Brown* to the law of race and marriage. In *McLaughlin v. Florida* (1964), the Court unanimously decided that a state cannot use a law that specifies race to keep people from living together. The case arose from the arrest of a white woman and a black man who, in view of a Florida law that kept them from marrying, lived together for a time without being married.

But as late as the *McLaughlin* decision, most of the Supreme Court justices were not yet ready to take on the question of interracial marriage itself. Most of the justices specified that they had reached their decision in that case—invalidating the Florida law and overturning the couple's convictions under it—"without expressing any views about the State's prohibition of interracial marriage."[16]

Two members of the Court, however, Justices Potter Stewart and William O. Douglas, went further and insisted that they could not "conceive of a valid legislative purpose . . . which makes the color of a person's skin the test of whether his conduct is a criminal offense."[17] Three years later, in *Loving*, their colleagues on the Court adopted the position that Douglas and Stewart had voiced. A unanimous Court applied the reasoning in *McLaughlin* to the facts in *Loving*.

It is time to return to the saga of Mr. and Mrs. Loving—to review their experiences in the late 1950s and detail the next few years, before their case reached the U.S. Supreme Court. Someone—the Lovings never knew who—complained to Caroline County authorities, who then took action. On July 11, 1958, Commonwealth Attorney Bernard Mahon obtained warrants for the arrest of Richard Loving and "Mildred Jeter," each for a felony associated with their marriage on June 2 in Washington, D.C. Late one night a day or two later, Sheriff Garnett Brooks and two officers went to make the arrests.[18]

The three law officers entered the Lovings' bedroom and awakened them that July night. "We were living with my parents," where "we had a guest bedroom downstairs," Mildred Loving later recalled. "I woke up and these guys were standing around the bed. I sat up. It was dark. They had flashlights. They told us to get up, get dressed. I couldn't believe they were taking us to jail."[19]

There was an interlude before they actually left the house. First, "I went upstairs, sat on the bed, talked with my mother," she remembers. "Make them go away," she pleaded to her mom. But the intruders had ascertained that the two were indeed living together as husband and wife. The couple did not share a racial identity, and yet they shared a bed. The men "explained we had broken the law," Mildred Loving said, and "they took us to jail." Richard was freed after one night, but Mildred, all alone in jail, was kept for several more days. Each posted $1,000 bail.[20]

The Caroline County grand jury brought indictments at its October term. At their trial on January 6, 1959, the Lovings pled not guilty at first and waived a jury trial. At the close of argument, they changed their pleas to guilty, and Circuit Court judge Leon M. Bazile sentenced them to one year each in jail. But he suspended those sentences "for a period of twenty-five years"—to 1984—provided that "both accused leave Caroline County and the state of Virginia at once and do not return together or at the same time to said county and state for a period of twenty-five years."[21] Samuel Christian Branaham would have recognized Virginia's mid-twentieth-century way of dealing with some black-white marriages—permitting the offenders to avoid prison if they agreed not to continue to live together in Virginia.

The suspended sentence did not mean that, after twenty-five years, the Lovings could move back to Virginia. One of them, it seemed, could live in Caroline County, Virginia, with impunity. Or, after twenty-five years, both could live there separately. As matters stood in 1959, however, if they ever attempted to live together in their native state, they faced trouble. If they were caught together in Virginia anytime during the next twenty-five years, they would each serve their suspended sentence. If they lived together in Virginia even after the twenty-five years had elapsed, they would face prosecution just as they had in 1958.

Richard Loving and Mildred Jeter, as the court knew them in Virginia, moved to Washington, D.C., where they resumed their identities as Mr. and Mrs. Loving, living at 1151 Neal Street Northeast with Mildred Loving's cousin Alex Byrd and his wife, Laura. Either Mr. Loving or Mrs. Loving could visit Caroline County, but both could not legally do so at the same time. Mildred Loving returned home to Virginia for the births of their three children—Sidney, Donald, and Peggy.[22] But the family had to live and work outside the state.

After four years of exile, the Lovings began to contest their fate. In 1963, Mildred Loving wrote to Robert F. Kennedy, U.S. attorney general, for assistance. As she recalled many years later, "I told Mr. Kennedy of our situation" and asked "if there was any way he could help us."[23] It was time, she felt, that her family move back home, and she had no doubt heard of a civil rights bill bobbing around in Congress, although the Civil Rights Act of 1964, when it became law the next year, left marriage as the one remaining pillar in the structure of Jim Crow.

The Justice Department redirected her letter to the National Capitol Area Civil Liberties Union with the suggestion that, though the federal government could not help the Lovings, perhaps the American Civil Liberties Union (ACLU) could. That organization had been pushing litigation since the *Perez* case in California in the late 1940s to rid the nation of miscegenation laws like Virginia's.[24]

ACLU member Bernard S. Cohen, a young lawyer practicing in Alexandria, Virginia, welcomed the opportunity to take the case. Years later, he recounted: How could he not? For one thing, he wanted to help make things work out for the young couple. For another, they were bringing the perfect test case for attacking the nation's miscegenation laws. Here were two people who clearly loved each other and wanted to live together and raise their family in familiar surroundings. The name of the case itself enthralled him: *Loving versus Virginia*.[25]

Thus the case of the Lovings made its way back into the courts. While it did, the Lovings returned home to the Caroline County area, though they faced uncertainty there and kept their sanctuary at the ready in Washington, D.C.[26] In November 1963, Cohen filed a motion in Caroline

County Circuit Court to set aside the original convictions and sentences. He knew that he would have to be creative to overturn a century's worth of adverse precedents. Of course, he deployed the Fourteenth Amendment's Equal Protection Clause to contest the constitutionality of Virginia's miscegenation statutes. He argued, too, that the suspended sentence "denies the right of marriage which is a fundamental right of free men"; that the sentence constituted "cruel and unusual punishment" in violation of the Virginia Constitution; that it exceeded the "reasonable period of suspension" permitted by Virginia law; and that it constituted banishment and thus violated due process.[27]

Judge Bazile was in no hurry to second-guess himself, so for some time nothing happened. In mid-1964, another young attorney, Philip J. Hirschkop, joined Bernard Cohen in the case, and, no action having been taken on the petition in state court, the lawyers began a class action in October 1964 in the U.S. District Court for the Eastern District of Virginia.[28] Cohen and Hirschkop requested that a three-judge court convene to determine the constitutionality of Virginia's miscegenation statutes and to enjoin the enforcement of the Lovings' convictions and sentences under those laws. Pending a decision by a three-judge panel, they requested a temporary injunction against the enforcement of those laws, which they said were designed "solely for the purpose of keeping the Negro people in the badges and bonds of slavery." District Judge John D. Butzner, Jr., however, saw no "irreparable harm" to the Lovings while awaiting the panel's decision and rejected a motion for a temporary injunction. With the federal panel due to meet soon, Judge Bazile finally set a date to hear arguments on Cohen's motion.[29]

In January 1965, six years after the original proceedings, Bazile presided at a hearing on the Lovings' petition to have his decision set aside. In a written opinion, he rebutted each of the contentions that might have forced reconsideration of their guilt. Pointing back to an 1878 Virginia Supreme Court decision, *Kinney v. Commonwealth*, he insisted that the Lovings' marriage was "absolutely void in Virginia" and that they could not "cohabit" there "without incurring repeated prosecutions" for doing so. Relying on the Virginia high court's earlier decision in *Naim v. Naim* (1955), Bazile noted that marriage was "a subject which belongs to the exclusive control of the States," and he noted that the U.S. Supreme Court had done nothing to overturn the Virginia decision or to undermine any other state's laws against interracial marriage.[30]

By way of conclusion, Bazile wrote, "Almighty God created the races white, black, yellow, malay and red, and he placed them on separate continents. And but for the interference with his arrangement there would be no cause for such marriages. The fact that he separated the races shows that he did not intend for the races to mix."[31] It is hard to know what to make of the judge's attempt at writing history and geography. After all, he was a Caucasian judge holding forth in Virginia, on a continent where "Almighty God" had placed the "red" race until Europeans moved there and forced Africans to settle there, too, and mingle among them.

The Lovings' case moved on from Bazile's court, for he had not had the last word. The Lovings were not giving up. First, lawyers for the state convinced the federal court that the case should next be heard in the Virginia Supreme Court. So the Lovings took their case to the state's highest court, and their lawyers and the state's rehearsed arguments that, both sides well knew, were likely to be heard again before long at the U.S. Supreme Court.

In mounting one of their arguments, Cohen and Hirschkop quoted from Perez v. Sharp, the 1948 California Supreme Court decision against the constitutionality of miscegenation laws: "If the right to marry is a fundamental right, then it must be conceded that an infringement of that right by means of a racial restriction is an unlawful infringement of one's liberty." They went on to assert, "The caprice of the politicians cannot be substituted for the minds of the individual in what is man's most personal and intimate decision. The error of such legislation must immediately be apparent to those in favor of miscegenation statutes, if they stopped to consider their abhorrence to a statute which commanded that 'all marriages must be between persons of different racial backgrounds.'" Such a statute, they claimed, would be no more "repugnant to the constitution"—and no less so—than the law under consideration. Something "so personal as the choice of a mate must be left to the individuals involved," they argued; "race limitations are too unreasonable and arbitrary a basis for the State to interfere."[32]

The Virginia Supreme Court largely adopted the brief of the state of Virginia as its opinion. On March 7, 1966, a unanimous court declared, "We find no sound judicial reason . . . to depart from our holding in the Naim case."[33] As far as the Virginia Supreme Court was concerned, the state law against interracial marriage was as sound in the 1960s as it had been in the 1880s.

The Lovings had exhausted their appeals in the Virginia courts, and their convictions remained intact. They were still not allowed to "cohabit as man and wife" in Virginia, so they appealed their case to the U.S. Supreme Court.[34]

The Lovings were reluctant parties to the law case that bears their name. This is not to say that someone had to convince them to bring the case, for they were committed to their marriage. Rather, they would much have preferred for the question never to have been raised back in July 1958. All they had ever wanted was to be left alone. Richard Loving, a private and taciturn man, explained their views in 1966, after the Virginia Supreme Court had rejected their position. "We have thought about other people," he told a reporter in Virginia, "but we are not doing it just because someone had to do it and we wanted to be the ones. . . . We are doing it for *us*—because we want to live here."[35] So they pressed on.

Cohen and Hirschkop, in their jurisdictional statement to the U.S. Supreme Court, pointed out why the case should be heard there: "The elaborate legal structure of segregation has been virtually obliterated with the exception of the miscegenation laws." They continued, "There are no laws more symbolic of the Negro's relegation to second-class citizenship. Whether or not this Court has been wise to avoid this issue in the past, the time has come to strike down these laws; they are legalized racial prejudice, unsupported by reason or morals, and should not exist in a good society."[36]

On December 12, 1966, the Court agreed to hear the case. Indicating that interest in the question went beyond black-white marriages and the law, the Japanese American Citizens League submitted a brief as a friend of the court. Cohen and Hirschkop, in their brief, reviewed the history of Virginia's miscegenation laws from the seventeenth to the twentieth centuries and characterized those statutes as "relics of slavery" and, at the same time, "expressions of modern day racism."[37]

In oral arguments on April 10, 1967, the ACLU lawyers made the case that Virginia's miscegenation laws could not pass constitutional muster. Hirschkop argued from the legislative history of the laws that their intent to secure the racial purity of the "white" race and their intent to demean and control black Virginians violated the Fourteenth Amendment. Cohen concentrated on the personal impact of the laws on the Lovings. With reference to the Equal Protection Clause of the Fourteenth Amendment, Cohen spoke of their right to marry, as he and they saw it, and their wish to live together in peace in Virginia. He referred to their terror and humiliation at being dragged out of bed and off to jail for living as husband and wife.[38]

With reference to the Due Process Clause of the Fourteenth Amendment, Cohen summarized some of the civil penalties (quite aside from the criminal penalties) that automatically attached to them under Virginia's laws. "The Lovings have the right to go to sleep at night," he declared, "knowing that should they not awake in the morning their children would have the right to inherit from them, under intestacy [in the absence of a will leaving them their parents' property]. They have the right to be secure in knowing that if they go to sleep and do not wake in the morning, that one of them, a survivor of them, has the right to social security benefits." The "injustices" that necessarily followed from the Virginia law, Cohen argued, "amount to a denial of due process," for those rights were being arbitrarily denied the Lovings.[39] Cohen wrapped up his argument by conveying to the Court the words of Richard Loving: "Mr. Cohen, tell the Court I love my wife, and it is just unfair that I can't live with her in Virginia."[40]

Two months later, on June 12, 1967, Chief Justice Earl Warren delivered the opinion of a unanimous Supreme Court. The Court rejected each of the state's arguments. Where the historical record, judicial precedents, and legal logic of the state's brief were incorporated in the decision of the Virginia Supreme Court, those of the Lovings' attorneys made their way into the decision of the U.S. Supreme Court. The decision of the Virginia appellate court in *Naim v. Naim* to the contrary, the chief justice wrote, the Tenth Amendment had to yield to the Fourteenth when it came to the claim of "exclusive state control" over the "regulation of marriage."[41]

As for the narrow construction of the Fourteenth Amendment, dependent as it was on the state's reading of the intent of the framers, the Court harked back to its statement in 1954 in *Brown v. Board of Education* that the historical record was "inconclusive." That Virginia's "miscegenation statutes punish equally both the white and the Negro participants in an interracial marriage" could no longer satisfy the standard of constitutionality. Should this Court "defer to the wisdom of the state legislature" on this matter? Warren gave the back of the hand to the state's contention that "these statutes should be upheld if there is any possible basis for concluding that they serve a rational purpose." The burden of proof rested on the state, for "the fact of equal application does not immunize the statute from the heavy burden of justification" required by the Fourteenth Amendment, particularly when racial classifications appeared in criminal statutes.[42]

The chief justice declared that "we find the racial classifications in these statutes repugnant to the Fourteenth Amendment, even assuming an evenhanded state purpose to protect the 'integrity' of all races." As Warren put it, "The clear and central purpose of the Fourteenth Amendment was to eliminate all official state sources of invidious racial discrimination in the States." Quoting from the *McLaughlin* case, he wrote: "Indeed, two members of this Court have already stated that they 'cannot conceive of a valid legislative purpose . . . which makes the color of a person's skin the test of whether his conduct is a criminal offense.'"[43]

Warren was sure of the Court's recent history in civil rights cases. "We have consistently denied the constitutionality of measures which restrict the rights of citizens on account of race. There can be no doubt that restricting the freedom to marry solely because of racial classifications violates the central meaning of the Equal Protection Clause." As for the Due Process Clause, the chief justice noted that "the freedom to marry has long been recognized as one of the vital personal rights essential to the orderly pursuit of happiness by free men." Connecting race with privacy, he explained, "To deny this fundamental freedom on so unsupportable a basis as the racial classifications embodied in these statutes, classifications so directly subversive of the principle of equality at the heart of the Fourteenth Amendment, is surely to deprive all the State's citizens of liberty without due process of law."[44]

Giving the Lovings and their lawyers everything they had asked for, the chief justice wrote that the Fourteenth Amendment "requires that the freedom of choice to marry not be restricted by invidious racial discriminations. Under our Constitution, the freedom to marry, or not marry, a person of another race resides with the individual and cannot be infringed by the State."[45]

Therefore, Chief Justice Warren concluded, "These convictions must be reversed."[46] Richard and Mildred Loving had a compelling case, able lawyers, and the good fortune to take their case to the U.S. Supreme Court at an auspicious time. They also had the commitment to see their case through. Ten days after their ninth wedding anniversary, the Court handed them the victory for which they had longed. It put an end to their banishment from Virginia and their odyssey through the judicial system. Not only could the Lovings live in Virginia without fear of prosecution for their interracial marriage, but laws similar to Virginia's fell in fifteen other states as well.

From their farm home in Bowling Green, east of Fredericksburg, Mr. and Mrs. Loving drove north to Alexandria for a news conference at their lawyers' office. There he said, "We're just really overjoyed." And she, "I feel free now." A photographer snapped a picture, law books in the background, of two happy people sitting close together, his arm around her neck. "My wife and I plan to go ahead and build a new house now," said Richard Loving the construction worker about the new home that Richard Loving the husband and father wanted his family to live in.[47]

The new house, in which the Lovings' three children grew up, symbolized the family's freedom to have a permanent dwelling where they could live in peace in their home state. As Mildred Loving later wrote, "The

Supreme Court decision changed our life a lot. We moved our family into our community in Caroline County without fear of going to prison."[48]

Other families, shook free of the law of interracial marriage, could make permanent plans. According to the *Loving* decision, race would no longer be the basis for county clerks to deny applications for marriage licenses. No longer could men or women, whether of European, African, or any other racial ancestry, be separated by the courts because of the racial identity of their partners in marriage. The penitentiary no longer awaited newlyweds for the crime of interracial marriage. Nowhere in the United States would such marriages be put on trial.

The major white newspapers in Virginia greeted the Supreme Court's ruling with equanimity, black newspapers with congratulations. Norfolk's two papers, the white *Virginian-Pilot* and the black *Journal and Guide*, illustrate the responses. "Anti-miscegenation laws go back three centuries," the *Virginian-Pilot* explained in an editorial on the decision. "In the beginning their purpose was to force mulattoes into the slave system, not to prevent what white-supremacists now call 'race-mongrelization.'" One might note, of course, that the seventeenth-century laws were in fact designed to achieve both objectives. The paper prophesied that "social discouragements to mixed marriages . . . will not quickly disappear," but it also suggested that "Virginia in recent years had allowed . . . its law to lose vitality." By that it meant to say that only black-white couples like the Lovings were challenged in court, though "the restriction they defied applied also to whites and members of brown and yellow races, including Chinese and Filipinos. But Virginia was inclined to arrest only whites and Negroes, although it withheld such marital civil rights as adoption, inheritance, and divorce from other racially mixed couples as well." The editorial concluded with a celebration of sorts that the topic of interracial marriage had now "been removed, as it had to be, from the field of jurisprudence."[49]

The *Journal and Guide* led off its front page with the headline, "Top Court Junks Marriage Bars," and printed an editorial on "Freedom of Choice at the Altar." That paper, too, predicted "no noticeable increase in the number of mixed marriages in Virginia," but it rephrased the explanation. "Prospective grooms" would continue to enjoy "the privileges of withholding their requests for the bride's hand," it said, and brides would retain "the privilege and authority to prevent mixed marriages simply by saying 'no.'" The paper nonetheless insisted on the importance of the court's ruling: "What makes this Supreme Court decision so desirable is that it lifts an onerous and brutalizing stigma from Negro Virginians by knocking down that psychological barrier which, in effect, told them and the world that no Negro is good enough to be the husband or wife of a white Virginian." And it saluted the Lovings: "They have done an incalculably great service for their community, their state, and their nation. Had they been less persevering, the legal battle to end Virginia's oppression on the marital front might have been forfeited long ago."[50]

The Supreme Court decision affected many couples in many states. In August 1967, Virginians were informed about "the first known partners to an interracial marriage in Virginia" since the *Loving* decision was handed down two months earlier. In a ceremony at Kingdom Hall Church, described as "a Negro Jehovah's Witnesses church" in Norfolk, a white woman, Leona Eve Boyd, married a black man, Romans Howard Johnson.[51] Thanks to the Lovings' persistence and the decision of the U.S. Supreme Court, the Johnsons had no need to leave the state to get married. Nor did they have to face the prospect of midnight arrest, felony conviction, or long-term exile. A federal court decision had forced a change in public policy in Virginia such that the Johnsons' decision, like that of the Lovings, was now a private matter. But it could be front-page news.

When Virginia newspapers reported the news in the year or so after the Loving decision, it sometimes included prominent items regarding interracial marriages. In September 1967, for example, the *Richmond Times-Dispatch* printed a page-one story that Margaret Elizabeth Rusk, daughter of Secretary of State Dean Rusk, had married a black man, Guy Gibson Smith, in California. And in June 1968, the *Richmond News Leader* told Virginians that, in Massachusetts, Donald Hasler, "who is white," had married Remi Brooke, the mixed-race daughter of Edward W. Brooke, a U.S. senator from Massachusetts.[52]

California and Massachusetts, though both had at one time maintained miscegenation laws, both abandoned them long before the Supreme Court decision in the *Loving* case. Thus the *Loving* decision had not changed the laws of those two states; it cannot explain the sites of interracial wedding ceremonies involving the daughters of Secretary Rusk and Senator Brooke. But at the time of the *Loving* decision, such laws were still on the books, and still shaped people's lives, in all eleven states of the former Confederacy plus five states of the Border South. Moreover, black-white couples from California or Massachusetts could not have freely moved to Virginia until the Lovings themselves could.

On July 14, 1968, thirteen months after the *Loving* decision, Marian E. Wright married Peter Edelman in Virginia, across the Potomac River from the District of Columbia. Wright was the first black woman to be admitted to the Mississippi bar, a friend of the Reverend William Sloan Coffin, Jr., and an aide to the Reverend Dr. Martin Luther King, Jr. Edelman, a white lawyer, had served as law clerk to Supreme Court justices Felix Frankfurter and Arthur J. Goldberg, as special assistant at the Justice Department, and as legislative researcher and speechwriter in Robert F. Kennedy's campaign for a U.S. Senate seat from New York. Coffin performed the ceremony, and Goldberg spoke as well.[53] Though a bittersweet time for all who attended—King and Kennedy had been assassinated only weeks before—a more graphic demonstration of how much had changed in the law of marriage could hardly be imagined.

Yet fossils of the old laws remained. The U.S. Department of Justice had to go to federal court in 1970 to have an Alabama law overturned that a local judge followed in refusing to provide a marriage license to a white man and a black woman.[54] In the 1970s and 1980s, especially in the South, a white woman, if she was divorced and had been awarded custody of her children, jeopardized that custody arrangement if she subsequently married a black man.[55]

Into the late 1990s, the state constitutions of South Carolina and Alabama still had provisions banning black-white marriages. Efforts were under way to remove those provisions, and the laws were no longer enforceable after 1967, yet such fossils served as reminders of a time, not so long ago, when race was so central a feature of American culture in general, and southern law in particular, that people could be arrested for marrying across racial lines. Repeal of Alabama's law, the last to go, was approved by the voters in November 2000.

As for Mildred Loving, she remained as private as possible and continued to shun the publicity that came with the events from her arrest in 1958 to the Supreme Court decision in 1967. She told an interviewer in 1994, some years after her husband's death and thirty-six years after the wedding that had brought such joy and trouble, "We weren't bothering anyone. And if we hurt some people's feelings, that was just too bad. All we ever wanted was to get married, because we loved each other. . . . I married the only man I had ever loved, and I'm happy for the time we had together."[56]

NOTES

1. Robert A. Pratt, "Crossing the Color Line: A Historical Assessment and Personal Narrative of *Loving v. Virginia*," *Howard Law Journal* 41 (Winter 1998): 236.

2. Peter Wallenstein, "Race, Marriage, and the Law of Freedom: Alabama and Virginia, 1860s–1960s," *Chicago-Kent Law Review* 70, no. 2 (1994): 389–406; Wallenstein, "Indian Foremothers: Race, Sex, Slavery, and Freedom in Early Virginia," in *The Devil's Lane: Sex and Race in the Early South,* ed. Catherine Clinton and Michele Gillespie (New York: Oxford University Press, 1997), 57–73.

3. Sidney Kaplan, "The Miscegenation Issue in the Election of 1864," *Journal of Negro History* 34 (July 1949): 274–343; Louis Ruchames, "Race, Marriage, and Abolition in Massachusetts," *Journal of Negro History* 40 (July 1955): 250–73; Peggy Pascoe, "Miscegenation Law, Court Cases, and Ideologies of 'Race' in Twentieth-Century America," *Journal of American History* 83 (June 1996): 44–69.

4. Peter Wallenstein, "Native Americans Are White, African Americans Are Not: Racial Identity, Marriage, Inheritance, and the Law—Oklahoma, 1907–1967," *Journal of the West* 39 (January 2000): 55–63.

5. *Pace v. Alabama,* 106 U.S. 583 (1883); *Plessy v. Ferguson,* 163 U.S. 537 (1896); *Buchanan v. Warley,* 245 U.S. 60 (1917); Peter Wallenstein, "Race, Marriage, and the Supreme Court—from *Pace v. Alabama* (1883) to *Loving v. Virginia* (1967)," *Journal of Supreme Court History* 2 (1998): 69–74.

6. *Loving v. Virginia,* 388 U.S. 1 (1967).

7. "Ruled a Negro, Man Must Quit White Wife," *Richmond Times-Dispatch,* 8 June 1938, 1.

8. "Racial Intermarriage Case Faces High Court," *Richmond Times-Dispatch,* 7 October 1954, 2; "Virginia Ban on Interracial Marriages Is Upheld," *Richmond Times-Dispatch,* 14 June 1955, 5.

9. *Naim v. Naim,* 197 Va. 80 (1955), 90; *Naim v. Naim,* 350 U.S. 891 (1955); *Naim v. Naim,* 350 U.S. 985 (1956); Gregory Michael Dorr, "Principled Expediency: Eugenics, *Naim v. Naim,* and the Supreme Court," *American Journal of Legal History* 42 (April 1998): 119–59.

10. *Calma v. Calma,* 203 Va. 880 (1962); Wallenstein, "Race, Marriage, and the Law of Freedom," 419–20.

11. *Loving v. Virginia,* 6n.

12. *Meyer v. Nebraska,* 262 U.S. 390 (1923); *Pierce v. Society of Sisters,* 268 U.S. 510 (1925); *Skinner v. Oklahoma,* 316 U.S. 535 (1942); William G. Ross, *Forging New Freedoms: Nativism, Education, and the Constitution, 1917–1927* (Lincoln: University of Nebraska Press, 1994).

13. *Griswold v. Connecticut,* 381 U.S. 479 (1965); *Roe v. Wade,* 410 U.S. 113 (1973); David J. Garrow, *Liberty and Sexuality: The Right of Privacy and the Making of* Roe v. Wade (New York: Macmillan, 1994).

14. *Brown v. Board of Education,* 347 U.S. 483 (1954); Richard Kluger, *Simple Justice: The History of* Brown v. Board of Education *and Black America's Struggle for Equality* (New York: Knopf, 1976).

15. Charles Whalen and Barbara Whalen, *The Longest Debate: A Legislative History of the 1964 Civil Rights Act* (Cabin John, Md.: Seven Locks, 1975); see also Steven F. Lawson, *Black Ballots: Voting Rights in the South, 1944–1969* (New York: Columbia University Press, 1976), ch. 10.

16. *McLaughlin v. Florida*, 379 U.S. 184, 196 (1964).

17. Ibid., 198.

18. *Loving v. Commonwealth* (Record No. 6163), Supreme Court of Appeals of Virginia, 2–4.

19. Phone interview with Mildred D. Loving, 7 January 1994.

20. Ibid.; Record No. 6163, 2–4.

21. Record No. 6163, 5–6.

22. Phone interview with Mildred D. Loving, 7 January 1994; interview with Mildred D. Loving, 12 August 1995; *Polk's Washington City Directory* (1962), 226, 950; "The Crime of Being Married," *Life Magazine*, 18 March 1966, 85–91.

23. Mildred D. Loving to Eleanor Rose, 31 January 1996. I thank Eleanor Rose for a copy of the letter.

24. "Anti-Miscegenation Case Move Rejected," *Richmond News Leader*, 29 October 1964, 21. At the time, no Virginia ACLU affiliate yet existed. The ACLU Archives (in the Mudd Library, Princeton University) demonstrate the organization's long-term commitment to eradicating the nation's miscegenation laws.

25. Interview with Bernard S. Cohen, 4 January 1994.

26. The Lovings are listed as late as 1967 as living at the home of Alex Byrd. Phone interview with Mildred D. Loving, 7 January 1994; *Polk's Washington City Directory* (1967), 827.

27. Interview with Bernard S. Cohen, 4 January 1994; Motion to Vacate Judgment and Set Aside Sentence, 6 November 1963, Record No. 6163, 6–7.

28. Interview with Bernard S. Cohen, 4 January 1994; phone interview with Philip J. Hirschkop, 18 August 1994.

29. "Pair Files Suit to End State Ban," *Richmond News Leader*, 28 October 1964, 23; "Anti-Miscegenation Case Move Rejected"; "Couple Begins Legal Attack on Mixed-Marriage Law," *New York Times*, 29 October 1964, 26; "Mixed-Marriage Ban Is Fought in Virginia," *New York Times*, 29 December 1964, 35.

30. Opinion, Record No. 6163, 10–12; *Kinney v. Commonwealth*, 71 Va. (30 Gratt.) 858 (1878).

31. Opinion, Record No. 6163, 15.

32. "Mixed Couple Case Delayed in Virginia," *New York Times*, 28 January 1965, 17; "U.S. Court Defers on Race Question," *New York Times*, 13 February 1965, 17; *Perez v. Sharp*, 32 Cal. 2d. 711, 734–35 (1948) (J. Carter concurring); Record No. 6163, 10.

33. *Loving v. Commonwealth,* 206 Va. 924 (1966), 929; "Ban on Interracial Marriages Upheld by Virginia High Court," *New York Times,* 8 March 1966, 26.

34. "Virginia Suit Scores Mixed Marriage Ban," *New York Times,* 30 July 1966, 9.

35. "The Crime of Being Married," 91.

36. Philip B. Kurland and Gerhard Casper, eds., *Landmark Briefs and Arguments of the Supreme Court of the United States: Constitutional Law* (Arlington, Va.: University Publications of America, 1975), 64:787–88.

37. "Supreme Court Agrees to Rule on State Miscegenation Laws," *New York Times,* 13 December 1966, 40; Kurland and Casper, *Landmark Briefs and Arguments,* 64:763.

38. Kurland and Casper, *Landmark Briefs and Arguments,* 64:960–72, 1003–7.

39. Ibid., 1005, 971.

40. Ibid., 971.

41. *Loving v. Virginia,* 7; Bernard Schwartz, *Super Chief: Earl Warren and His Supreme Court—A Judicial Biography* (New York: New York University Press, 1983), 668–69.

42. *Loving v. Virginia,* 8–9.

43. Ibid., 10–12.

44. Ibid., 11–12.

45. Ibid., 12.

46. Ibid.; "Justices Upset All Bans on Interracial Marriage," *New York Times,* 13 June 1967, 1, 28; "Miscegenation Ban Is Ended by High Court," *Richmond Times-Dispatch,* 13 June 1967, 1, 4.

47. "State Couple 'Overjoyed' by Ruling,"*Richmond Times-Dispatch,* 13 June 1967, B1; "Mrs. Loving: 'I Feel Free Now,'" *Richmond Afro American,* 17 June 1967: 1–2; Simeon Booker, "The Couple That Rocked Courts," *Ebony* Sept. 1967, 78–84.

48. Mildred D. Loving to Eleanor Rose, 31 January 1996.

49. "A Unanimous Court," *Virginian-Pilot,* 13 June 1967, 14.

50. "Top Court Junks Marriage Bars," *Norfolk Journal and Guide,* 17 June 1967, 1; "Freedom of Choice at the Altar," *Norfolk Journal and Guide,* 17 June 1967, 6.

51. "Caucasian, Negro Wed in Norfolk," *Richmond Times-Dispatch,* 13 August 1967, B2.

52. "Miss Rusk Weds Negro," *Richmond Times-Dispatch,* 22 September 1967, 1; Deborah L. Kitchen, "Interracial Marriage in the United States, 1900–1980" (Ph.D. diss., University of Minnesota, 1993), 140–44; "Mixed Couple Ends Honeymoon," *Richmond News Leader,* 24 June 1968, 2.

53. "Aides to Robert Kennedy and Dr. King Are Married in Virginia Ceremony," *New York Times,* 15 July 1968, 23.

54. *United States v. Brittain*, 319 F.Supp. 1058 (N.D. Ala. 1970); Wallenstein, "Race, Marriage, and the Law of Freedom," 433–34.

55. Renee Romano, "'Immoral Conduct': White Women, Racial Transgressions, and Custody Disputes," in *"Bad Mothers": The Politics of Blame in Twentieth-Century America*, ed. Molly Ladd-Taylor and Lauri Umansky (New York: New York University Press, 1998), ch. 12; *Palmore v. Sidoti*, 466 U.S. 429 (1984); Derrick A. Bell, Jr., *Race, Racism and American Law* (2d ed. (Boston: Little, Brown, 1980), 53–80.

56. Pratt, "Crossing the Color Line," 244.

11

RACE, AFFIRMATIVE ACTION, AND HIGHER EDUCATION ON TRIAL

Regents v. Bakke

Howard Ball

Dawn, October 12, 1977. Hundreds of people lined up at the U.S. Supreme Court building, waiting to enter the Court to hear the oral arguments in the case of *Regents of the University of California Board v. Allan Bakke*. That evening, all three television network anchors led off the news with comments about *Bakke*. Walter Cronkite on CBS news said, "The Supreme Court heard arguments in a controversial case that could produce its most important civil rights ruling in two decades." On ABC News, Harry Reasoner began, "Good evening. One of the most important civil rights cases in two decades, the Allan Bakke reverse discrimination suit, was argued before the Supreme Court today." At NBC, David Brinkley called the *Bakke* case "one of the most difficult the Court has had in years."

For millions of Americans watching television that night, it was difficult not to grasp the fact that an extremely important event was taking place in the Supreme Court. With massive television, radio, press, and news magazine coverage of the *Bakke* case, the public was inundated with terms such as *preferential treatment, affirmative action,* and *reverse discrimination.* By the time the Court's decision was announced on June 28, 1978, most Americans had a perception of the controversial public policy called affirmative action. However, there was dissonance between the public policy and public opinion. Polling data collected by Gallup and other organizations showed that most Americans opposed preferential treatment for racial and ethnic minorities. At the time of oral arguments in *Bakke,* in October 1977, the Gallup Poll indicated that 83 percent of Americans were opposed to *any* preferential treatment not based on merit.

The polling results of the American National Election Studies (NES) the following year echoed these findings, that most Americans polled believed that university admissions committees should admit applicants based solely on ability and that only about 11 percent support preferential treatment for minority applicants. When polled by the race of the respondent, 52 percent of whites strongly supported university admission based on ability, while only 28% of African Americans agreed with the use of that measure. Only 2 percent of the white cohort supported preferential admissions processes for minority group members, while 24 percent of African Americans strongly supported affirmative action.

For all observers, the *Bakke* case epitomized the societal clash—political, moral, and legal—between the value of *meritocracy/race neutrality* and that of *racial balance/equality of opportunity*. The debate raised a series of questions about getting ahead in American society. Does one make it in America by virtue of one's merit, character, intelligence, and virtues? Or does one make it by virtue of special treatment afforded that person because of membership in a racial or ethnic group that has been severely disadvantaged throughout American history? How long must society compensate historically disadvantaged groups? Finally, and most specifically, *Bakke* raised a question that has been hotly debated since the John F. Kennedy Administration: Can a university, in implementing an equal opportunity admissions program for members of historically disadvantaged and discriminated-against groups, engage in an unconstitutional "reverse discrimination"?

The U.S. Supreme Court became embroiled in these discussions when a 32-year-old man, Allan Bakke, a National Aeronautics and Space Administration (NASA) engineer working in California, decided that he wanted to become a doctor. Because his family lived near the University of California, Davis (UCD), campus, he wanted to attend its medical school.

The medical school at UCD, one of five in the state, opened in 1966 with forty-eight entering students. There were no systemwide admissions standards; each of the medical schools established its own standards and procedures. For its first four years, when UCD medical school had no special admissions program, only 3 percent of its applicants were minorities. In 1970, concerned about the school's lack of diversity, the UCD administration established a "special" preferential admission program. Its general objectives were to "enhance diversity in the student body and the profession, eliminate historic barriers for medical careers for disadvantaged racial and ethnic minority groups, and [to] increase aspiration for such careers on the part of members of those groups."[1] Sixteen percent of places, or eight seats out of fifty for first-year medical students, were set aside for successful disadvantaged minority applicants.

All candidates for admission to the UCD medical school were asked to indicate on their application for admission whether they wished to be considered for admission under the Special Admission Program or under the Regular Admission Program. To be considered for admission through the special program, an applicant had to be an "economically and/or educationally disadvantaged person."

Under the Regular selection process, if an applicant's grade point average (GPA) was less than 2.5, there was summary rejection. Of those applicants who had better than a 2.5 GPA, 40 percent were invited to the campus for interviews. Admissions committee members served as the interviewers. They examined the applicant's personality, motivation, and other nonstatistical characteristics. Afterward, the interviewer reviewed the entire file and graded the applicant, using a 1–100 scale. All the interviewers based their "benchmark scores" for each applicant on the interview, the overall GPA, the scores on the Medical College Admission Test (MCAT), letters of recommendation, and extracurricular experiences.

If an applicant chose to be reviewed under the special program, the file was sent to a special subcommittee of the UCD admissions committee, consisting primarily of white and minority faculty members and minority medical students. The subcommittee reviewed the files the same way the regular admissions committee did. However, the standard of review was different: there was no minimum GPA requirement for minority applicants. There was also no comparison of the cohort admitted in the Regular process with the cohort recommended under Special admission. These realities led to highly significant statistical differences between those admitted to the medical school under the Regular as opposed to the Special admission process. In the two years Bakke unsuccessfully sought admission as a Regular applicant, 1973 and 1974, these differences were stark (see table 1).

Allan Bakke was born in Minnesota in February 1940. He graduated from the University of Minnesota in 1962 with a degree in mechanical engineering. After one year of graduate work, Bakke honored his ROTC obligation by serving as an officer in the U.S. Marine Corps from 1963 to 1967, including a combat tour in Vietnam. After his discharge, Bakke began work as a research engineer at NASA's Ames Research Center, south of San Francisco. He received his master's degree in mechanical engineering in June

TABLE 1   Bakke's Scores Compared with Medical School Applicants,
1973 and 1974

	MCAT Science (percentile)	MCAT Verbal (percentile)	MCAT Quantitative (percentile)	MCAT General Information (percentile)	Undergraduate GPA
Regular Admission	83	81	76	69	3.5
Special Admission	35	46	24	33	2.6
Bakke	97	96	94	72	3.44

1970. In 1972, after taking some science preparatory courses, he applied for admission to UCD's medical school.

When Bakke first applied to the medical school at UCD, the application packet contained his MCAT scores; transcripts from other schools he had attended; community and extracurricular activities information; work experience; two letters of recommendation; and his personal statement explaining why he wanted to become a physician. In 1973, Bakke's application was one of 2,464 received by UCD's medical school, which would select only 160 to make its first-year class of 100. The following year, 3,737 applicants sought the school's 100 seats. As was the case in the nation's law schools, the number of applicants interested in attending medical school in the 1970s grew exponentially. Accompanying this extraordinary increase in applications for admission—with no expansion of facilities and faculty—most of these predominantly white schools established preferential admissions policies in order to increase the number of qualified minority students. This led to some Regular applicants being rejected in favor of admitting the sixteen Special, that is, minority, applicants.

In 1973, all eleven medical schools to which Bakke applied—Minnesota, Stanford, UCD, UC-Los Angeles, San Francisco, Bowman-Grey, Cincinnati, Georgetown, Mayo Clinic, South Dakota, and Wayne State—rejected him. Bakke's age was given as the major factor in their decisions not to admit him. For example, Dr. Theodore West, the UCD interviewer, recorded that Bakke was "a well-qualified candidate for admission whose main handicap is the unavoidable fact that he is now 33 years of age."

In August 1973, Bakke reapplied for early admission to UCD's medical school. More than 3,100 nonminorities applied for 84 available seats. In late September 1973, he was informed that he was not admitted under early admissions, nor was he placed on their waiting list. (In fact, twelve other nonminority applicants with scores higher than Bakke's did not make the alternates list. Thirty-two nonminority applicants with scores higher than Bakke's were also not admitted to the UCD medical school.) On April Fool's Day 1974, he was informed that he was again rejected by the UCD medical school.

After his second UCD rejection, Bakke sought the legal assistance of Reynold Colvin, a 57-year-old well-established lawyer in San Francisco. Colvin had been an attorney in the city since 1941. He was also an active member of the Jewish community and the president of the San Francisco chapter of the American Jewish Committee. He filled the "Jewish" seat on the city Board of Education, serving a stint as its president.

In building his case against the allegedly discriminatory UCD admissions policy, Colvin chose not to focus on the enormous quantitative disparities between Regular and Special admittees of UCD or how Bakke's qualifications were categorically better than most of the admittees, whether minority or nonminority. Instead, he argued that the setting aside of sixteen seats for minority applicants was an illegal and unconstitutional racial quota, one that was prohibited by both the Fourteenth Amendment's Equal Protection Clause as well as Title VI of the 1964 Civil Rights Act. Again and again, Colvin argued one theme: racial preferential treatment, however positive, however laudatory the rationale for the special privilege, was nevertheless an unconstitutional racial quota. Whether it was called a special program, or an affirmative one, or benign, or remedial, or a compensatory program, at bottom, such programs were all based on the use of an illegal racial quota. These color-conscious admissions mechanisms, he argued, were barred by federal statute and by the Fourteenth Amendment.

When the legal arguments began in the California courts, Donald Reidhaar, the general counsel for the University of California nine-campus system, marshaled the support of a three-person legal team to help him prepare the defense of the UCD preferential admissions process. His essential argument was that there was nothing illegal or unconstitutional about the UCD's creation of a benign, nondiscriminatory preferential admissions program for minorities. When race is used in such a positive manner to overcome the vestiges of slavery and race discrimination, Reidhaar contended, it was constitutional.

In his *Bakke* briefs and oral argument, Reidhaar maintained that the 16 percent of seats set aside for qualified disadvantaged minority students was not a "quota," but a "goal," one of many implemented by the university to diversify higher education. If there were fewer qualified candidates in a given year, Reidhaar noted, then the unfilled seats reverted to qualified Regular applicants, but this had not happened since the program's inception in 1970.

On June 20, 1974, Colvin brought suit on behalf of Bakke in Yolo County Superior Court. Judge F. Leslie Manker, a 67-year-old retired Superior Court judge, was asked to come out of retirement in order to hear the case because the two sitting judges were swamped with cases. Colvin's legal complaint requested that Bakke be admitted to the UCD medical school because the Special Admission Program had "reduced the number of places" for which he could compete, thereby denying him a place in the first-year class because of his race. He argued that the UCD special admissions process was racially discriminatory and therefore in violation of the U.S. Constitution's Fourteenth Amendment; the California Constitution's Article I, Section 21; and Title VI of the 1964 Civil Rights Act.

The UCD legal counsel argued that the preferential program was consistent with the federal civil rights act because it successfully addressed past generations of racial discrimination in the admissions process. Reidhaar asked the judge to issue an order declaring that the Special Admission Program was constitutional and not in violation of Title VI of the 1964 act.

The burden of proof fell on Colvin and his client. They had to successfully show that (1) Bakke would have been admitted to the UCD medical school had there been no Special Admission Program in place and (2) the Special admission process was arbitrary, capricious, and fraudulent. Colvin requested an order from the judge compelling the UCD medical school to admit Bakke. Judge Manker had two questions to answer: (1) Was the Special Admission Program constitutional? (2) If not, should Allan Bakke be admitted to the medical school by court order? In late November 1974, he ruled that the Special Admission Program was a racial quota and ran afoul of the Fourteenth Amendment, the state constitution, and Title VI. "The use of this program did substantially reduce plaintiff's chances of successful admission to medical school for the reason that, since 26 places . . . were set aside for this special program [in 1973 and 1974], the plaintiff was in fact competing for one place, not in a class of 100, but in a class of 84, which reduced his chances for admission by 16 percent."[2] He did not, however, order UCD to admit Bakke; instead, he ordered the UCD admissions committee to reconsider Bakke's application without regard to his or any other applicant's race.

In May 1975, Reidhaar appealed Manker's ruling to the California Supreme Court. Colvin also appealed because the judge did not issue an order calling for the UCD medical school to enroll Allan Bakke. The California Supreme Court was, at the time, perceived as the most liberal appellate state court in America. Many assumed that it would overturn the Yolo County judge's ruling. They were mistaken.

In March 1976, oral arguments took place in the state supreme court. Eight public organizations filed briefs with the state supreme court: six civil rights organizations, such as the NAACP, supported the UCD position; a few organizations sided with Bakke (including the Anti-Defamation League of B'nai Brith, the American Jewish Congress, and the American Federation of Teachers [AFT]). The battle lines were drawn with civil rights groups and the medical and legal profession on one side and Jewish organizations and teachers' unions, who had historically opposed the use of "quotas," on the other.

The question of law before the court was "whether a racial classification, intended to assist minorities but which also has the effect of depriving those who are not so classified of benefits they would enjoy but for their race, violated the constitutional rights of the majority." A half year later, in mid-September 1976, in a 6 to 1 vote, the court affirmed Manker's ruling that preferential admissions policies violated the Equal Protection Clause of the Fourteenth Amendment. The majority said, "The Equal Protection clause applies 'to any person,' and its lofty purpose, to secure equality of treatment to all, is incompatible with the premise that some races may be afforded a higher degree of protection against unequal protection than others."[3]

Chief Justice Stanley Mosk, a well-known and highly respected jurist, authored the opinion. He wrote that he Special admission plan "violates the constitutional rights of non-minority candidates because it affords preference on the basis of race to persons who, by the University's own standards, are not as qualified for the study of medicine as non-minority applicants denied admission. . . . Regardless of its historical origin, the equal protection clause by its literal terms applies to 'any person.'"[4]

The solitary dissenter, Justice Matthew O. Tobriner, wrote a 57-page opinion noting that *all* minority applicants accepted by the UCD in the two-year period "were fully qualified for the study of medicine." He maintained that the UCD program did not violate the Constitution and that there was a rational relationship between the program and the goals of the state. "Two centuries of slavery and racial discrimination have left our nation an awful legacy, a largely separated society, in which wealth, educational resources, employment opportunities—indeed all of society's benefits—remain largely the preserve of the white-Anglo majority."[5]

The majority opinion sent the case back to Judge Manker to determine whether or not Bakke would have been admitted in either year without the special admissions program. The medical school administrators quickly conceded that Bakke "came extremely close to admission . . . even with the Special admissions program being in operation."[6] This answer led the California Supreme Court to amend its earlier ruling; it ordered Bakke's immediate entry into the UCD medical school.

The regents immediately appealed to the U.S. Supreme Court, and implementation of the admit order was delayed by the U.S. Supreme Court in November 1976, pending the outcome of the legal request filed by the regents. They asked the U.S. Supreme Court to review the California Supreme Court's decision because "[Davis and other professional schools as well as Allan Bakke] have a strong interest [in finding out] whether the special admissions program at the Davis medical school and other similar programs are, as held by a majority if this [California Supreme Court], unconstitutional."[7]

The constitutional question posed by the regents in their petition to the justices went to the core of the affirmative action in higher education controversy:

> When only a small fraction of thousands of applicants can be admitted, does the Fourteenth Amendment's "Equal Protection" clause forbid a state university professional school faculty from voluntarily seeking to counteract the efforts of generations of pervasive discrimination against discrete and insular minorities by establishing a limited special admission program that increases opportunities for well-qualified members of such racial and ethnic minorities?[8]

Colvin's brief urged the U.S. Supreme Court not to hear the case and to let the California Supreme Court's decision stand because the California Supreme Court acted "and did so by way of a reasoned application of prior constitutional decisions."

The U.S. Supreme Court discussed the question of whether to hear the *Bakke* appeal on three separate occasions in December 1976 and January and February 1977 before deciding to hear, discuss, debate, and then rule on the constitutionality of preferential admissions processes based on race and ethnicity. By this time, Allan Bakke was nearly thirty-eight years old. His last hope for admission into UCD's medical school and for the resolution of the moral, political, and legal issue of racial quotas rested with the nine men who sat on the Supreme Court.

Oral arguments in the case of *Regents v. Bakke* took place on October 12, 1977. Typically, they hold little public interest and attract very little public attention. The sparse audience usually consists of persons whose seats have been reserved by one of the sitting justices, members of visiting school and college groups, representatives of special interest groups, and visitors touring the Court that day. Seldom was the 400-seat (100 of which are unreserved) courtroom filled to capacity. The *Bakke* oral argument was very different. The courtroom was filled to capacity with people drawn to the debate because of their intense interest in the subject matter. Due to the importance of the case, the Court gave each side double the regular amount of time (one hour rather than one half hour for each side) to present their arguments. Afterward, the justices met in their secret Friday conference session, where they began the process of arriving at a decision in *Bakke*.

Usually at the end of a conference session there is a Court majority. Either the chief justice or, if he is not in the majority, the senior associate justice assigns the writing of the opinion to one of the justices. Not so in the *Bakke* case; the views expressed did not command a majority along one line of argument—they were badly split. Although Chief Justice Warren Burger decided that there would not be a decisive vote in conference on the case until later in 1978, the flood of memos gave the justices a lot to digest as well as a clear sense of how eight of them lined up. (So wordy were the justices in discussing the issues in *Bakke* that Justice Lewis Powell wrote that "my first impulse is to 'cringe' when I see another [memo].")[9] The ninth justice, Harry A. Blackmun, was being treated for prostate cancer at the Mayo Clinic in Minnesota and did not circulate his views on the matter until he returned to Washington in early 1978.

Initially, six of the justices were convinced that they would have to deal with the constitutional question at the heart of the case. If not, Powell wrote to his colleagues, "We will have resolved finally nothing."[10] Burger and the recently appointed justice, John Paul Stevens, were the only ones who urged avoidance of the constitutional issue from the beginning. They did not want the Court to decide the case by interpreting the Fourteenth Amendment's Equal Protection Clause.

Justices William Brennan, Byron White, and Thurgood Marshall agreed with Powell's observation, as did, initially, Justices William Rehnquist and Potter Stewart. Brennan believed that a tough standard, "strict scrutiny," should be applied in cases in which race was used to stigmatize and demean, not in those, like the UCD case, where race was used to remedy past discrimination.

Rehnquist and Stewart disagreed with Brennan's view. For them, "strict scrutiny" must be applied in all cases where there is a "difference in treatment of individuals based on their race or ethnic origin."[11] He rejected Brennan's contention that the Fourteenth Amendment (and Title VI) "protects only minorities." For Rehnquist, "the *thing prohibited* [in the Constitution and in the statute] is discrimination on the basis of race, *any race.*"[12]

The justices had to answer four questions in deciding the case:

1. Should *Bakke* be decided on statutory grounds, that is, did the medical school's Special admission policy violate Title VI of the 1964 Civil Rights Act?

2. Should *Bakke* be decided on constitutional grounds, that is, was the UCD Special Admission Program in violation of the Fourteenth Amendment's Equal Protection Clause?

3. If such a "reverse discrimination" case was to be decided on constitutional grounds, what was the appropriate standard of measurement of constitutionality to be used by the Court: "Strict scrutiny," "rational relationship," or some other intermediate standard?

4. What was the relationship between the protection afforded an individual in Title VI and the Fourteenth Amendment's Equal Protection guarantee? Were they saying the same thing? Did one dominate the other?

Chief Justice Burger's views on *Bakke*, put forth in a memo dated October 21, 1977, set the tone for months of circulating memoranda and draft opinions before the announcement of the decision in late May 1978. We must find a way, he wrote, "to affirm the California Supreme Court without putting the states, their universities, or any educational institutions in a straitjacket on the matter of broader based admissions programs." Courts do not belong in the business of "establishing fixed ground rules for educators. . . . We have far more competence to say what cannot be done that what ought to be done." For him, the most important part of the Court's ruling would be "to structure and shape a result so as to confine its impact and yet make it clear that the Court intends to leave the states free to serve as 'laboratories' for experimenting with less rigidly exclusionary methods of pursuing social goals."[13]

By late May 1978, the Court, although badly split, had arrived at the time of public pronouncement of their decision in *Bakke*. Six opinions were written: two four-person opinions written by Stevens and Brennan, the critically important opinion written by Powell, and separate opinions written by Marshall, Blackmun, and White.

In an opinion joined by Burger, Rehnquist, and Stewart, Justice Stevens concluded that Bakke was excluded from UCD in violation of Title VI of the 1964 Civil Rights Act. Differing dramatically from the other five justices, the Stevens cohort rejected *any* use of race as a factor in admissions processes at colleges and universities. For Stevens (who later changed his position on affirmative action), it was "perfectly clear that the question whether race can ever be used as a factor in an admissions decision is not an issue in this case, and that discussion of that issue is inappropriate."[14] They avoided a decision in *Bakke* based on the Court's interpretation of the Constitution's Fourteenth Amendment, maintaining that there was no need for the Court to reach the constitutional question if the case could be resolved through statutory construction. Since Title VI's "plain meaning of the words" forbids the use of racial quotas and the use of race even as one among many factors examined in the admissions process, they believed an interpretation of the Constitution's language was necessary.

Five justices did reach the constitutional questions associated with *Bakke*: Brennan, writing for Marshall, Blackmun, and White, and, writing separately, Powell. The Brennan opinion was a milestone in that, for the first time, four justices jointly created or subscribed to a major change in the meaning of the Fourteenth Amendment. The quartet, after Herculean cobbling by Brennan, supported the view that the judgment of the California Supreme Court should be reversed in all respects. Brennan wrote that "government may take race into account when it acts not to demean or insult any racial group, but to remedy disadvantages cast on minorities by past racial prejudice."[15]

In the *Bakke* case, Powell stood alone. Because there were two four-person blocs in disagreement with each other, his was the fifth and deciding vote. Whichever way Powell went on the question of affirmative action, his opinion would settle the issue of affirmative action in higher education. His opinion satisfied, in part, the other eight justices. All eight concurred in part and dissented in part with Powell's opinion. He explained the Court's unusual voting in the first sentences of his opinion:

> I believe that so much of the judgment of the California court as
> holds petitioner's special admissions program unlawful and
> directs that respondent be admitted to the Medical School must
> be *affirmed*. For the reasons expressed in a separate opinion, my

Brothers THE CHIEF JUSTICE, MR. JUSTICE STEWART, MR. JUSTICE
REHNQUIST, and MR. JUSTICE STEVENS concur in this judgment.

I also conclude that the portion of the court's judgment
enjoining petitioner from according any consideration to race in
its admissions processed must be *reversed*. For reasons expressed in
separate opinions, my Brothers MR. JUSTICE BRENNAN, MR. JUSTICE
WHITE, MR. JUSTICE MARSHALL, and MR. JUSTICE BLACKMUN concur
in this judgment. *Affirmed in part and reversed in part.*[16]

Powell presented his justification next. The UCD Special Admission
Program unconstitutionally denied Bakke equal protection, and therefore
the California Supreme Court order admitting Bakke to the medical school
was valid. The use of numbers, quotas, or set-asides may be justified, he
wrote, only in situations where there was proof in the record that the
institution receiving federal funds had indeed discriminated against applicants on the basis of race or color. This was not the case with UCD; it had
no record of intentionally discriminating against minorities.

But Powell also concluded that universities and colleges could develop
an admissions formula that took the race of an applicant into account
and offered Harvard College's admission program as an example of an
institution of higher education that took race as a positive factor in the
admissions process. In addition, he concurred with Justices Brennan,
White, Marshall, and Blackmun that Title VI did not "control" in the case.

The three justices who joined Brennan's opinion all wrote separately
to express their views about affirmative action. Marshall's lengthy separate opinion recapitulated the shameful history of three centuries of "denial of human rights" to African Americans. Recent history, Marshall
wrote, demonstrated that "the position of the Negro today in America is
the tragic but inevitable consequence of centuries of unequal treatment.
Measured by any benchmark of comfort or achievement, meaningful
equality remains a distant dream for the Negro."[17] He continued:

The racism of our society has been so pervasive that *none*,
regardless of wealth or position, has managed to escape its
impact. . . . If we are ever to become a fully integrated society,
one in which the color of a person's skin will not determine the
opportunities available to him or her, we must be willing to take
steps to open these doors. I do not believe that anyone can truly
look into America's past and still find that a remedy for the
effects of that past is impermissible.[18]

Blackmun's brief concurring and dissenting opinion in the case grati-
fied Marshall immensely. Blackmun, who missed the first months of the
Court's *Bakke* discussions because of illness, noted the impossibility of a
race-neutral university affirmative action program. He spoke about a time
in the future when affirmative action programs would be

> unnecessary and a relic only of the past. Then persons will be
> regarded as persons, and discrimination of the type we address
> today will be an ugly feature of history that is instructive but is
> behind us. . . . In order to get beyond racism, we must first take
> account of race. . . . And in order to treat some persons equally,
> we must treat them differently. We cannot—we dare not—let the
> Equal Protection Clause perpetrate racial supremacy.[19]

White's short opinion focused on the question he had raised in October 1977: Does a private person have a cause of action under Title VI?
White, the only justice to address this technical and somewhat anachro-
nistic issue, believed that one does not and wrote separately to express
his disagreement with the Stevens quartet.

The Court decision, which set aside the UCD Special admission process because it was based on the use of an unconstitutional racial quota
and ordered Bakke admitted to the medical school, triggered an avalanche
of media coverage. Conservative newspapers trumpeted the fact that the
UCD affirmative action plan was invalidated by the Court. "WHITE STUDENT
WINS REVERSE BIAS CASE; Justices OK Some Racial Preferences," shouted the
Chicago Sun-Times headline. The *Wall Street Journal* stated correctly, in its
fashion, that *Bakke* was "The Decision Everyone Won."

Liberal newspapers focused on the other side of the *Bakke* opinion. "HIGH
COURT BACKS SOME AFFIRMATIVE ACTION BY COLLEGES, BUT ORDERS BAKKE ADMIT-
TED," headlined the *New York Times*, while the *Washington Post* stated in
bold letters: "AFFIRMATIVE ACTION UPHELD: Court Orders School to Admit
Bakke, Curbs Racial Quotas." *Time* magazine put it simply and accurately:
"Quotas No; Race, Yes."

The Court's decision allowed all the pressure groups who participated
in the case to claim victory. The Anti Defamation League, B'nai Brith,
called *Bakke* "a significant victory in the effort to end racial quotas in
college admissions," while the ACLU, though concerned about the decision "sapping the will of officials responsible for achieving racially integrated enrollment," breathed a sigh of relief because "it is not the disaster
we might have had." A vocal critic of the Court and of the *Bakke* decision

was Robert H. Bork. His response, published in the *Wall Street Journal*, was sharp and to the point: All those who supported the UCD plan, including those sitting on the Court, were "the *hard-core racists* of reverse discrimination." The Fourteenth Amendment, he argued, was a color-blind clarion call for an equality of merit.

At the White House, however, U.S. Attorney General Griffin Bell took a much different position. After speaking with President Jimmy Carter, he said, "[Our] general view is that affirmative action has been enhanced" and that there would be no immediate changes in the 110 federal programs that grant some form of preference to persons on the basis of membership in a disadvantaged racial or ethnic group."[20] Eleanor Holmes Norton, chair of the U.S. Equal Employment Opportunity Commission, said that "*Bakke* doesn't dismantle affirmative action and it doesn't take employers off the hook. As a law-enforcement official, I have to say that the *Bakke* case has not left me with any duty to instruct the EEOC staff to do anything different or to recommend a change of policy to the Commission."[21]

Back on the UCD campus, both sides claimed victory. The vice chancellor said that the Special Admission Program would be overhauled when UCD receives "definitive guidelines from the university's general counsel." And a UCD lawyer said that "at the very least, the Court repudiates the California Supreme Court's simplistic position that race cannot be taken into account."

A happy Reynold Colvin said that *Bakke* had set reasonable parameters for affirmative action programs: "The decision is not the end of the road for affirmative action. [It] sets an outer limit and the case stands on its own facts. A quota is not the same thing as affirmative action." He also read a message from Allan Bakke, now thirty-eight and reclusive, that said, "I am pleased and, after five years of waiting, I look forward to entering medical school in the fall."[22]

The question left unanswered was: What impact would *Bakke* have on a university's ability to diversify its student population to overcome three centuries of racial segregation and discrimination? *Bakke*'s implementing population, the admissions directors of America's higher education institutions, had no problem carrying out the perceived mandate of the Court. Within days of the decision, they met with their legal counsel to modify their school's diversity admissions plans to comply with the Judgment for the Court.

What effect has *Bakke* actually had on efforts to diversify colleges and universities over the past two decades? Scholars have analyzed enrollment data since *Bakke* in an effort to answer this question. And the answer, as the United States enters the twenty-first century, is that *Bakke* has had a dramatic, positive impact on the diversification of undergraduate, graduate, and professional schools. The decision immediately terminated the use of quotas or set-asides based on race or ethnicity and, for a brief time, served as a restraint on diversification. However, by the end of the twentieth century, an analysis of enrollment data showed that the case has been invaluable in the diversification of college and university campuses at the undergraduate and graduate levels. Even though it has been challenged in a number of states, and the Fifth U.S. Circuit Court of Appeals, in *Hopwood v. Texas* (1996), effectively nullified its impact in Texas, Louisiana, and Mississippi, it is still the law of the land in forty-six states. (California and Washington State, in the late 1990s, passed initiatives that ended all affirmative action programs in those states.)

The legitimatization of affirmative action practices by *Bakke* led to dramatic improvements in student diversity. Between 1988 and 1995, overall African American enrollment increased more than 30 percent. The number of degrees earned by African Americans during this same period increased 34 percent for bachelor's degrees and more than 40 percent for master's degrees. Growth in Hispanic American enrollment has been even more dramatic, increasing by more than 50 percent. Diversification in medical and law schools has also been quite spectacular. From 1988 to 1995, minority first-year enrollments in medical schools increased by 40 percent; Hispanic American (including Puerto Ricans) enrollments increased by more than 43 percent. By 1995, minorities accounted for almost 15 percent of the total enrollment in U.S. medical schools. These figures were replicated for minority enrollment in U.S. law schools. Without a doubt, the *Bakke* decision was received positively by its implementing public. Inroads were made in the effort to provide equal educational opportunities for formerly disadvantaged minorities.

However, the issue is not at rest. Conservative legal organizations, believing that *Bakke* was wrongly decided, continue to challenge higher education affirmative action programs that use race as one of a number of positive factors in the admissions process. In early 2001, in U.S. District Court in Michigan, two federal judges reached opposite conclusions about the University of Michigan's use of race in admitting students. Judge Patrick Duggan, in the case of *Gratz v. Bollinger, President, University of Michigan*, validated the university's use of race in its undergraduate admissions process. However, on March 27, 2001, Judge Bernard A. Friedman, in a case involving the university's law school admission process, *Grutter v. Bollinger*, ruled that the use of race was unconstitutional.

There is no doubt that the U.S. Supreme Court will be asked to review these cases.

While the U.S. Supreme Court's ruling in *Bakke* encouraged America's universities and colleges to diversify racially and ethnically, the affirmative action in higher education question will probably be revisited by the nine men and women a quarter of a century later. And there is the possibility that a new U.S. Supreme Court majority in, say, 2005 will overturn *Bakke*. The Court in 2002 is different from the 1978 High Bench: different justices with a much more conservative view of affirmative action programs in employment. (See, for example, Justice Sandra Day O'Connor's majority opinion striking down governmental affirmative action contacting programs, in *Adarand Construction Company v. Pena*, 1995.) Since 1978, *Bakke* has been a benchmark case for affirmative action in higher education. Most university educators await the future with great trepidation.

NOTES

1. *Regents v. Bakke* (1978), Justice Powell's Judgment for the Court.
2. Ibid.
3. Ibid.
4. Ibid.
5. Ibid.
6. Ibid.
7. Ibid.
8. Ibid.
9. Lewis F. Powell, Memo to the Conference, 21 January 1978, Lewis F. Powell Papers, Washington and Lee University, Lexington, Va.
10. Lewis F. Powell, Memo to the Conference, 5 January 1978, Lewis F. Powell Papers, Washington and Lee University, Lexington, Va.
11. William J. Brennan, Memo to the Conference, 15 November 1977, William J. Brennan Papers, Library of Congress, Washington, D.C.
12. William J. Brennan, Memo to the Conference, 10 November 1977, William J. Brennan Papers, Library of Congress, Washington, D.C.
13. Chief Justice Warren Burger, Memo to the Conference, 21 October 1977, William J. Brennan Papers, Library of Congress, Washington, D.C.
14. John P. Stevens, Memo to the Conference, 9 October 1977, Thurgood Marshall Papers, Library of Congress, Washington, D.C.
15. *Regents v. Bakke*, Brennan, concurring and dissenting.
16. *Regents v. Bakke*, Justice Powell's Judgment for the Court.
17. Thurgood Marshall, Memo to the Conference, 13 April 1978, Thurgood Marshall Papers, Library of Congress, Washington, D.C.

18. Ibid.

19. *Regents v. Bakke*, Blackmun, concurring and dissenting.

20. Press release, Attorney General Griffin Bell, 29 June 1978, Department of Justice, Washington, D.C.

21. Remarks by Eleanor Holmes Norton, EEOC, 30 June 1978.

22. Raymond Colvin, quoted in the *Los Angeles Times*, 29 June 1978, p. A1.

12

BLACK AND WHITE
The O. J. Simpson Case

Walter L. Hixson

The O. J. Simpson case was the most sensational criminal drama in American history. Never before had such a volatile mixture of celebrity, murder, media, glitz, sleaze, grandstanding, incompetence, and injustice come together in a series of judicial proceedings that seemingly would not end. More than a mere media event, however, the Simpson case illuminated the status of race relations in the United States. Its disturbing outcome revealed just how deeply divided Americans remained over issues of race and justice.

Public awareness of the case began on Sunday evening, June 12, 1994, when the bodies of Nicole Brown Simpson and Ronald W. Goldman were discovered at her residence at 875 Bundy Drive, a busy north-south artery in the heart of the Los Angeles suburb of Brentwood. Word quickly circulated that the female victim was the former wife of the actor and former football star Orenthal James "O. J." Simpson. Goldman, a waiter at the restaurant where Nicole had dined earlier in the evening, was a friend who was returning a pair of glasses she had left at the eatery. Three Los Angeles Police Department (LAPD) detectives—Mark Fuhrman, Philip Vannatter, and Tom Lange—proceeded to the O. J. Simpson estate two miles away on Rockingham Drive, an address that Fuhrman knew from a previous domestic violence call. Simpson, who had divorced his first wife, Marguerite, with whom he had two children, Jason and Arnelle, had lived at the estate since 1977. That same year, he began dating Nicole, who was eighteen years old at the time. She moved into the Rockingham home in

1979. In 1985, with Nicole pregnant with Sydney, the first of the couple's two children, she and Simpson had been married.

With Fuhrman leading the way on the warm June evening, the cops arrived at Simpson's estate, where they immediately noticed a single car, a white Ford Bronco, parked somewhat askew, as if hurriedly, outside the gates. After conferring, the detectives made a crucial decision to enter the Simpson estate. If the police considered Simpson a suspect, they were required to obtain a search warrant before entering the premises. The police officers later testified that they did not at that time consider Simpson a suspect, statements that were almost certainly false since it is a venerable axiom of police work that when a woman dies the first suspect to be considered is her partner, since as many as a third of all female homicide victims are killed by their husband or boyfriend. Moreover, since Fuhrman knew about the history of domestic violence in the home, Simpson would be an obvious suspect. The cops justified their decision to enter the grounds by insisting that Simpson was not a suspect and that their primary concern, given the crime scene they had witnessed on Bundy, was to ensure that there were no other Simpson-related victims inside the Rockingham gates.

Simpson was not present at the estate, but police did find Kato Kaelin, a young man sleeping in a guest house. Under questioning, Kaelin recalled that at about 10:45 P.M. he had responded to a loud thump outside his room wall, on the other side of the window air conditioner. He remembered this because he had experienced the natural California initial reaction to a shaking wall: fear of an earthquake. On the ground outside the wall from which the sound heard by Kaelin had emanated, Fuhrman found a dark leather glove, matching one the police had seen at the Bundy crime scene.

The LAPD officers soon learned that Simpson had flown to Chicago that evening for a golf tournament sponsored by Hertz Rent-a-Car, which had long employed Simpson as the "superstar of rent-a-car" in a series of well-known television commercials. Detective Ron Phillips telephoned Simpson to inform him that his ex-wife "had been killed." "Oh my God, Nicole is killed?," Simpson responded.[1] Simpson declared that he would catch the next available flight to Los Angeles. As Phillips hung up, he realized that Simpson had not asked how or even when his wife had been killed.

By the time Simpson arrived back at his home, shortly after noon the following day, he was clearly the number-one suspect in the murder case. The police assumed that this was a fairly typical case in which a husband, or ex-husband, consumed with rage, had murdered his former spouse.

Acting on Vannatter's orders, police handcuffed Simpson, but soon freed him after his attorney, Howard Weitzman, assured them that his client had no intention of fleeing and planned to cooperate in the investigation. By that time, however, photographers and cameramen had captured pictures of Simpson in handcuffs. The media frenzy had begun. Word quickly spread across the country that Simpson had been arrested as the suspect in the murder of his ex-wife.

Noting a bandage on Simpson's left hand, Vannatter asked Simpson if he would agree to come to the police station to make a statement. After conferring with Weitzman, Simpson agreed to a tape-recorded interview with Lange and Vannatter. Although the LAPD treated Simpson with deference befitting his status as a Hollywood celebrity, the 32-minute police interview produced devastating evidence against Simpson. The former football star offered contradictory explanations as to how he cut his finger, at first stating that it happened at home the evening before, when he was rushing to get ready to fly to Chicago. Moments later, Simpson said he suffered the cut in Chicago, on broken glass in his hotel room, when he received the news of Nicole's death. He had no alibi for his whereabouts from 9:35 to 10:55 P.M., when a limousine driver picked him up for the trip to the airport. During the time the murders had taken place, Simpson admitted to dripping blood around his home and driveway. Simpson's police interview, characterized by halting and contradictory statements, served to confirm police suspicions that he had killed his wife.

Despite the consensus that there was probable cause to arrest Simpson and charge him with murder, the LAPD and the Los Angeles district attorney's office decided to wait a few days to marshal evidence, including the results of blood tests. Simpson's new attorney, Robert Shapiro, negotiated with the district attorney's office to ensure that Simpson would be allowed to attend his ex-wife's funeral, which he did together with his children on June 16. At Shapiro's request, Simpson privately underwent a lie detector test, which he failed miserably. A psychiatric evaluation revealed that Simpson might be approaching an emotional breaking point.

No turn in the Simpson case would be more shocking or bizarre than what happened on Saturday, June 18. After being informed of his imminent arrest, Simpson went into flight with his close friend and former football teammate, A. C. Cowlings, in the white Ford Bronco. Police soon spotted the Bronco heading north on a Los Angeles freeway. An almost surreal chase scene unfolded in a city that had invented the chase scene. At the wheel, Cowlings turned on his emergency flashers. At one point, when police drew their guns and began to approach the Bronco at a red light, Cowlings quickly called 911 on his cellular phone to explain that a despondent Simpson had a gun to his own head. Cowlings convinced the police to back off and turned the Bronco toward the Simpson estate.

As television helicopters hovered over the Bronco, all three national networks broke into regular programming to cover what became the most watched television event of the year. Crowds gathered at the roadside and on bridges along the Bronco's route. In a harbinger of the racial divide that would open over the Simpson case, a crowd comprised mostly of sympathetic African Americans gathered along the highways and at Simpson's driveway at Rockingham to shout, "Free the Juice."

After spending the weekend in jail, Simpson was arraigned on Monday, June 20. Appearing depressed, he muttered an unenthusiastic "not guilty" plea. Despite Simpson's morose appearance, the district attorney's office realized that the accused man remained a popular public figure. Sports fans knew him as the winner of the prestigious Heisman Trophy as a running back at the University of Southern California. After playing in the 1969 Rose Bowl, Simpson was the number-one pick by the Buffalo Bills in the annual National Football League draft. In 1973, he became the first running back ever to amass more than 2,000 yards rushing in a single season. After a sterling football career, Simpson employed his sculpted good looks and ebullient personality to garner a fortune in endorsements, most notably in the Hertz commercials. He had carried the Olympic torch in the 1984 Los Angeles summer games and established himself as a popular broadcaster of sporting events for two major networks. A brilliant businessman and self-promoter, Simpson was worth an estimated $11 million a year before the murders. He seemed to have put behind him a difficult childhood spent in a rough neighborhood of San Francisco, where he had been a juvenile delinquent, engaging regularly in shoplifting, fights, and other criminal activity. Even then, Simpson had risen to the top—as a gang leader—and later boasted that he was the "Al Capone" of his neighborhood. Now known to the public simply as "O. J.," the use of initials conjuring up an image of affection, Simpson appeared regularly in movies, including the series of comedic *Naked Gun* spoofs in which he played Nordberg, a brain-dead police officer.

The prosecutors realized that Simpson's public persona could be a serious obstacle, since public perception would play as significant a role as the actual evidence. To combat Simpson's appeal, Gil Garcetti, the elected district attorney of Los Angeles County, and prosecutor Marcia Clark began to offer statements and leak information to condition the public to see the other side of O. J. Simpson—a chronic wife beater who had finally resorted to murder. One of the tactics employed by the district attorney's office was to release to the public a 1989 tape of a 911 call made by a terrified Nicole Brown Simpson during an incident of spousal abuse that took place at 4 A.M. on New Year's Day at the Simpson home. On the tape, the sounds of screams and slaps could be heard. After arriving at the scene, police were told by a housekeeper that there was no problem at the home, whereupon a blond woman wearing only a bra and sweatpants emerged from behind some bushes, screaming, "He's going to kill me! He's going to kill me!" Her face was cut and an eye had been blackened. She told the cops that Simpson had hit and slapped her and pulled her hair. Simpson then emerged in a bathrobe, screaming that he no longer wanted Nicole in his bed. He denied beating her, stating that he merely had pushed her out of bed.

Simpson reacted with astonishment when the police informed him that they would have to arrest him as in connection with the incident of domestic violence. After all, he explained, they had been to the estate for the same reason many times before—including a 1985 call to which Mark Fuhrman had responded. Simpson insisted that he had done nothing wrong and that the incident was "a family matter." When the cops asked him to prepare to accompany them to the police station, he instead hopped in his Bentley and fled the scene, successfully evading four police cars. Nicole attempted to drop the matter the next day, but after looking into the history of abuse, prosecutors were determined to pursue the case. Simpson pleaded no contest in return for a probated sentence and community service, which he promptly skirted by arranging for a fundraiser to be organized. He also avoided counseling sessions that were typically required in spousal abuse cases.[2]

O. J. and Nicole's relationship continued to sour before ending in divorce in October 1992. On the eve of the murder, the relationship deteriorated further over financial disputes and O. J.'s feeling that Nicole was trying to minimize his access to their children, Sydney and Justin, although he enjoyed regular visitation. Five days before the murders, Nicole Brown informed a Santa Monica battered women's shelter that Simpson was stalking her.

As the prosecution began to present this evidence to a grand jury, Simpson's formidable defense team objected. Shapiro had now been joined by high-profile attorneys F. Lee Bailey and Alan Dershowitz, a Harvard law professor well known for his defense of such wealthy celebrities as Klaus von Bulow and Mike Tyson. These men understood that the outcome of a trial can often be determined by the legal maneuvering that occurs before the courtroom proceedings actually take place. The defense pressed for a hearing to be scheduled as soon as possible, in the hope that the prosecution would have to present a hastily prepared case to which they would then be committed in the subsequent criminal trial.

Although it is normal practice to file a case in the district where a crime occurs, the Simpson case would not be heard in Santa Monica Superior Court, which has jurisdiction over Brentwood. Prosecutor Garcetti mistakenly believed that once the prosecution had begun to present a case before the grand jury, which met in the downtown Los Angeles Criminal Court Building, the criminal case had to be continued downtown. Months later, it would become obvious that the problem with conducting Los Angeles County Superior Court Case BA#097211, *The People v. Orenthal James Simpson*, in downtown Los Angeles was that a predominantly African American jury would prove so suspicious of the official version of events that it would overlook the evidence against Simpson.

Racial perceptions could hardly be ignored in any case involving an African American defendant and the LAPD. Like most American cities, Los Angeles had a long history of racial tensions and police violence against African Americans. The 1965 Watts riot, in which thirty-four people were killed and rioters and police did $35 million in property damage, began with an altercation between police and a black motorist charged with drunk driving. Strained relations endured between blacks and the LAPD, a gigantic and quasi-military force headed by a series of police chiefs who, if not outright racists, were at best insensitive to injustices against the African American community. Race relations between the police force and African Americans hit an all-time low in the early 1980s when, in an effort to combat a crime wave fueled by drug trafficking and gang warfare, the LAPD went on a collective rampage against the black community. The police victimized thousands of innocent people through illegal raids, beatings, and frame-ups. Some of the cops carried out their mission in cruel and sadistic fashion, yet few were brought to justice for their crimes.

On March 3, 1991, however, when a citizen with a video camera taped police administering a brutal beating to a black suspect, Rodney King, the issues of police brutality and racism became prominent national stories. On April 30, 1992, violent riots once again erupted in Los Angeles when a predominantly white jury in Simi Valley, where the case had been tried, acquitted the white police officers of brutality charges in the King incident. A distinguished national commission concluded that the LAPD frequently employed excessive force against blacks and that racism and bias were rife among its rank and file. The King incident was atypical only because it had been captured on videotape; such incidents of white on black police brutality were routine in Los Angeles.

The subsequent outcome of the Simpson case stemmed directly from the profound mistrust on the part of the black community of not only police but also the entire criminal justice system in Los Angeles and the United States as a whole. While the Simpson *crime* had no apparent connection with race, the Simpson *case* would be decided in a community and nation riven by racial tensions. Many African Americans, both in Los Angeles and nationwide, immediately rallied around Simpson. The *Sentinel*, the African-American newspaper of Los Angeles, decried the handcuffing of Simpson after his return from Chicago as an example of the LAPD's desire to seize upon a black suspect. The African American community in Los Angeles knew that other black sports stars, including Hall of Fame baseball player Joe Morgan and Olympic track star Al Joyner, had been wrongfully detained by the LAPD in past incidents solely on the basis of their race.

Nationally, the victimization of African Americans by predominantly white police forces was recognized as a sign of institutionalized racism. Hundreds of thousands of black men across the country had been pulled over on roads and highways by police, not for DWI (driving while intoxicated) but for DWB—driving while black. While most whites remained indifferent to such discrimination, African Americans were targeted for crimes and incarcerated at alarming rates. In the wake of efforts to crack down on drug offenders in the late 1980s, the U.S. prison population soared from 900,000 in 1987 to 1.4 million inmates in 1994, almost half of whom were black men. African Americans routinely received harsher sentences than whites, with an especially noteworthy disparity between blacks convicted for possessing crack cocaine and white offenders convicted for powdered cocaine offenses.[3]

Nothing better symbolized white phobias of blacks as criminal predators than the infamous 1988 campaign commercial launched by Republican candidate George H. W. Bush against Massachusetts Democrat Michael Dukakis. The national television advertisement focused on the case of Willie Horton, a convicted black rapist who had been paroled during Dukakis's term as governor only to perpetrate violent crimes again. The political commercial angered blacks and white liberals but seared into the national consciousness the perception of blacks as violent offenders who should be caged. Despite widespread condemnation of the Willie Horton incident, *Time* magazine placed a surreal darkened mug shot of Simpson on its June 18 cover. Invoking stereotypical nineteenth-century depictions of African Americans as violent, unpredictable, and animalistic, the cover outraged African Americans, and millions of others, across the nation.

By the time the preliminary hearing began on June 30, the Simpson case had become inextricably linked with one of the most explosive issues in American history: race relations. Unprecedented media attention enveloped the Simpson case, and the trial was conducted in a heavily mediated carnival atmosphere. Already in the 1990s Americans had been mesmerized by a series of sensational celebrity crime cases, some of which had been broadcast live on national television, including the William Kennedy Smith rape case in Florida and the Los Angeles trial of the Menendez brothers for the murder of their parents. Sensational criminal cases involving prominent blacks—heavyweight boxer Mike Tyson for rape and pop icon Michael Jackson on accusations of child abuse—preceded the Simpson case. Not only did these and other stories dominate local and national news, but tabloid journalism and "reality TV" shows such as "COPS," "America's Most Wanted," and "Hard Copy" had also brought images of crime to Americans on a constant basis. Fueled by the national obsession with crime, celebrity, and race, the Simpson case morphed into a compelling daily national soap opera. Cable networks such as CNN and Court TV, boasting millions of subscribers, provided "gavel-to-gavel" coverage, while Simpson case chat lines and web sites sprung up on the Internet. The Simpson case, in short, became a heavily mediated national obsession.

Crucial to the unprecedented public access to the Simpson trial was the presence of cameras in the courtroom. After the Warren Court barred cameras from legal proceedings in the 1965 *Estes* decision, a new Supreme Court ruling in 1981 effectively reversed the decision by leaving the matter to the discretion of individual states. Under California law, cameras could be allowed into the courtroom, thus enabling blanket coverage of the Simpson case.

On July 8, a judge concluded the preliminary hearing by ruling that sufficient evidence existed for Simpson to stand trial for murder. Simpson's friends and advisers concluded that he lacked an experienced defense attorney who could sway a jury in the upcoming murder trial. Ultimately, the rather obvious choice for this role was Johnnie L. Cochran, Jr., the most prominent African American defense attorney in Los Angeles. Although Cochran did not invent the Simpson team's race-based defense, which had already begun to unfold under Shapiro, he alone turned it into an art form. Cochran had already spearheaded several successful defenses of African American clients by seizing upon illegal activities and racism on the part of the LAPD, and he knew precisely how to win over predominantly black juries. In addition to Cochran, two more high-profile attorneys with national reputations for freeing wrongly convicted defendants completed the defense team. Barry Scheck and Peter Neufeld, experts on the use of DNA blood evidence, were hard at work in what would become a successful effort to convince the jury that the incriminating blood evidence against Simpson was somehow tainted.

The media dubbed Simpson's coterie of attorneys, the most powerful legal talent with an array of investigators and expert witnesses, the "Dream Team." The same media representatives who had once peppered Gil Garcetti with hostile questions about the district attorney's initial kid-glove treatment of the celebrity suspect now depicted the defense attorneys in glowing terms. Media coverage, which had become more favorable to the defense, played a critical role in the evolution of the murder trial.

The defense continued its momentum by winning a decisive battle over jury selection, which is often more important in trials than the evidence presented. Nationally known consultants on jury selection revealed that race would play a dramatic role in jurors' perceptions and that African Americans, particularly females, were inclined to be far more sympathetic than whites to Simpson. The defense used the jury selection process to seek as many African American, and particularly African American female, jurors as possible, while Marcia Clark, the chief prosecutor, ignored consultants' warnings, based on questionnaires and analysis of mock jurors, that African American women were turned off by Clark's assertive style and her aggressive, rapid-fire pattern of speech. During the screening process, the defense blatantly eliminated as many prospective white jurors as possible, particularly white males, whom the consultants' analyses showed were those most likely to convict. Cochran showed himself to be a master of spin by charging publicly that it was the prosecution that was pursuing a racial agenda by screening out blacks. In reality, both sides were fully aware of the racial divide, but only the "Dream Team" placed race at the forefront of its courtroom strategy.

After more than two months of jury selection, twelve jurors and an additional twelve alternates were chosen, of whom fifteen were African American, including eight women. By comparison, Los Angeles County as a whole was 11 percent black. Only two of the jurors were college graduates. Most relied on television, and often tabloid television, for their news and information rather than reading newspapers and news magazines.

Some believed that use of force was acceptable within the family. Many had acknowledged negative perceptions of the LAPD and thought that O. J. Simpson was less likely to be guilty because he was a sports hero. No wonder Johnnie Cochran later wrote that the day of final jury selection marked one of his great triumphs in the case.

Despite having lost the battle over jury selection, the prosecution nonetheless entered the case with a high degree of confidence. They believed that the physical evidence of Simpson's guilt, based largely on DNA tests, ultimately would prove decisive. Since its introduction into forensic science in 1987, DNA testing has been particularly effective in solving cases of rape and murder in which evidence remained in the form of blood or semen. When such evidence could be matched with an individual's unique genetic code, DNA had the potential to remove virtually all doubt from a criminal case. In the Simpson case, the blood evidence at the Bundy crime scene, at Simpson's Rockingham home, and in the Bronco had left the defendant's genetic fingerprints all over the crime. DNA tests confirmed that the blood found inside and outside of the Bronco matched Simpson's type and those of his victims. They also confirmed that the glove found behind the guest house on Simpson's estate matched the mixture of the defendant's blood and that of his two victims. Socks found in Simpson's bedroom contained one spot that matched his blood and another that matched that of his ex-wife, Nicole.

The evidence demonstrated not merely that Simpson was guilty beyond a reasonable doubt, the American legal standard, but that in reality there was virtually no doubt at all. DNA tests confirmed that the blood drops the killer had left while leaving the crime scene matched Simpson's type and excluded well more than 99 percent of the human race. There was a 1 in 57 *billion* chance that blood on the rear gate at Bundy belonged to someone other than Simpson. Furthermore, the defendant had motive: his rage against his ex-wife, for whom he had bought everything, from a luxurious home and cars to enlarged breasts, and who had totally rejected her ex-husband in the days before the murder. Simpson also had opportunity: no one could account for his whereabouts at the time of the killings. Simply put, if the case went forward on its merits, Simpson was a condemned man. The rather obvious defense strategy, then, was to do everything they could to take the case away from its merits and to provide an alternative issue—LAPD racism and planting of evidence—to seize center stage in the nationally televised courtroom drama. As this strategy emerged, Clark summoned Christopher Darden, a close friend and, more important, an African American lawyer, to work with her on the case. Older and far more accomplished than Darden, Cochran ruthlessly depicted the young black prosecutor as little more than an "Uncle Tom." In arguments before Judge Lance Ito with the jury dismissed, the two black attorneys argued bitterly over whether race should be allowed to dominate.

At issue was the defense effort to ask LAPD detective Mark Fuhrman whether he had ever used the term *nigger* to describe African Americans. Darden argued that use of the word should be excluded because it would "inflame the passions of the jury." If Cochran were to be allowed "to play this race card," Darden contended, "the entire complexion of the case changes. It is a race case then. It is white versus black . . . us versus them, us versus the system." The young prosecutor had clearly perceived the defense strategy and its potential effectiveness, but Cochran lashed back with venom. Simpson's lead attorney charged that Darden's comments were offensive and that he wanted "to apologize to African-Americans across this country" for Darden, whom he dismissed as an "apologist" for Fuhrman and the racist LAPD. Darden and the prosecution lost the battle when Ito ruled that Fuhrman could be asked whether he had ever used the word *nigger*. Lacerated by Cochran's personal attack, Darden remained wounded, defensive, and often ineffective throughout the rest of the trial.[4]

The clash over the word *nigger*—and Ito's dubious decision to allow it to be invoked—set the stage for race, rather than murder, to become the centerpiece of the Simpson murder trial. By the time the trial opened in Los Angeles Superior Court on January 2, 1995, the race-based defense of the "Dream Team" was firmly in place. As the trial proceeded, "gavel-to-gavel" television coverage by the networks, CNN, and Court TV converted seemingly minor developments into supposedly major turning points. Scores of attorneys assumed roles as expert commentators, and even Judge Ito joined the attorneys in pandering to the television cameras. Ito granted press and television interviews and posed for pictures with souvenirs and stacks of fan mail he had received. He also entertained celebrities and talk show hosts in his chambers and offered courtroom passes to his favorite Hollywood stars. It was one thing to be star struck, but it was quite another to prove unable to conduct courtroom business in an efficient manner. The longer the case dragged on, more and more side issues and irrelevant information entered the record, and the core reality of the case, the massive hard evidence against Simpson, became more obscure.

By early March, the prosecution had managed to introduce damaging evidence of a history of Simpson's physical abuse of Nicole during their marriage. During cross examination, however, Cochran managed to depict the murders as a drug hit and, through the words he used in formulating his questions, also implied that Nicole had been sexually insatiable and habitually targeted black men as the object of her desires. All of this played well with the jury, which also proved susceptible to the theory of an LAPD conspiracy against Simpson. Cochran raised myriad issues with Detective Lange about police handling of evidence, going out of his way repeatedly as he framed questions to draw the jury's attention to the fact that Lange resided in Simi Valley, a conservative, predominantly white, suburban community where an overwhelmingly white jury had exonerated the officers who beat Rodney King.

The turning point in the Simpson case came with the swearing in of Detective Mark Fuhrman. The 43-year-old officer, a Marine combat veteran of Vietnam, had long been targeted as the centerpiece of the race-based defense theory of an LAPD effort to frame Simpson for murder. The "Dream Team" seized upon LAPD records of a psychological evaluation that bolstered the depiction of Fuhrman as, in Shapiro's words, a "bad cop" and a "racist cop." The assessment found that Fuhrman coveted the "big arrest" and that he seemed to enjoy opportunities to use violence against "low class" (and often black) people. Evidence also emerged that Fuhrman had engaged in racist talk, including resentment of black men who dated white women. Fuhrman blatantly lied when asked if he had "addressed any black person as a nigger or spoken about black persons as niggers in the past ten years?"[5] Together with other police lies—notably the absurd claim by Lange, Vannatter, and Fuhrman that they had not initially considered Simpson a suspect—as well as procedural errors, these missteps would give a jury sympathetic to Simpson the opportunity to set him free.

The prosecution still had plenty of compelling evidence to present. Clark summoned her best witness, limousine driver Alan Parke, who had taken Simpson to the airport on the night of the murders. Parke was clear and objective and, remarkably, had even spurned offers to sell his story to the tabloids. As he had done in the preliminary hearing, Parke testified that he had arrived at Simpson's estate at 10:25 P.M. on the night of the murders. He saw no white Bronco and no one answered the doorbell. Parke then saw a well-built African American man jog across the lawn and up to the front door. Moments later, he rang the doorbell again and Simpson answered, explaining over the intercom that he had overslept, was taking a shower, and would be down in a few minutes. When Simpson emerged, he insisted on handling a black duffel bag himself. Never seen again, the black duffel bag presumably contained the weapon and other incriminating evidence that Simpson disposed of later. As they pulled out of Simpson's driveway, Parke testified, he found his view obstructed by a vehicle that had not been there before: Simpson's white Ford Bronco. Cochran could do nothing to challenge the incriminating circumstantial evidence of Simpson's guilt offered by Parke.

With Parke's testimony having stabilized its case, the prosecution now presented the decisive DNA evidence. The Simpson attorneys understood, of course, that the DNA evidence could be marshaled to demonstrate Simpson's guilt beyond a reasonable doubt and knew that the only way to challenge it was by mounting an all-out assault on the handlers of that evidence. The architects and executioners of this portion of the defense case were Scheck and Neufeld, who exploited a series of procedural and handling errors to argue that some of the DNA evidence against Simpson had been contaminated and was therefore invalid. The defense declined to challenge other DNA evidence linking Simpson's blood with the defendants but charged that this blood had been planted by the LAPD. Scheck introduced photographic evidence that purported to show there had been no blood on the back gate at Bundy the morning after the crime, though, in fact, myriad witnesses had seen it that morning. Scheck was on target, however, when he pointed out that LAPD criminalists had erred in allowing the blood to remain on the gate for days before testing it. Similarly, Scheck argued that socks found in Simpson's house, which contained incriminating spots of both his and Nicole's blood, had been planted.

The defense bolstered its conspiracy theory through its own witness, Dr. Henry Lee, director of the Connecticut state forensic science laboratory. In a phrase that resonated with the jury, Scheck led Lee to declare that there was "something wrong" with the blood evidence in the case because of contamination. Day after day, Scheck emphasized the "something wrong" theme and the contamination of the blood samples. But a DNA expert, New York attorney Harlan Levy, has explained, "DNA is far more robust, and less subject to contamination, than the [Simpson] defense suggested."[6] The jury failed to understand, and the prosecution failed to explain to them, that *contamination would have made a match less likely.* That is, had the blood samples been contaminated, the contamination could have impeded a match but could not produce a false positive result. Contamination would make it more difficult to determine whose blood was in the sample; it could not make a sample of blood bear the DNA of O. J. Simpson. The torturously slow and detailed prosecution presentation of the evidence and the complexity of the issue, combined with Scheck's relentless assault and repeated charges of conspiracy and cover-up, raised enough questions with the receptive Simpson jury to call into question the credibility of the very evidence that in reality proved the defendant's guilt beyond doubt.

The pattern of overwhelming evidence of Simpson's guilt blowing up in the prosecution's face continued with the infamous Aris Isotoner leather glove. One glove had been left at Bundy; the other was found by Fuhrman behind Kaelin's cottage at Rockingham. Christopher Darden botched this compelling evidence by deciding on the spur of the moment, in direct contradiction of agreed-upon prosecution strategy, to have Simpson try on one of the gloves in court. Simpson, a decent actor, strained and kept a straight face as he mumbled "too tight" loud enough for the jury, and millions of Americans watching on television, to hear. "Expert" analysts, talking heads, and tabloid reporters converted this inconsequential bit of courtroom theater into a major disaster for the prosecution. While media coverage gave enormous publicity to the botched effort to have Simpson try on the glove, it devoted far less attention to prosecution witness Richard Rubin, a real expert on the gloves, who calmly explained the impact of the shrinkage and of the layer of latex and concluded that "at one point in time those gloves would be actually, I think, large on Mr. Simpson's hand." Indeed, when Darden brought out a new pair of the gloves, they fit nicely, but the damage had already been done. The most famous line of Johnnie Cochran's summation had been written: "If it does not fit, you must acquit."[7]

The prosecution had still more compelling evidence to present, but it was questionable at this point how much the jurors, already languishing in the prolonged confinement, were willing to hear. A shoe expert testified that the killer was over six feet tall and wore $160 Bruno Magli shoes, size twelve, the same size that the six foot three Simpson wore. Impressions from the shoes had been found at the murder scene and on the rug on the floor of the Bronco as well. Chillingly, a print from the same shoe had been identified on the back of Nicole's dress, where the killer placed his foot when he lifted her head to slit her throat.

Hair and fiber experts testified that hair in the blue knit cap found at the scene matched Simpson's, as did hair found on Ron Goldman and deposited by "direct contact." Experts testified that they found Nicole's hair on the bloody glove left at Rockingham. Fibers from Goldman's shirt were found on each of the gloves. Fibers matching those in Simpson's Bronco were found at the scene. Cumulatively, the evidence was devastating and would have required an implausible conspiracy among officials, many of whom did not even know each other, in order to manufacture it.

By mid-summer, with Ito already having allowed the case to drag on for half a year, the prosecution made the decision to wrap up the presentation of evidence against Simpson. The decision meant that the prosecution rested without presenting any information about the infamous Bronco chase, seen by millions, and Simpson's "suicide note." Why would Simpson write what his own attorney at the time described as a suicide note if he were not guilty? Why did Simpson take with him a passport, fake goatee and mustache, changes of clothes, and $9,000 in cash if he had not been running from something? Even more inexplicable was the decision not to introduce the 32-minute statement Simpson gave the day he flew back from Chicago, in which he sounded edgy, defensive, and contradictory.[8] On July 5, 1995, after 92 days of testimony, 58 witnesses, 488 exhibits, and the expenditure of at least $6 million in public funds, Clark stood before Ito and declared: "The People rest."

Given the poor performance by the prosecution, the defense might have been wise to consider presenting only a modest case of its own. Instead, Cochran summoned a series of witnesses, many of whom backfired. One, Laura Hart McKinny, played a key role in the defense campaign to put the LAPD rather than Simpson on trial. McKinny had once lived in Los Angeles pursuing of a career as a screenwriter and during the mid-1980s had made twelve hours of tapes with an Los Angeles policeman she had interviewed to gain insight into cop culture. The officer was Mark Fuhrman.

On the subpoenaed tapes, Fuhrman repeatedly used the term "nigger" and also admitted to manufacturing and planting evidence against defendants he "knew" to be guilty. He also described in detail systematic police abuse and torture of black gang members. The defense knew it was but a small step to convince the jury that with such characters prevalent in the LAPD, an otherwise implausible theory of planted evidence against Simpson might gain credibility and set their client free.

After a full year in court, closing arguments finally were heard, and it was Clark's final opportunity to change the momentum of the trial. She should have demonstrated the compelling evidence against Simpson and the dubious defense conspiracy theory but instead appeared disorganized, imprecise, and inarticulate when attempting to highlight Simpson's guilty behavior and present evidence that should have been introduced earlier. In sharp contrast with the weary and disorganized prosecution effort, Cochran displayed style, flair, and confident aggression in his closing statement, arguing that the police and a racist justice system, rather than his own client, were on trial. Emphasizing the alleged LAPD "rush to judgment," Cochran argued that the racist cops had been out to frame an innocent man, a role model for African Americans. By effectively telling the jurors they could ignore the evidence in the case since it had been gathered by the LAPD, Cochran came very close to encouraging jury nullification, which occurs when a panel deliberately chooses to ignore the evidence in a case in order to render a verdict that satisfies their sentiments or emotions rather than the facts.

By the time the case was finally turned over to the fourteen remaining Simpson jurors, they had lived apart from their communities and families for almost ten months. They had heard eleven defense attorneys and nine prosecuting attorneys and had listened to an astonishing 16,000 objections. The issue of race had been at the forefront of their minds from the outset. They knew that they were the survivors of a selection process in which both sides had impaneled and dismissed prospective jurors on the basis of race. During the long trial, as alternates replaced ten jurors for a variety of reasons, charges of racism surfaced repeatedly. The Simpson case began with eight black jurors and ended with nine, none of whom could be expected to ignore the pressure from the African American community to free the former football star. The stunning rapidity with which the jurors reached their verdict clearly revealed that their minds were made up and that they had barely deliberated, if at all. They spent less than two hours discussing the evidence before asking for verdict forms and voting for acquittal.

An unprecedented 150 million viewers worldwide—the most ever to watch a television event—tuned in to hear the jury render its verdict of "not guilty" on Tuesday, October 3, 1995. Simpson clenched his fist in victory, while a smiling Johnnie Cochran gripped the powerful athlete's shoulder. The prosecution sat in stunned silence. Kim Goldman, the sister of victim Ron Goldman, sobbed on her father's shoulder as he shook his head in anger and disbelief. Across the nation, Americans had divergent emotional responses to the jury's verdict. The unrestrained jubilation of African Americans contrasted sharply with the anger expressed by most whites over the injustice of Simpson being set free. According to one poll, 85 percent of blacks concurred with the verdict compared with 32 percent of whites. The reaction to the Simpson verdict revealed evidence, shocking to many whites, of the profound alienation of African Americans from the justice system.

Racial dynamics dictated the outcome of the Simpson trial. The African American majority seized the opportunity that the prosecution and Ito, through his weak administration of the case, had given them to respond to the chants of "free O. J." No one, aside from Cochran, understood the racial dynamics of the case better than Darden, who later declared that from the outset of the proceedings he "could see in [the jurors'] eyes the need to settle some score."[9] Well before the drug wars of the 1980s, the LAPD had been infamous for riding roughshod over civil rights in the African American community, and the total absence of LAPD credibility was the main reason for Simpson's acquittal. The time had now come to lash out against the system, and the chief beneficiary of that backlash was Simpson. In retrospect, the reaction of the African American community and the decision of the jury are understandable. The justice system had been made to work for a black man in a celebrated case. African Americans knew all too well that police harassment, violence, and tampering with evidence against African Americans were everyday occurrences in the United States. Why weren't those whites who protested the outcome of the Simpson case upset that African Americans suffered daily injustices under the law?

The African American jurors knew that the cops were lying when they said Simpson was not a suspect after going over the wall at Rockingham. The black community resented a judicial system that winked at cops who routinely planted evidence and lied, especially in cases of search and seizure, to implicate alleged criminals.[10] The irony of the Simpson case was that a pampered and narcissistic celebrity—a man who had long since distanced himself from the black community—had become the focal point of an African American struggle for equal protection under the law. The case might well be cited for the salutary effect of calling attention to racial inequality under the law, but Simpson himself was no hero to the black community.

Yet, to many African Americans charges that Simpson gained his freedom by playing the "race card" had little resonance. After all, the race card in American jurisprudence had always been played from a deck stacked against *them*, not in favor of a black defendant. Although many African Americans view white racism as the main problem of the criminal justice system, the dynamics are rapidly changing. It is true, as already noted, that a disgracefully high number of African American young men are in prison and on death row. Most of the crimes that land people in prison are committed by African Americans, but most of those crimes are also intraracial—directed against black victims. Authoritative studies have shown, however, that African American defendants are less likely than white defendants to be convicted by juries of violent crimes. Across the country, prosecutors are reporting more difficulty obtaining convictions against African Americans based on testimony by white police officers.

Juries increasingly practice nullification. As legal scholar Susan Estrich has noted, "The Simpson case, for all its uniqueness, captured too well the ills of the system; it is in all the ways that it is *not* unusual that the case teaches us the most."[11]

In the final analysis, the Simpson affair was far more than a murder case, and public fascination with the event reflected more than a media driven desire for the salacious details of sex, sleaze, and murder. The trial became something of a national referendum on race and power relationships in the United States. The lesson that a majority of African Americans took from their awareness of the nation's history of racist criminal justice and applied to the trial was the need to side with one of their own against a system that historically had repressed people of color. The striking juxtaposition of anger and celebration on the part of whites and blacks, respectively, points to the ultimate significance of the Simpson case. Despite meaningful progress in race relations since the civil rights movement of the 1960s, the Simpson case illuminated the profound divisions that remained in American society. Even as a multicultural society emerged in America at century's end, the conclusion reached by a federal commission analyzing race riots in the mid-1960s still resonated: in 1967, the Kerner Commission had declared that the United States consisted of two nations—one black, one white—separate and unequal. The Simpson case traumatized Americans, not simply because of the verdict that was rendered but because the heavily mediated national drama underscored deep divisions over race. These divisions not only undermine the administration of justice, but if left unbridged also will remain a menace to domestic tranquility.

NOTES

1. Jeffrey Toobin, *The Run of His Life: The People v. O. J. Simpson* (New York: Random House, 1996), 39.

2. Ibid., 51–58.

3. Samuel Walker, *Popular Justice: A History of American Criminal Justice*, 2d ed. (New York: Oxford University Press, 1998), 211–43.

4. Christopher A. Darden, *In Contempt* (New York: Harper, 1996), 247–52.

5. Toobin, *Run of His Life*, 148–55, 319–27.

6. Harlan Levy, *And the Blood Cried Out* (New York: Avon, 1996), 187–225.

7. Toobin, *Run of His Life*, 362–68.

8. Vincent Bugliosi, *Outrage: The Five Reasons Why O. J. Simpson Got Away with Murder* (New York: Norton, 1996), 110–93.

9. Darden, *In Contempt*, 3.

10. Alan Dershowitz, *Reasonable Doubts: The Criminal Justice System and the O. J. Simpson Case* (New York: Simon and Schuster, 1996), especially 46–68.

11. Susan Estrich, *Getting Away with Murder: How Politics Is Destroying the Criminal Justice System* (Cambridge, Mass.: Harvard University Press, 1998), 5.

SUGGESTED READINGS

Ball, Howard. *The Bakke Case: Race, Education, and Affirmative Action.*
Lawrence: University Press of Kansas, 2000.

Carter, Dan T. "A Reasonable Doubt." In *Race and Criminal Justice*, 16–27.
Vol. 8 of *Race, Law, and American History: 1700–1990*, edited by Paul
Finkelman. New York: Garland, 1992.

———. *Scottsboro: A Tragedy of the American South.* Baton Rouge: Louisiana
State University, 1969.

Dreyfuss, Joel, and Charles Lawrence III. *The Bakke Case: The Politics of
Inequality.* New York: Harcourt Brace Jovanovich, 1979.

Fehrenbacher, Don E. *The Dred Scott Case: Its Significance in American Law
and Politics.* New York: Oxford University Press, 1978.

Finkelman, Paul. Dred Scott v. Sandford: *A Brief History with Documents.*
Boston: Bedford, 1997.

Goodman, James. *Stories of Scottsboro.* New York: Pantheon, 1994.

Irons, Peter. *Justice at War.* New York: Oxford University Press, 1983.

Johnson, Jack. *The Autobiography of Jack Johnson—In the Ring and Out.* New
York: Citadel, 1992.

Jones, Howard. *Mutiny on the* Amistad: *The Saga of a Slave Revolt and Its
Impact on American Abolition, Law, and Diplomacy.* New York: Oxford
University Press, 1987.

Kennedy, Randall. "Dred Scott and African American Citizenship." In
Diversity and Citizenship: Rediscovering American Nationhood, edited by
Gary Jeffrey Jacobsohn and Susan Dunn. Lanham, Md.: Rowman &
Littlefield, 1996.

Lofgren, Charles A. *The* Plessy *Case: A Legal-Historical Interpretation.* New
York: Oxford University Press, 1987.

McClain, Charles, ed. *Asian Americans and the Law.* New York: Garland,
1994.

McLaurin, Melton A. *Celia: A Slave.* Athens: University of Georgia Press,
1991.

Morrison, Toni, and Claudia Brodsky Lacour, eds. *Birth of a Nation'hood: Gaze, Script, and Spectacle in the O. J. Simpson Case*. New York: Pantheon, 1997.

Patterson, James T. *Brown v. Board of Education: A Civil Rights Milestone and Its Troubled Legacy*. Oxford: Oxford University Press, 2001.

Pratt, Robert A. "Crossing the Color Line: A Historical Assessment and Personal Narrative of *Loving v. Virginia*." *Howard Law Journal* 41 (winter 1998): 236.

Schuetz, Janice E., and Lin S. Lilley, eds. *The O. J. Simpson Trials: Rhetoric, Media, and the Law*. Carbondale: Southern Illinois University Press, 1999.

Tateishi, John. *And Justice for All: An Oral History of the Japanese American Detention Camps*. New York: Random House, 1984.

Wilkinson, J. Harvie. *From* Brown *to* Bakke: *The Supreme Court and School Integration, 1954–1978*. New York: Oxford University Press, 1979.

Williamson, Joel. *New People: Miscegenation and Mulattoes in the United States*. New York: Free Press, 1980.